D1132128

HUNTINGTON LIBRARY PUBLICATIONS

ALBERT GALLATIN OSBUN

TO
CALIFORNIA
AND
THE SOUTH SEAS

The Diary of Albert G. Osbun
1849-1851

EDITED BY JOHN HASKELL KEMBLE

1966

THE HUNTINGTON LIBRARY
San Marino, California

The publication of this volume has been assisted by the James Irvine
Foundation Publication Fund of the Huntington Library.

CONTENTS

◎

MAPS

INTRODUCTION

THERE IS no such thing as a "typical" California Gold Rush journal. Archer Butler Hulbert attempted a synthetic account of an overland journey to the mines and succeeded in describing a sort of "three-ring circus" in which almost every possible adventure and experience befell the party which he created. Every journal and the experiences which formed the basis of every journal reflected individual and unique happenings, and it would be pointless to try to select one which was a common denominator. Certainly the journey of Albert Gallatin Osbun from Ohio to California and then to the South Seas does not fit a usual pattern at many points. A physician, the right-hand man of a fairly large-scale operator in placer mining, and the collector of a cargo of provisions with the hope of making a "killing" on the San Francisco market, Dr. Osbun was remarkable at almost every turn. His journal throws light on phases of the Gold Rush, of life in San Francisco in 1849 and 1850, and on Pacific Ocean commerce which is of real interest and importance. Furthermore, he emerges from his narrative as a person worth knowing, a man who consciously and unconsciously reveals much that is amusing and significant about human character.

Albert Gallatin Osbun was born at Cadiz, Ohio, on December 2, 1807, the son of Samuel and Hannah (Ross) Osbun. He attended Jefferson College at Canonsburg, Pennsylvania, just up the Monongahela River from Pittsburgh, graduating with the Class of 1826. Manuscripts of two orations survive from his college days. One of these, entitled "On the Importance of Some Kind of Religion in a Government," is dated September 27, 1826, and may have been delivered at his commencement. In 1824 Jefferson Medical College was established in Philadelphia under the aegis of the parent college.

Albert Osbun was matriculated at the medical college, and his correspondence with his sister indicates that he was in Philadelphia from December 1829 until about the end of March 1830. Whether this was his only period of attendance at the college is not certain. He did not receive a medical degree from it. According to the Jefferson College list of graduates, he studied medicine in his home town, Cadiz, with Dr. Wilson, and practiced medicine in Wheeling, Virginia, beginning in 1829.

The full order of events in Dr. Osbun's life from 1828 until 1849 is not clear, and probably it is not important that it be made so. In 1833 he married Elizabeth Frances Hawkins, who was born in Washington County, Pennsylvania, in 1812. The Osbuns had six children: Sarah (Sallie), Samuel, Charles, Albert, William, and Mary Frances. A case book containing notes on forty-five obstetrical cases indicates that Dr. Osbun was practicing on the Stillwater Creek in the western part of Harrison County, Ohio, not far from Cadiz, his birthplace, in 1840 and 1841. At least at the end of this period, Dr. Osbun was engaged in business, since on April 6, 1849, on the eve of his departure for California, a partnership with Samuel Mitchell and Aaron Kelley under the firm name of Mitchell, Osbun & Co. in Wheeling, Virginia, was dissolved.

The circumstances of the journey to California, or rather of the decision to undertake it, can only be surmised. During the winter of 1848-1849 the excitement over gold in California rose to a high pitch in the United States. It seemed to a good many that if they did not reach the streams of the Sierra Nevada foothills at the earliest possible moment they might be too late. Thus, the route overland from the Missouri River to California had the very real disadvantage that it would not be open for travel until the late spring, and this meant a wait of nearly half a year. The alternatives lay in two sea routes, one by way of Cape Horn and the other by the Isthmus of Panama. The latter offered the greater promise of early arrival in California, although it was fraught with unknown hazards of tropical travel and with uncertainties regarding connection at Panama, on the Pacific side of the isthmus, with a vessel for San Francisco.

Dr. Osbun's sister, Sarah or Sally, had married Wilson Shannon, an attorney and politician of St. Clairsville, Ohio, close to Cadiz and to Wheeling. Shannon, five years Osbun's senior, had enjoyed an active and generally successful political career. He had been Governor of Ohio, 1838-1840 and 1842-1844, and after an unsuccessful effort at election to the United States Senate in 1842 he had served, apparently with little distinction, as United States Minister to Mexico in 1844-1845. He had evidently become a man of some wealth, for he now embarked on the venture of financing a large party of prospective gold miners from Ohio to California. What the details of the organization were is not clear. Shannon apparently paid the passages of twenty-five men to California and furnished provisions and equipment for their mining operations. Whether he was to receive all the gold which the men of the party found and pay them a daily wage in return or whether the men were to share on some proportional basis in the takings of the whole group is uncertain from the fragmentary evidence to be found in the diary of Dr. Osbun. In any event, this was an interesting instance of a large mining company, not the more familiar mutual or joint-stock association, but rather financed by an individual. The party seems to have stayed together fairly well through the late summer and fall of 1849 and only broke up in the winter of 1849-1850.

Shannon, Osbun, and two others went out as an advance party, leaving Ohio on April 9, 1849, just three days after Osbun had dissolved his business partnership. Osbun was then forty-one years of age. Proceeding to New York by stage and railroads, the four took passage in the steamer *Crescent City* from New York for Chagres, on the Caribbean side of the Isthmus of Panama. Apparently Osbun and Shannon had first-class tickets and the other two members of the party traveled in the steerage. After reaching Chagres, making their way up the river to the head of navigation, and continuing to Panama overland, the party had a wait of somewhat over three weeks before the steamer *Oregon* was ready to take them to San Francisco. They arrived there on June 13, 1849.

After a brief stay the party went by boat to Sacramento and then continued by water and land to the Yuba River, where they began mining operations. The main body of the party arrived on the Yuba on September 23. They had come from New York via Cape Horn in the ship *John G. Coster*, departing from New York February 24 and arriving in San Francisco August 6. The next three months were ones of almost constant movement. Shannon was away from his men a good deal of the time, obtaining supplies in Sacramento and San Francisco and apparently entering into California politics as well as beginning a law practice of his own. In Shannon's absence Osbun acted as his deputy and seems to have been in charge of operations.

The reader of the diary cannot avoid being impressed by the restlessness of the group, or at least of the leaders. No sooner had the party established itself in diggings than Osbun would remark that they were too late or in the wrong place, and laborious preparations for a move would begin. Shannon took an option to buy Pierson B. Reading's ranch on the upper Sacramento River, and in the autumn of 1849 the party moved from the Yuba to the new location. It appears that they were repeatedly in country which was in the future to yield a rich harvest of gold, but whether because of inexperience, lack of skill and persistence, or general ignorance of the most effective placer mining methods in this fairly early period, the results of the Shannon party were disappointing.

Some indications as to the organization of the party are contained in the diary entries made by Osbun at the time the party was disbanding. Apparently the men had given bonds to Governor Shannon to cover the amount of their passage money, which he had paid. Now they agreed to dissolve if he would return their bonds and pay them a dividend on the gold which they had taken. A few men dissented from the arrangement and agreed to pay the cost of their transportation—apparently $200—as soon as they were able. Presumably they would also expect a larger dividend of gold or perhaps the full payment of what they had gathered. Fragmentary records in the diary lead to the conclusion that detailed daily records of the gold taken by each man had been kept.

Osbun returned to San Francisco in January 1850 in poor health and somewhat dispirited. In conjunction with a Mr. Perry, whom he had met in the mines and now again encountered keeping a hotel or boardinghouse in San Francisco, he conceived the idea of chartering a vessel and making a voyage to the Pacific Islands to collect a cargo of provisions which could then be sold to advantage on the San Francisco market. Every move in this direction seemed to take time, and many obstacles presented themselves, but Osbun and Perry persisted and succeeded in chartering the American brig *Rodolph*. Perry eventually took command of her, although there is no clear indication what his previous seagoing experience had been.

After a trip to Stockton with a cargo of lumber, which the brig's owner insisted that she make, *Rodolph* sailed out into the Pacific at the end of April 1850. The expedition called at Fanning Island, at various islands in the Samoa Group, and at Wallis Island, and finally made its way up to Pearl and Hermes Reef—the last in hopes of locating sea turtles. Pigs, yams, coconuts, and chickens were the chief goods sought. For a variety of reasons Osbun felt that the brig was equipped with the wrong trade goods, that the natives met were not dealt with skillfully, and that the trip as a whole was not much of a success. He himself seems to have gotten a good deal of enjoyment out of the voyage despite recurrent bouts with seasickness. He tried his hand—unsuccessfully—at cooking for the crew, but in the main went as a passenger and was only active when it was time to go ashore to trade. *Rodolph* returned to San Francisco on September 9, 1850, and although there is in the diary no full account of the financial results of the expedition, Osbun gives the impression that it was a money-losing venture.

Toward the end of October 1850 he headed for home. Sailing from San Francisco in the bark *Eureka* for Realejo, Nicaragua, and Panama, the vessel made an uncommonly long passage and eventually landed her passengers at Acapulco. From here Osbun and a party of friends took animals for the trip across Mexico to Vera Cruz. The diary breaks off at Puebla de Cocula, about two thirds of the way from Acapulco. There is a brief fragment apparently written on shipboard at the mouth of the Mississippi, and it is to be assumed that Osbun landed at New Orleans and made his way home up the Mississippi and Ohio rivers by steamboat.

Presumably Dr. Osbun remained in the vicinity of his original home in eastern Ohio for the next sixteen years. Meanwhile Shannon had come home from California and reentered politics in Ohio. In 1853-1855 he served as a member of the House of Representatives, and in 1855 was appointed Territorial Governor of Kansas by the Buchanan Administration. He retired in 1857 but remained in Kansas, engaging in the practice of law for the rest of his life. Osbun, who had been connected with a large paper- and straw-manufacturing plant in Wheeling, Virginia, came to Kansas on a visit in 1857 and decided to remain and make his home there. He purchased a quarter section of land in Bourbon County, near Fort Scott, in 1858. His family had all joined him by 1860. Dr. Osbun died at Fort Scott on April 7, 1862, of "typhoid pneumonia." He was then just over fifty-four years of age.

The narrative of Dr. Osbun's journey to California, his experiences in the mines, and his voyage to the South Seas is contained in the diary. This fills 218 pages in a volume approximately 10 x 8 inches, which was obviously rebound long after the diary itself was written, and 25 pages in a smaller notebook in original boards and with the remaining pages blank. The diary is published in full here. In addition, letters from Dr. Osbun and other members of the party which were published in the *Belmont Chronicle*, his hometown newspaper, are published here insofar as they add directly to an understanding of the diary or fill out the narrative.

The Osbun diary has presented few serious difficulties to the editor. At some points, particularly on the early pages, torn edges have made it necessary to supply obliterated words in order to make a connected narrative. Dr. Osbun wrote a clear hand, and there are not many instances in which it has been difficult to be sure of what he meant to say. In transcribing the diary no changes have been made in spelling. Where a wrong name has been given or an obvious slip has been made, the correct form has been supplied in square brackets. This has been kept at a minimum, however, and when Osbun's spellings, even though incorrect, do not obscure his meaning, they have been allowed to stand. As with many nineteenth-century writers—and others of later date as well—Osbun's punctuation was frequently capricious and sometimes makes his meaning difficult to grasp. The editor has freely repunctuated the text where the author's meaning, upon careful study, seemed clear but where the punctuation as he had it was confusing. Insofar as birds, beasts, fish, and plants are concerned, the editor has sought the counsel and advice of those who were wise in these special fields. In many instances, Osbun's descriptions were apparently too general to make any sort of satisfactory identification possible. Where the scientists consulted have been willing to hazard guesses or to make positive identifications, these have been included in the footnotes. Where no footnotes occur in connection with flora and fauna mentioned, the reader may assume that no identification of any certainty at all was forthcoming.

Footnotes have been kept at a minimum. At the end of the text are three appendixes: persons, places, and ships. At this point identifying notes have been gathered as far as locations and identities could be established, rather than placing this material in footnotes. Names of persons and places are listed in these appendixes as they are spelled in the text. If they are incorrect, the proper form is supplied in the note following the initial entry. If undue and cumbersome scholarly paraphernalia have been avoided by this, the editor's aim has been achieved.

The manuscript of the Osbun diary and related papers have been placed on indefinite loan in the Henry E. Huntington Library at San Marino, and it is through the generous permission of Kathryn C. (Mrs. Lloyd V.) Powell, Dr. Osbun's great-granddaughter, that the diary is published here.

Many individuals and institutions have been of assistance in the preparation of the Osbun diary for publication. In the identification of ships and places, the staffs of the Social and Economic Branch of the National Archives and Records Service, Washington, D.C., the Marine Historical Association, Mystic, Connecticut, and the Peabody Museum, Salem, Massachusetts, have helped generously and effectively. The Cincinnati Historical Society made available its file of the *Belmont Chronicle* and permitted materials bearing on the Shannon party to be copied. The following persons gave counsel in the identification of flora and fauna mentioned in the diary: Rimo Bachigalupi, Jepson Herbarium, University of California, Berkeley; Peter Hillier, M.D., Pasadena; Carl L. Hubbs, University of California, San Diego; Myron Kimnach, Henry E. Huntington Botanical Gardens, San Marino; and Kenhelm Stott, Jr., Zoological Society of San Diego. The Automobile Club of Southern California generously agreed to construct the map of the California gold regions. William H. Newbro, Manager of the Public Relations Department, and Forrest M. Burke, Assistant Manager of the Map Department, gave this matter their enthusiastic and skillful attention. My friends John Goodman of Beverly Hills, California, and Colonel Fred B. Rogers of San Francisco were both repeatedly of great assistance in the identification of ships and places mentioned in the diary. Finally I wish to mention the unfailing enthusiasm and the splendid assistance given me by the editorial staff of the Huntington Library, especially Mrs. Nancy C. Moll and Mrs. Anne W. Kimber.

JOHN HASKELL KEMBLE
Pomona College

San Marino, California
December 8, 1965

TO CALIFORNIA AND THE SOUTH SEAS

1

OHIO—PANAMA—SAN FRANCISCO

©

[*Monday,*] *April 9th, 1849.* After having made all necessary preparations for [going to] California, Gov. Shannon & myself left St.
Clairsville this morning. ([I already] had removed my Family untill
my return) to be absent from 1 to 3 [years].

[*Tuesday,*] *10th.* Left Wheeling with Jas. Barnett & Jno. Harding
at 6 oclock A.[M.] for N. York via Balt. & Philada. from which place
we expect to emb[ark on one] of Steam Ships to Chagris, in New
Greneda.[1]

[*Wednesday,*] *11th.* This morning early we were landed at Cumberland, & to[ok one] of Steam Cars, upon the Balt. & Ohio Road &
arrived in Balt. early in the [evening].

[*Thursday,*] *12th.* This morning left Balt. at 9 oclock A.M. on Rail
road, & arrived [at Philadelphia] at 3½ & left immediately on Rail
road for N. York where we arrived [at] 8 P.M. & took lodging at the
Boarding house of Mrs. Vandiver N[o. 328] P[earl Street.][2]

Tuesday, 17th. Having spent our time here very busily in laying
in [such stores] as we supposed we would need, we this day left this

---

[1]The journey from Wheeling to Cumberland was made by stage on the National
Road, a distance of 130 miles. The Baltimore & Ohio R.R. was in operation for the
178-mile run from Cumberland to Baltimore. From Baltimore the travelers would
have taken the Philadelphia, Wilmington & Baltimore R.R.; and from Philadelphia
to Jersey City there was through service over the Philadelphia & Trenton, New
Brunswick & Trenton, and New Jersey railroads.

[2]Franklin Square Hotel, 328 Pearl St., Elizabeth E. Vanderveer, proprietor.

3

port upon the Ste[amer] Crescent City, at about half past 1 oclock, amid the cheering of an [immense] multitude of people, who as usual assemble to witness the departure of vess[els for] California. In order to insure our passage upon the Pacific, we conside[red it] more prudent to purchase Steamer tickets for that portion of our trip & accordingly we bought [two cab]in tick[ets] & 2 steerage, for which we were compelled to pay a p[remium of] $260. We paid for the two former $260 each, & for the two la[tter] [MS torn]. [We] went aboard without our dinners, & being compelled to run about [locating & col]-lecting together our goods, & having eaten but little breakfast [we were very hungry]. About half past 2 dinner was announced. I d[id] it full honor, but it proved to be the last meal that [I had for some time]. The wind soon blew up to quite a gale, & [when we were entire]ly out upon the wide deep ocean, I commenced [feeling ill].

[Wednes]day, 18th. I arose this morning quite sick. We were en-[tirely ou]t of view of land. I undertook to remain upon deck, but ha[d to spend] the most of the day in my state room. It still continued [to blow a] gale. At noon to day we had travelled 170 miles [from New York].

Thursday, 19th. Still quite sick. The wind not blowing quite So [hard, I spent] more time upon deck. At noon we found ourselves [in lat.] 34°23′ [sic]. Longitude 72°30′. Distance 215 miles.

Friday, 20th. At noon found us in Lat. 34°47′. Longitude 72°12′. Dist. 216 m[iles].

Saturday, 21st. At noon found us in Lat. 26°42′. Long. 72°26′. Dist. 246 miles.

Sunday, 22d. At noon found us in Lat. 22°45′. Long. 72°52′. Dist. 239 miles.

Monday, 23d. At noon found us in Lat. 19°05′. Long. 74°27′. Dist. 235 miles.

Tuesday, 24th. At noon found us in Lat. 16°08′. Long. 77°10′. Dist. 238 miles.

4

Wednesday, 25th. At noon found us in Lat. 12°25'. Long. 78°41'. Dist. 240 miles.

[We] now passed the Island of Cuba upon our right, the Island of [Santo Dom]ingo on the left, & Jamaica also on the right.

Thursday, 26th. This morning at 9 oclock we cast anchor off about two [miles f]rom Chagris, & in full view of the Coast for a considerable distance [to the] South. Here I was much disappointed. I expected to see a low [lying s]hore, full of Fever & Ague. On a high & projecting prominence of rock [stands the C]astle or Fort of Chagris, a verry ancient building filled with monstr[ous guns] rendered useless by age, but still guarded by some 8 or 10 of the nat[ives].[3] I did not vi[sit] it but understand that the woodwork of their massive [carriages is ent]irely decayed, & immense stores of Powder, spoiled from a [long neglect]. [The vil]lage of Chagris cannot be seen from our Anchorage [but it is across the river] & far below the above Castle. We were visit[ed by men from] the town who came out in their Canoes, to seek p[assengers].

The Steamer Orus when we stopped was [up the] river with a load of Passengers that landed the day before from a Steamer from N. Orleans. In a short time however she hove in sight wending her way down the Chagris to her landing. As she did not come out we concluded a contract with a couple of Yankees to convey us to Gorgona with our baggage for $10 each, in a whale boat. We after dinner entered their boat with them, & went out to the village.

Being verry anxious to go ahead, & the prospect being verry poor for the delivery of our goods on shore to night, our boat with Barnett started late to the Steamer for our Baggage. With great difficulty & danger they procured it & brought it ashore. It being after night we concluded to remain here untill morning & be off by the first dawn of day. After supper which we obtained in the tent of an old Marylander, we crossed over to the village, to see what the Natives were about, as we understood a regular Fandango was to pass off during the evening. A death & burial had occurred to day, which prevented the Fandango. They were busy going through their ceremonies, first a serenade with torches, & then their chaunts &c. at the church. We went to their church & took our stand at the door. As the natives

---

[3]Fort San Lorenzo as Osbun saw it was a structure dating largely from only the 17th and 18th centuries.

passed out, they crossed the foreheads of each of us, their fingers being moistened with the holy water. The population here are either
entirely Negro blood, or where it preponderates. Many Indians & a
few Spaniard. Their dress is altogether white, & mostly linen, & look
verry clean. Labourers, both among the male & female, wear nothing
but a small cloth around the Pelvis. Children are entirely naked.
Their houses are, if enclosed at all, enclosed with reeds, but many
of them have but corner & centre posts, with a high straight roof covered with Palm leaves.

They generally sleep up stairs. They appear to be a very indolent
people, spend their time in walking about, lounging in their hammocks, & cockfighting. And withal, they appear to me to be a verry
happy race of People.

Friday, 27th. I arose this morning before day (having slept upon
a hard table 12 inches shorter than my body) tolerably well refreshed,
benefitted more perhaps by having my feet once more on *Terra firma*
than any thing else. Having no water on this, the North side of the
river, we could get nothing to eat, untill we could procure some from
Chagris. This detained us untill a late hour in the morning. We however got our baggage all aboard & shoved off all in fine health &
spirits. We started with two men at the Oars, & Barnett as steersman.
The river here was a delightful stream & verry deep.

It continued so the whole day, & the scenery which bordered it,
Birds, fruits, in fine every thing connected with the trip reminded me
more of the fairy land of romance, than reality. I had no idea that a
country so rich, in every thing to charm the senses of man, existed
any where upon the face of this globe. I would not undertake to describe what I have to day seen. The cocoa nut, the palm tree & several varieties of the clematis were all that I could name among the
vast number of elegant trees & vines, that constantly crowded themselves upon our view.

What Slander! was the constant exclamation of our company, has
been heaped upon this river in the States, & how different from our
expectations.

Not an alligator or venimous reptile of any kind has been seen by
any of us this day. We stopped several times to pluck & taste the delicious looking fruits that hung in great profusion along the shore, &
also to shoot some birds, that we might examine their rich plumage.
We stopped at a village called Gitune, where a native oarsman was

procured, to assist in pulling up our Boat. About one mile above this place & 8 miles from Chagris we stopped at a spring, & partook of a Dinner made up of sea crackers, Boiled ham & water. This meal, tho seemingly poor, was to us rich indeed. We passed this evening the landing spot of the Steamer Oris, which is at this time the head of navigation & is only 16 miles from Chagris. We kept still ahead of her, she having most of our steamer passengers aboard of her. We proceeded about 3 miles above & landed an hour before sundown, pitched our tent on the left bank of the river, & put up for the night. Before day a most tremenduous howling commenced in the woods, all around us. We concluded that all the Tigers & Lions & Leopards of the Isthmus had gathered around us, perhaps to devour us. A native, before we left Camp, informed us they were not *Tigers* but *Monkeys*.[4] If so there must have been hundreds upon hundreds within hearing distance.

Saturday, 28th. After breakfast, at sunrise, we struck our Tents & were soon again upon the waters of the beautiful Chagris. We were here overtaken by a party of 2 Ladys & their husbands, fellow passengers on their way to San Francisco, both married just before their departure.

The natives generally work entirely naked upon their canoes. To these young married Ladies, this spectacle must have been interresting. To day the difficulties in rowing our boat have greatly increased. Many rapids occur in the river, which make it necessary for our oarsmen, who have now taken to the pole, to jump into the river, & pull us through. To day we saw two Alligators, & shot them both, one about 2 feet long, & the other 12. We also saw Monkeys upon the trees, & an immense number of Parrots, of various kinds, & other new & splendid birds. This evening we pitched our tent at the residence of a *Padre*, 37 miles from Chagris.[5]

Here was the first improvement we came across that looked like farming since we came into the country. Fine large herds of cattle filled the fields, & they all looked fat & sleek. The *Padre* was absent & we spent a pleasant evening with his household. The whole of this country appears to be infested with ants of every habit & variety.

[4]Howling monkeys; genus *Alouatta*.

[5]This may have been at the village of San Pablo, which was 36.5 miles up the Chagres River from its mouth.

7

There are several varieties that build their nests upon trees, similar in appearance to the nests of hornets, & from 2 to 6 feet in length. Others live in the earth & throw up immense mounds of it. We frequently see their roads, worn like the paths of school children.

We had great difficulty to night in finding a place free from these roads large enough to pitch our tent upon. Several of the Orus crew overtook us here, having travelled late, so that we had a company of 3 tents besides our own. Our location proved with all our care to be an unfortunate one. Jno. Harding had taken a bag of bread for his pillow, & placed it over a nest of small red ants, which we had not observed. About midnight we were all aroused by his cries, the d——d ants were eating him up. Upon examination his head was literally covered with them, & also the bread bag. The poor fellow did moan most pitifully. After he got them cleaned off pretty well he went to the boat & spent the balance of the night in it.

Sunday, 29th. The monkeys gave us another Serenade during the night & this morning. We arose at the break of day, & got our negro landlady of the Padre's house (who is himself we understood as dark as the ase of Spades) to make us some coffee & chockolate for breakfast, after which we struck our tents, & were soon again upon the water.

We met to day many canoes loaded down with gold & silver on its way to England, entirely in the possession of the natives & unguarded. The natives are remarkable for their honesty. Not a single instance has occurred in which they have proved themselves dishonest, or unworthy of their trust. About 9 oclock we landed at the anxiously looked for village of Gorgona, which we find situated upon the right bank of the river, & elevated high above its low water mark. This village has a much better appearance than Chagris. Many of its houses are closed & daubed with clay, having doors & windows, & several apartments inside. The roofs are however all covered with palm leaves. Its population is about 800.

We pitched our Tent immediately upon the commons, but before we had our baggage all conveyed to it, a heavy shower of rain came up, & wet considerable of our baggage. This rendered our situation very unpleasant, the rain having ran in upon us & under us. This was the first shower of rain we have seen since we left home, & we took it to be a commencement of the rainy season in this region. After all was over, we concluded to strike our tents & take up lodging with the alcalde of the village. There we were verry comfortable, the only annoyance being a lot of New York Yankees who by the bye annoyed me more during our whole trip than all other troubles & annoyances put together.

They think they are smarter & better bred than any other people. This gives them the impudence & forwardness of the Devil himself. They supposed their accomplishments in the arts of singing & Dancing could not be surpassed, & hence we were daily compelled to listen to their nonsensical airs having not one note of genuine music about them. This with their constant halloing & bellowing about the Boat annoyed verry much many of the passangers. We here secured board & lodging in rooms seperate before they found out the house. When they came they asked for board & lodging, & hence concluded as they were the salt of the earth, they [were] entitled to & would have the best rooms in the house. We claimed our rights promptly & sternly & they gave way. But they outgeneraled us at breakfast. We had a table expressly prepared for our party, & before it was ready & while we were in our rooms, they seated themselves at it, & devoured the victuals as fast as they were placed upon the table. We discovered the Alcalde was much hurt about it. We told him to let them alone, & not disturb them. He then took us to his private room, prepared another meal, & we eat undisturbed.

The country for some distance back has been getting more & more hilly or as it is here called mountainous. The soil is verry rich & productive—producing vegetation of every variety that belongs to the climate.

The Chagris river is verry crooked, running in all directions of the compass, the valleys verry wide, no hills being perceptible ¾th the distance to this place. And if the country was in the possession of Yankees, & cleared up, would certainly be one of the ritchest countries, & most productive, upon the face of the Globe.

Monday, 30th. About 8 oclock this morning, after having contracted for the delivery of our baggage in Panama, we all started on foot for that far famed City. We supposed our Baggage would weigh about 1000 lbs. & agreed to pay $40 for its transportation.

The cost of a mule for riding is $10 & we considered by making a two day trip of it, it would not fatigue us, & not being in any hurry, we could make it a trip of pleasure. The distance across has been variously computed; that generally received is 24 miles. We found it verry hot walking during the forenoon. We however walked verry slow, & at about 4 oclock P.M. arrived at what is called the half way house, distance 13 miles. This camp is situated upon the highest ground over which the road runs between the two oceans, & is the summit level of the Rail roads. We here supped & breakfasted most sumptuously on Beans, fat, pork & sea buiscuit, for which we paid 50 cts. per meal, & 25 cts. for the priviledge of laying on the ground under their tent.

A company of Engineers from N. York were encamped within one half mile of us, locating the rail road.[6]

Tuesday, May 1st, 1849. This morning as soon as we swallowed our Coffee, Beans & pork, we set out upon our Journey, a good deal the worse of the beans & pork, several of the company having used them rather liberally for this climate. Doct. Weeks was taken during the night with severe diarrhoea, which alarmed him considerably. We did not proceed far before he was compelled to hire a mule. This day was verry hot. Shannon & myself, finding ourselves getting considerably fatigued & overheated, hired a mule & rode time about, when within 4 or 5 miles of the city, where we all arrived about 3 oclock. We looked around for a suitable Hotel to stay it [sic], & decided to put up at the Oregon House, situated upon the Plaza outside the wall. Board $8 per week or $2 per day.

The road over which we have passed from Gorgona has been generally good & pleasant. Occasionally we decended into steep but not deep ravines where the path was narrow, & worn & washed deep into the earth, sometimes deeper than our heads, but we found none of it muddy or swampy & verry little rock, & none of those dangerous precipices which we have read so much about. About 4 or 5 miles from the city commences a turnpike about 6 feet wide, & laid with boulders as the streets of our cities. We however avoided it, finding it verry hard to walk upon.

We understand that there are here about 2000 Americans waiting for a passage to California, & that there are here sailing vessels sufficient to take off from 12 to 1500. But no word from Steamers.

[6]A party of engineers under the direction of Col. C. W. Hughes of the U.S. Topographical Corps left New York for the Isthmus of Panama on Jan. 22, 1849. The survey for the Panama Railroad was completed by June of that year, and the road itself was constructed between Dec. 1, 1849, and Jan. 27, 1855.

Wednesday, May 2d. To day we all cleaned up & put on our best bib & tucker & sallied forth to see & be seen. The Gov., Weeks & myself called upon the Consul, & also upon Col. Weller & learned that they looked confidently for 2 or 3 of the Steamers in a very short time. We concluded after this interview to await their arrival, with as much patience as possible.

Thursday, 3d. To day rumors of sickness & death among the Americans flew through the city & filled the minds of many with great fear. One of the passangers upon the Crescent [City] has died, another who came upon the N[ew] O[rleans] Steamer also, & one of the natives; all said to die from Cholera. Other deaths also reported. We concluded this evening we would move to the Island of Tobago & there await the arrival of the Steamers. The Gov. & Dr. Weeks accordingly went down this evening in a canoe to make arrangements for our reception as soon as we could get there tomorrow.

Friday, 4th. About noon we settled our fare at the Hotel, contracted with a native to take us down, & had all things aboard, with provisions to last several days, & were ready to shove off, just as the Gov. & Dr. approached the landing on their return. They made a verry unfavorable report of the health & comforts of the Island, & completely knocked into pie this calculation. We now concluded to rent a room in the city & commence housekeeping. After some search we found one that pleased us tolerably well, & accordingly moved bag & baggage to it. We agree to pay for the room, table & water cask $1.00 per day. Having no cots, or matrasses or [blank in MS], we spread our tent upon the tile floor, & covered it with our Gum Blankets, & had a comfortable night's rest.

Saturday, 5th. This morning after early breakfast, I went to market, to procure some fresh Fish & Eggs but failed entirely in getting any thing. Having rather poor fare for dinner, the Gov. & Weeks dined out. We made ours of Tea, Bread & Bologna Sausage.

Getting this afternoon somewhat uneasy about the early arrival of the steamers, we held a consultation about the propriety of disposing of our tickets & going up upon a sail vessel. Called upon a Broker to see what we could sell for, & finding the prospect rather dull for making a saving sale, concluded to postpone the further consideration of the matter untill Monday, & see what 48 hours would bring forth. Barnett & myself concluded we would take a stroll a couple of miles into the country, & see if it afforded any game. We went out in a westernly direction & found the country a mass of tangled under-brush, vines & briars, & entirely impassable unless where there were paths. We found the woods filled with Pheasants, differing much tho from ours, being more like a verry Turkey & about the size of our own Pheasants. We succeeded in killing two. Returning past the cemetery, we beheld what was to us a novel sight indeed. We first met a com-pany of Boys hallooing & laughing at the top of their voice, then an-other lot of young men laughing & talking & playing upon violins, flutes & a Tamboreen. Next [came] the corpse of a native apparently about 12 years of age, borne by 4 young men, in a coffin covered with scarlet cloth, the lid being raised 3 or 4 inches. The corpse was cov-ered with flowers. And next was a Padre clothed in his broad rimmed hat & black gown, accompanied by a number of older persons, prob-ably relatives of the child. We turned back, determining to see the end of the farce. They moved untill they came to the gate, when they set down the coffin, took off the lid, and with hats off went through some ceremonies of chaunt, &c. After this the carriers closed up the coffin, took it within the gate & we supposed placed it within a vault, none entering but the carriers.* The whole company, Padre and all, were Negroes, or the mixed population of the country.

The young men & musicians left in a row among themselves before the ceremonies were over. This we afterwards understood was the usual way in which they buried children. No females were present. About nine oclock this evening, the town was thrown into a great up-roar by two reports from cannon at sea. In an instant it seemed that thousands of human beings were upon the streets, yelling, hollowing, & huzzaing. It was soon ascertained that the Steamer Oregon had arrived from California to make her second trip. She was indeed a welcome visiter, not only to us, but to many, many others who have been waiting here for her for many weeks, & some for months. This night was spent by many in frolic and jollification. I did not, in con-sequence of the noise, get to sleep untill after midnight.

Sunday, 6th. We arose this morning in fine spirits, much pleased with ourselves for not having disposed of our tickets, & consider we

*I have since learned that the corpse is taken from the coffin & deposited in the earth without box or anything of the kind, the earth being thrown directly upon the body. The coffin and flowers are kept for the purpose of carrying bodies to the burial ground.

are still in luck. Went to market, got 4 or 5 Doz. Oysters for 10 cts. which proved to be verry good, & some Sweet Potatoes, also a couple of Hams at 25 cts. per lb. & some dried beef 15 cts. We dined to day most sumptuously upon our Pheasants. About one oclock, the city was the scene of another excitement, tho not so great as the one of the past night. Another Steamer hove in sight, which proved to be the Panama, the 3d steamer of the line, on her way from New York to take her place. A goodly number are also here, holding tickets for berths upon her, that greeted her arrival with much enthusiasm.

This afternoon Weeks and myself took a stroll through the suburbs of the City, & fell into truly what may be called a Den of iniquity, nothing else than a pit for cockfighting. We were told the Priests & Padres generally attend these places of amusement held every Sunday afternoon. We witnessed a vast amount of severe excitement, among the owners & betters, but no quarrelling or fighting. A Judge occupies a high seat in the midst of them & by the tap of his bell announces the commencement of the fight & also the conclusion. His decision is final, & universally obeyed without a grumble. We witnessed 4 or 5 fights & both cocks were either generally killed upon the spot or mortally wounded. They seldom fought longer than 1 minute. They fought with a sharp cutting knife, called slashers, fastened to one leg. I left much disgusted with this barbarous sport. Barnett is complaining this evening, & seems quite unwell.

Monday, 7th. Barnett has been verry unwell all day & seems much discouraged. He complains of sick stomach & headache. I have given him nothing but soda. There seems to day to be much uneasiness among the steamer ticket holders. The Californias claim as their tickets are the oldest, they are entitled to be off first. The Oregons, that as their tickets call for the 2d trip of the Oregon, & she being here to make it, no other tickets can supersede theirs.[7] The agents withhold a decision, & all parties are held verry uneasy. It is supposed by some that the two Steamers can take all who hold tickets here. It has rained every day since we have been here, from 1 to 2 hours, and the Ther-

[7] By "Californias" Osbun meant the men who held tickets for passage in the steamer *California* of the Pacific Mail Steamship Co. She had made the first trip from Panama to San Francisco, sailing Jan. 31, 1849. Her crew deserted her in San Francisco, and she also lacked coal for a return voyage to Panama. She finally sailed south on May 1, and from Panama for San Francisco again on June 24. "Oregons" refers to men who held tickets for the Pacific Mail steamer *Oregon*.

13

mometer stands in the morning & evening at 80° & at noon 85°, with not one half degree's variation.

At noon today a Mr. Wheeton from Allegheney, Pa., joined mess with us. This evening 3 deaths is reported among the Americans, from fever. I believe there are many sick persons among the Americans, but originating almost altogether from imprudence.

Tuesday, 8th. This morning Barnett is much better. In the afternoon John & myself took a hunt, in our usual hunting grounds. We killed one Pheasant, & scared up a Fawn, but could not get a shot at him. It rained verry hard to day. Thermomemeter, 79° —85° —80°.

Wednesday, 9th. Barnett, John & myself took a long hunt to day, but was unsuccessful. We saw many Pheasants, but could not get a shot. We have discovered in all our rambles, in the midst of the thickest woods & largest timber, the ruins of ancient buildings, arches, gateways, & wells, which tells us that all these plains now covered with timber & underbrush was once in the highest state of cultivation. In all my walks I have seen but one snake. Lizards are verry numerous from 1 foot in length down to 1 In. They are a verry harmless reptile. I saw a verry singular species of frog; it was small, black, shining with white spots. There was no rain to day. Thermometer 80°—85°—80°.

Thursday, 10th. Having all our water to buy at the rate of a bit for each 3 Galls., we filled up our water cask the day before yesterday with rain water in order, as we supposed, to save a little & to get purer water.[8] But to day we discovered it was full of waggle tails & had to throw it, & commence the use again of the native water.

The whole of the city is supplied with water carried upon the backs of the natives & of mules, a distance of from 1 to 2 miles. And they pay for it at about the above rate. A want of decision, or a desire to mislead the minds of ticketholders, has prevented the agents from announcing their conclusions regarding the course they intend pursuing. To some they make one statement & to others & [sic] contrary one.

Fearing that all will not get off, & our tickets being of the latest date, we to day addressed a letter to the Agents stating our great desire to be off, & the importance of our departure, &c., &c. We re-

[8]A "bit," also called a *real,* was one eighth of a Spanish dollar.

cieved the verbal answer that is [sic] was their opinion that the two Boats will be able to take off all the ticket passengers. At a large meeting held this evening, contradictory statements were ascertained to have been confidentially made by the Agents. Another meeting was determinioned upon to be held at 9 oclock in the morning, at which time some course of proceeding would be determined upon by which to bring the agents to a decision.

Friday, 11th. This morning a notice from the agents was posted up announcing the conclusion that in the Panama, all the Panama tickets would be taken, & as many of the California as would make up her complemement. In the Oregon, all the Oregon tickets would be recieved & the balance of the load made up of the California. This decision was well received, because it was founded in right & justice. But it seems the Agents had not gumption enough to make it. They called upon a Mr. King, an eminent Lawyer here from Georgia, who is here on business for H. & Aspinwall connected with the rail road.[9]

This evening Barnett & myself concluded we would take a measurement of the city by stepping, & make a plat of it. This is pretty much of an undertaking, but having nothing to do, we will go through with it.

Saturday, 12th. I had forgotten to mention that on Thursday my Thermometer was broken, but no person did it. This is to me a great misfortune. I can get none here, & I wish to keep an account of the heat of this climate. Up to the date of of its loss however there was but little variation. It ran from 80° to 85°, & I judge at this season of the year it may be considered as the regular & correct degree of heat. Barnett & myself put in most of the day examining the city & stepping the width of its streets & the size of its squares. We find it will make us well acquainted with every nook & corner of the city. This day has been spent more quietly by the Americans here than any day since our arrival. Tuesday is the day announced for the departure of the Panama, & the Oregon 3 or 4 days afterwards. This day is the birth day of Dr. Weeks. The Doctor placed upon our table a bottle of good

[9]This was probably Thomas Butler King (1800-1864). He was in Panama at the time and made the trip north to San Francisco in the steamer *Panama* sailing May 18 and arriving June 4, 1849. "H. & Aspinwall" refers to the New York firm of merchants and shippers formed by William Edgar Howland and William Henry Aspinwall. Howland and Aspinwall were prime movers in the establishment of the Pacific Mail Steamship Co. and the Panama Railroad Co.

15

French brandy, & we took a little cautious Jollification on the occasion. This evening we concluded to take a walk among the gambling establishments here, of which there are a verry respectable number for this City. And we concluded also that it was our duty to break up some of them. So we made up a purse of *12 dimes*, put it into the hand of Barnett, & put out. The first establisment we entered was an apartment back of an eating house, in which there was 2 Roulette tables, 1 sweat board, 1 Faro bank, & 1 Monte board. The room was literally jammed full of gamblers. Every table save one Roulette was full & in active operation. To this one we drew up & marked it as the one whose time was short. Barnett squared himself up at its foot, the Gov. on his right, Weeks behind him, & I on his left. Down went a dime bet upon the red column. There my good fellows take that if you can, was the silent exclamation of our brave crew. I had forgotten John. He placed himself at the wheel to detect roguery, to [keep] their cheating propensities at bay, & to see that all the operations were conducted fairly & honorably. Away went the ball in one direction & the wheel in the opposite. It rolled & rolled, & made several attempts to get home, but it seemed to us it would never nestle itself. Finally it succeeded, after keeping us seemingly an age in breathless anxiety, & settled upon the black.

Gone! gone! our dime was lost. Had we gained on this bet, we would have gained 3 for the one. Nothing daunted, & looking at the glorious result as undoubted, we renewed our bets with increased risk. Down went a dime upon the same red column, and another upon one of 4 numbers. Whirl again went the wheel, & the ball, & down she settled upon the red, & upon one of the 4 numbers. This placed in Barnett's hands 3 dimes upon the red, & 6 upon one of the 4 numbers. Hah! my good bankers, thought we, now has commenced your certain destruction. Another bet upon the red & won, another upon the black & won. Barnett's hands were now fast filling up. It being his first attempt at gambling, he was verry slow & awkward in his movements. He could scarcely gather up his winnings as fast as won, they being all in 5 & 10 cent pieces. It was really amusing to watch him. He continued to bet, but his luck seemed to forsake him. One continued loss after another, with only an occasional win, soon emptied his hands, so that in a verry short space of time after this turn of luck, all our bright prospects [vanished]. We gave [the game] up, deeply impressed with the great uncertainty of the result of all great undertakings.

Sunday, 13th. To day we feasted upon Oysters & Eggs the [first] costing us about 4 doz. for 5 cts., the latter costing 25 cts. per doz. We are becoming verry fond of the Plantain. We eat it fried in slices after frying ham, & find it agrees with us well. This afternoon several of our company made a short visit to the Cock pit.

The present city of Panama has been built up entirely since the destruction of Old Panama. The old city from the best information I can collect was commenced by [Pedro Arias de Avila] a few years after the discovery of the Pacific by Bilboa. He, finding Porto Bello verry unhealthy, petitioned the Government of Spain for the priviledge of moving the colony to a point on the Pacific where they could have better health & from which they could better extend their discoveries on the Coast of the Pacific. This was in about the year 1520. Government granting it, they selected a point 5 or 6 miles north of this place & called it Panama. It prospered & became a verry wealthy city, altho its houses were generally built with reeds. It contained many churches, & a splendid Cathedral built of stone, the ruins of which are still standing. In about the year [1671] its wealth attracted the attention of pirates, & a company of 8 or 900 headed by Sir Geo. Morgan, whose headquarters were upon the island of [Jamaica], crossed over the Isthmus, attacked & entirely destroyed it, leaving it in ashes.[10] They obtained an immense treasure in Gold, Silver &c. Instead of rebuilding on the old ground, the present site was selected & built up after the same manner & with the same materials as the Old City. About the year 1770 it was again destroyed by fire, & then rebuilt with stone as we at present find it. The present city was built on a neck of land running out into the bay & is walled in by an immense stone wall, & is washed on 3 of its sides by the sea. On the west, & the side we approach & enter the city, is a double wall & a ditch or canal between, running from the bay on one side to the bay on the other. It was besieged by Bolivar & taken in 1824, & its walls & buildings much injured. The city now may be said to be in ruins but its ruins show that it was once a city of wealth & splendor. The number & splendor of the Churches & Monasteries show that it was under church dominion, & that perhaps of the most rigid kind. What its population was during its period of prosperity I could not ascertain, but learn that it has been declining for many years. At present it has

---

[10]The expedition which sacked Panama was led by Henry Morgan, who was not knighted until later. It consisted of about 1,200 men.

17

about 7000 natives & from 2 to 3000 Americans on their way to California. By looking at the map it will be seen that about ⅓ of its area is in entire ruins being darkened to show the location & about ⅓ the balance of the city is going fast into the same condition.[11] But if the Americans should proceed with the rail road, the locating of which they are now busily engaged & which I have no doubt will be completed, then we shall see Panama take a new start & again become a city of importance. Its present population consists mostly of Negroes & Indians & their mixtures, with a verry few Spaniards. They are a lazy, indolent people & will do no work unless their immediate wants require it. Almost the only mechanics I see among them & that work any are Shoemakers & Tailors & they seem to be verry industrious & constantly at work. Their whole passion seems to consist in Cock-fighting & gambling. Every dwelling almost seems to have a collection of Cocks training for this amusement & large sums of money are bet upon the results of these fights. Government seems here to patronise gambling, which no doubt partly accounts for the indolence of the people. The Churches, Monasteries & the College of the Jesuits, now in ruins, are well worth examination for the splendour of their architecture & the magnificence of their design. I spent several days wandering through & around them. In passing around I observed, under several of the Churches, openings passing into cellars or pits used for casting the bodies of dead children into. I looked into one & saw the bodies heaped up upon one another just as cast in from the opening. In another place, near a prison & church connected, I observed 13 sculls built in the wall with the masonry. They, I understood, were the sculls of a portion of the Buccaneers or Pirates beheaded for the crime of destroying old Panama.

Wednesday, 23d May. Having nothing to note since the 13th, I now commence, as we are taking up the line of March, to record our movements. On Monday our ticket holders, having nothing positive from the agents regarding our day of departure, became verry restless. They concluded to hold a meeting at 10 oclock by a public notice. But before the hour arrived it was announced by a bill posted at the office of the Agents that on Tuesday the baggage would be recieved on the Oregon & the Passengers on Wednesday. We accordingly on yester-

[11]The reference here is evidently to the map of Panama which Osbun drew during his stay. Only a part of this has survived.

day sent aboard all our baggage except our Carpet Bags containing a little cloathing to do us on the way. And to day about 2 oclock we were safely deposited on the steamer Oregon, with the exception of a good wetting that fell from a cloud whilst on the way out. Yesterday after packing up our cooking utensils, we dined at an eating house, where [we had] some Bean Soup, & which came near doing me great injury. Diarrhoe came on me from it to day, & this evening vomiting followed, with rapid purging so that this night I put in, a verry sick man.

Thursday, 24th. Our vessel raised anchor & paddled off about 8 oclock last evening. I am now verry sick & have been upon my back the whole day. I feel to night verry weak, & verry much reduced. Sailing upon the *Pacific* I consider not a verry desireable *amusement*. I find a great number of the passengers sick to day. The Gov. & Barnett are both casting overboards. And it appears singular that so many are sick, & the ocean so quiet. Not a white cap or wave of any height seems to disturb its quiet surface. Our location at noon to day is Lat. 7°90′. Long. 81°26′. Dist. 140 miles.

Friday, 25th. I am still verry sick, tho my diarrhoea being checked the sickness is now altogether seasickness. Barnett also looks verry bad, [illegible word] verry sick; the Gov. is improving. We sailed W. by N. & in sight of land all day, & at noon are in Lat. 8°6′. Long. 84° 16′, & have sailed since noon Yesterday 233 miles.

Saturday, 26th. Still sick. Our general course has been NW. by W. At noon we are in Lat. 9°33′, Long. 87°30′, & distance 212 miles.

Sunday, 27th. Still quite sick, altho I put in the whole day on deck. We had a service at half past 10, after the Episcopalian form, read by a Col. Allen. I perceived his socks were marked "Col. A." From this you can judge of his manner & style. The exercises were prefaced by remarks intended to be suited to the occasion. The music was indeed excellent. We have many excellent singers aboard & old ocean was made ring with most enchanting music. We have no land in view to day. At noon are in Lat. 11°28′, Long. 90°35′. Dist. 216 miles.

Monday, 28th. My health is now improving, & also Barnett's. The bal[ance] of our company are in fine health & spirits. An accident

19

serious to life came near occurring upon our ship to day. About two oclock it was discovered by the smell & by the bursting of scales from the boiler, that it was empty of water, & burning, & just on the point of bursting. The valves were immediately opened & the fire put out, & all done just in time. We were perhaps from 60 to 70 miles from shore & had the accident from bursting occurred & the Ship not blown to atoms, it would even have been doubtful that many of us could have been saved. We have boats & Gum Mattrasses sufficient aboard to save all, but in the confusion of such an occurrance, not half could or would avail themselves of their advantages. The ship is now moving under the action of one engine & gets along at but a slow pace.[12] At noon & before the accident, we were in Lat. 12°56' & Long. 94°0' & Distance 218 miles.

Tuesday, 29th. I arose verry early this morning, & feel pretty well. Our engineers worked during the whole night at the boiler; and at about 8 oclock this morning they had all again in order & we were soon under full headway. Since the accident we have travelled at about half speed & stopped entirely several hours during the night. There has been much severe talk to day among the timid & fault finding portion of our passengers against the conduct of those concerned in managing the engine, & on this occasion there was no doubt some good ground for them to indulge their propensity.

To day several birds alighted, completely exhausted, upon the mast & rigging of the Ship. They were called South American Crows, & were about the size of our crows but were webfooted. A passenger ran up the ropes & caught one, but came near paying dearly for his rashness. Just as he caught it, it darted at his eye with his bill & struck close to the ball, making a severe wound. I think our crew is now generally in good health, Barnett & myself being among the latest of the sick.

Our Latitude 14°48'—Longitude 95°56'. Dist. 159 miles.

Wednesday, 30th. This morning we find ourselves in full view of a range of mountains along the shore, and will now remain in full view of land perhaps the whole distance to San Francisco. This has been to

---

[12]This episode is not mentioned in the engineer's log of *Oregon* which is in the M. H. De Young Memorial Museum in San Francisco. In fact, there is no entry at all for May 28, 1849, although the log is very regular with entries for every watch on all days before and after.

me a verry interresting day. I now feel *myself* once more, & for the first time since my departure from Panama have taken up my pen to bring up my journal. The mountains as viewed from the ship show the peculiar features of the mountains of this region of our Continent. On Saturday we passed through a shoal of whale, supposed to be from 80 to 100, & from 60 to 80 feet in length. They appeared to us to be enjoying themselves verry much; we could see their spouts in all directions. There was great excitement among to [sic] passangers, & it was indeed an interresting & beautiful sight. About 2 oclock to day we entered the Bay of Acapulco & cast anchor near the town & fort. We remained here about 4 hours. Most of the passengers went ashore & purchased fruits from the natives, but owing to the great rush & confusion attending the visit, I concluded to remain aboard & be an eye witness to the scene.

The inhabitants here are nearly altogether Indian, a few Spaniards & a few mixed. They brought out melons, &c. & disposed of them readily & at fair prices. I paid 6 cts. for a large glass of a drink called Pulque, verry sweet & pleasant, & much celebrated. It is made from the Cactus.

Our Steerage passangers are much dissatisfied with their fare. They represent their treatment & fare to be more like unto Hogs than of human beings. There are about 230 of them confined closely to the steerage, not being allowed the privilege of any other part of the vessel. But little attention is paid to cleanliness by a majority of them, & as they have to do their own cleaning, they must become verry filthy. Their food is cooked for them, & cast out upon a board all together, where each man goes up to & cuts off or pours out what he wants & retires to his bunk & devours it. Old strong salted meat & sea buiscuit with black bitter coffee & no sugar is the general bill of fare. Here an opportunity is given them to procure something more palatable for themselves & they are making good use of their time; all are coming in heavily laden with fruits, fresh water & bread. What makes their situation hard & more unpleasant is they cannot, even for money, procure any thing to eat better than their allowance from the Boat.

Barnett during his sickness has fared better than is usual. I had victuals brot to my berth & he would visit me & partake. This is the only manner he could get any thing palatable to eat. The bay & harbor of Acapulco must certainly be one of the finest in the world. It is not large but seems to be sufficiently deep & extensive for safety. It makes its entrance safe & winds around like a horse shoe, so that it becomes entirely surrounded by high mountain. There is here a walled fort with soldiers, & a clean neat looking town, much in advance of the population of Panama in every respect. Still we see no cultivated fields, no evidences of agriculture, high lofty peaks of mountain rising up suddenly in the rear of the town.

The bay is filled with verry fine fish. We procured some for cabin use. We find here several sail vessels filled to overflowing with passangers, on their way for Gold, having put in for provisions & water. We also find some 15 or 20 Americans, waiting for a passage on our Steamer, having travelled across from Vera Cruz, but we could not take them. At noon we are in Lat. 16°40′, Long. 99°39′, & Dist. 242 miles.

Thursday, 31st. This day we have sailed the whole day in full view of shore, & have feasted our eyes upon its magnificent scenery. High & lofty peaks of mountain rise towering one above another to an immense height, whilst clouds float along regularly far, far beneath their conical peaks. At noon our course N.61°W. & in Lat. 17°44′–Long. 103°25′. Dist. from Acapulco 151 miles.

June 1st, 1849. To day we were much amused at a race between a drove of fish, a species of Porpoise from 6 to 10 feet long, & the boat. We observed them ahead of us for some time before we came upon them, & percieved they were in great numbers. We soon came along side, which made them increase their speed, so that for a long distance it seemed that neither could get ahead. They appear to be a fish that always swim near the surface, & occasionally dart from the water, & blow, like as many scared hogs. They suddenly gave up the race, wheeled to right & left us at a right angle. It seemed that the alarm was communicated to each one of the Co. at the same instant. They all wheeled, & swam as suddenly & regularly as if the word of command had been given & heard. They continued in the same direction as far as we could follow them with the eye. Our course N. 53°W. Lat. 20°07′; Long. 105°40′. Dist. 241 miles.

Saturday, 2d. Last evening at about 9 oclock we arrived at the city of San Blas. This city is situated at the mouth of the Rio Grande [de Santiago]. It contains a population of about [blank in MS]. It is a miserable looking place. Its location is upon sand, a few feet above the level of the sea, & during the rainy season is partly inundated. There appears to be here quite an extensive low flat valley, now filled with ponds of water covered with a green scum. There has been no rain here for 6 months, & they are now looking for the commencement of the rainy season. And so soon as it commences, the inhabitants leave their town & move into the interior, with the exception of a few poor families. It is considered during the rainy season to be one of the most sickly locations in this whole region of country.

Here we expect to remain 3 days to replenish our stores, it being a point for the deposit of Coal. The town is constructed generally after the usual mode of this climate, in reeds, & Palm or Cocoa leaf roofing. There are however quite a number of their houses plastered with clay & mortar & covered with tile. The old town situated upon a high bluff rock, 1 mile back, has been the former seat of the aristocracy of the town & country, but it is now mostly in ruins. It is a most delightful spot, & was in former times the residence of the Governor. We paid it a visit & enjoyed ourselves much with the delightful prospect, & invigorating sea breeze, which its elevated position afforded us. Here in the suburbs some of our party gathered Oranges, Tamarinds, Banana & other native fruits, growing in abundance around the town. Here is located a cathedral, the only church I observed in any part of San Blas. Returning to the lower town I saw a verry large green chameleon, the first one I have ever seen. I also see a species of Cactus 3 & 4 sided such as we cultivate in pots, growing in the woods to the height of 20 to 25 feet. They have a market here all the time. It appears to be coming in all the time from the country, & consists of Tomatoes, Oranges, Limes, Banana, Onions verry fine, Pine Apples, Water & Musk melons, a large red watery & tasteless plumb, Tamarands, Chickens, Plantain &c. The demand by Americans being just now so great has made rather a scarcity, & increased the price. I bought 50 pretty good oranges for 37½ cts. Pine apples bring from 50 to 75 cts. Melons about the same price as at home. We have had great difficulty to pay for our purchases, the natives utterly refusing to take any money but Spanish or Mexican.

On Sunday evening a circus performance was exhibited in the town by Mexicans, which I understand went off pretty well. I did not visit it. Sunday is here their great day for Gambling & amusements, their streets being lighted up & tables spread with the choicest provisions of their country, all along the sidewalks. On Monday Barnett & myself took an excursion across the narrow neck of land that makes in to the left of the harbour. We found it a high ledge of trap rock covered with bushes, & upon its extreme surface is the ruin of an old fortification, now grown up & covered with vines & bushes, the woodwork having almost entirely decayed, & the cannon half consumed with rust. I brought away a specimen of the rock. The tide rises here about 12 feet. On Monday evening a vessel arrived 11 days from San Francisco, & reports 80 vessels in the Harbor, much sickness in the mines, provisions & goods low price, & plenty of Gold in the diggins, but that few who dig for it succeed, on account of the labour, difficulty & privations that are connected with it.

Tuesday, 5th. Last night about 2 oclock we again got under way being almost worn out by the delay. This day we have sailed the whole day out of view of land, crossing the mouth of the Gulf of California. Our vessel, from the roughness of the sea, has tossed & pitched verry considerably, so much so that many are getting sick. I have myself eaten no dinner. Our course today N. 76°W. Lat. 21°58′, Long. 106°54′ & Distance 119 miles.

Wednesday, 6th. I feel to day not sick exactly but sufficiently disturbed to keep me from enjoying my victuals. The sea still continues verry much disturbed, & I find a great change in the air. The thermometer has fallen to 75°, it having ranged from 80° to 85° ever since we left Panama. Course N. 75°W. Lat. 22°42′. Long. 109°56′. D[istance] 174 [miles].

Thursday, 7th. It has grown verry cold. Passangers who had deserted their berths, & hung their Hammocks, & fixed their beds upon deck have fled & taken their berths inside. Summer cloathing has been laid aside & a great scrambling among trunks & travelling bags, for woolen cloathing & overcoats. I have myself suffered verry considerably. Barnett was offered a berth in the Pantry on Tuesday & accepted it. He concluded it was better to work for nothing & get good fare, than live in the steerage & be a *Gentleman.* He set in without making a contract as to wages, & appears much pleased with his berth. Thermometer 65°. Course N. 52°W. Lat. 24°29′. Long. 112°24′. Dist. 174 miles.

Friday, 8th. Our course to day N. 53°W. Lat. 27°00′. Long. 114°20′ & dist. 183 [miles]. Cold has increased. Thermometer this morning 58°. We have passed to day through several shoals of the sulphur belly whale.

Saturday, 9th. Our course N. 27°W. Lat. 29°19′. Long. 115°50′. Dist. 160 [miles]. Two months since this day, we left our homes, & expected at that time to have been at the end of our journey long ere this. But considering all things we have done well to be now so near the end. Thermometer 58°.

Sunday, 10th. Our course N. 18°W. Lat. 31°50′. Long. 116°48′. We are now at noon 50 miles from San Diego. Course N. 11°W. We have passed this [day] along the coast in sight of & generally close to shore. The country presents a verry barren appearance, verry rough & mountainous, occasionally rising in high conical peaks beyond the clouds. We had service performed by Col. Allen as on last Sabbath. This evening at 6 we entered the bay of San Diego & left 12 or 15 passengers & baggage, all belonging to Col. Weller's party. We did not go up as high as the town, located at the head of the bay, it being some 5 or 6 miles up, and were on that account deprived of a sight of it, but we had a full view of the Bay. It is certainly a most excellent harbour. We enter it by a narrow neck & afterwards swells out considerably, & presents a calm unruffled surface, & so situated that it can seldom be disturbed by storm. We saw here immense numbers of the Grey Pelican, sitting about on the sand, & fishing for food. We have also seen immense quantities of a sea plant called Kelp floating upon the surface of the water, like long vines with broad & long lanceolate leaves, some of them 30 or 40 feet long. They are attached to rocks deep down in the sea. It is the plant from which Iodine is usually obtained, & presents a verry handsome appearance as it floats upon the water. We remained here only about one hour. A Spaniard came aboard here who reports the arrival of a large body of Americans here, who crossed on foot from Vera Cruz, and also that rich deposits of Gold have been found 60 leagues back, near Puebla los Angelos, & that this company will stop.[13] Also that a vein of Coal has been discovered 2 miles back. Also that letters have just been recieved, stating that the deposits at [San] Francisco are giving out, & the people quarrelling much among themselves. These reports are entitled, all of them, to but little notice.

---

[13]There is also a reference to this report of a gold discovery near Los Angeles in a letter from Charles Frederick Winslow to Charles G. and H. Coffin and C. B. Swain, dated San Francisco, June 18, 1849, and published in "Nantucket to the Golden Gate in 1849," *California Historical Society Quarterly,* XXIX (1950), 14.

Monday, 11th. Course N. 50°W. Dist. 138 miles from San Diego. Lat. 34°08′, Long. 119°05′. This morning & during the night verry cold & foggy. Thermometer 50°.

Tuesday, 12th. Course N.[blank in MS] W. Dist. [blank in MS], lat. [blank in MS], long. [blank in MS]. Still a strong wind from NW. & cold. Still sailing along shore, in full view of high barren mountains, with occasional slopes covered with their grass & herds of Cattle.

Wednesday, 13th. During the night, the fog being verry dense, to avoid shore our ship had sailed too far out. She now occupied 2 hours steering direct for land, with still a verry dense fog, before we came to land. And fortunately & accidently our first view of land through the fog was a short distance below the Bay. We were however surely apprised of our nearness to it, by the appearance of thousands of Ducks, the Sprat Barrows called, swimming & luxuriating upon the surface of the troubled sea. Soon we made our entrance within the Golden Gates of the Bay. On our right stands an old fort having full command of the entrance, N. S. E. & West. It is now in ruins. And in a verry short time were in full view of the Harbour, covered with Ships & vessels of every description numbering about 100. And also of the long looked for City of San Francisco. Our cannon was fired & anchor cast about 2 miles out from the landing, about 9 oclock A.M. The Captain, Gov. & some others went ashore immediately, the object of the Capt. being to get a conveyance to take us ashore with our luggage. On account of high wind, but one load was landed, & we remained aboard all night, our baggage not being aboard of the launch.

2

SAN FRANCISCO—BENICIA—SACRAMENTO
YUBA RIVER

©

Thursday, June 14th, 1849. Being anxious to get my feet upon Terra Firma once more, after Breakfast I went ashore & took a general survey of the city. We selected a site for our Tent upon the beach on the southern edge of the town. I dined at the Boarding house of Mrs. Robinson, & took tea at a Restaurant. Our baggage not getting ashore, I sought lodging & obtained it, after much searching, in a Tent occupied by some of our travelling companions, & put in a most miserable night. I kept on all my cloathes even Cap & Boots, & had a Blanket to cover me. And withall, I thought I came near freezing. I believe I never slept colder in my life.

Friday, 15th. Our baggage was landed about 8 oclock this morning, & we immediately pitched our tents, carried up our baggage & went to work getting our breakfast. Being verry tired I kept quiet the balance of the day.

Saturday, 16th. I have formed a poor opinion of the climate of San Francisco. A strong NW. wind commences in the morning & increases in strenght until evening when it gradually abates. The whole country around is a barren desert of sand, & this wind keeps the atmosphere filled with it. I suffered much in both my eyes & lungs. So unpleasant was it to me that I have avoided being out as much as I could consistently with my curiosity. Barnett, myself & Mr. Northrop, a young Gentleman from New Haven sent out by a mining company from New York (& who are now on their way here by the Cape), as Geologist & assayer, took a stroll to day in the neighbourhood to hunt & examine the country in the vicinity of the town. High hills rise up immediately back of the town from which we had a most delightful view of the

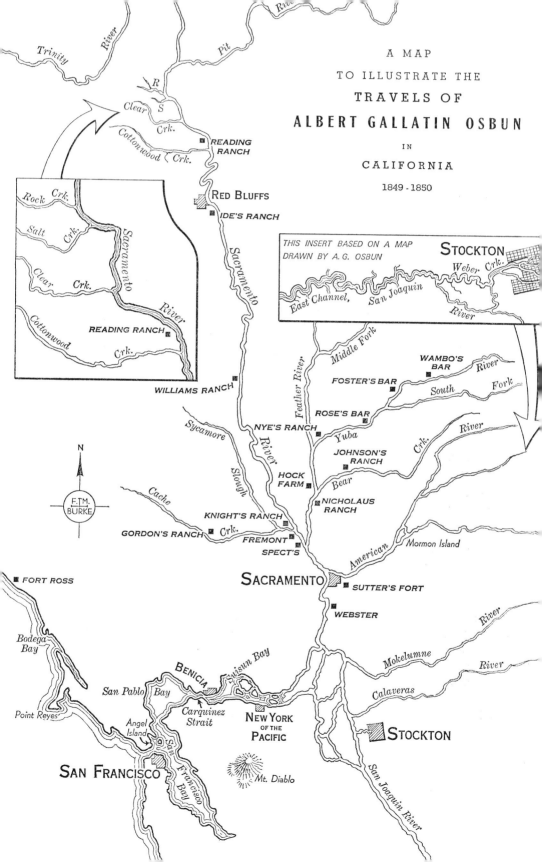

country back & of the Bay. The country appears a continuous succession of barren hills of sand, & never can be used for agricultural purposes. The bay is certainly a most magnificent sheet of water, & covered as it is with so many vessels at anchor, give the place an appearance of business in amount far short of the amount actually done.

We saw a Rabbit just like the rabbit of our own region, & a flock of Quails, [one] of which we killed. It differed in colour from ours, being dove coloured on the head, & had a different head dress more like the feather of the peacock. We returned & found the Gov. had concluded to start at 8 oclock in the morning for Sacramento City, & had engaged our passage on a Whale boat. Price $16 for each with 100 lb. baggage. The extravagant accounts heard in the States of business & Gold here we find all confirmed & we can no longer doubt its existence & in large quantities. Buying gold dust appears to be a part of the business of every business man here. We see the card of "Gold dust bought here" upon every man's door, & a pair of Gold Scales upon every counter. No trading in Butter, eggs & chickens in the stores here, no handling of clover seed & oats & dried fruit by the merchants. The prices of labour & merchandise is as often made in ounces & half ounces as in Dolls. & cents. At auction sales, ounces & half ounces are often bid, which means 8 or 16 dolls. Labouring hands get from [?] dolls. to ½ oz. a day & Carpenters from 10 dolls. to 1 oz. Barbers charge 1 Doll. for a shave & 2 for cutting hair. Boarding is from 1 oz. to $20 per week. Sailors upon the Bay & River get from $100 to $200 per month; Cooks from 100 to $120; Clerks from 150 to $200.

Rents, City lots & houses are also extravagantly high. An ordinary lot will bring $20,000 & one house built for a Hotel of ordinary size rents out its rooms for $27,000 per year. A small house with from 3 to 4 rooms of meanest structure & no out door convenience will rent from 4 to $5,000. The demand for houses is so great that at least one half of those erected at present are studs planked & covered & enclosed with canvass. These prices are paid & taken on long leases which proves that these prices are paid in the full expectation of no falling off. Strangers cannot be accomodated, more than one half of them, with lodging. The Restaurants will feed all at from 37 cts. to $8 per meal, but not lodge, so that the floors of near every house in the city are nightly strewed with travellers.

Tents are necessarily resorted to & are used by at least one half the population. It is computed that there are here about 400 houses enclosed & covered with wood, about 400 enclosed & covered with canvass, & about 800 tents. Merchandise at retail generally sells verry high, & at wholesale on an average as low as in our eastern cities. There are here several Wholesale Auction Stores where whole Cargoes are disposed of as with us. There has been several Cargoes of Chinese goods sold at verry low prices. The sum of the whole matter is that labour & all things necessarily produced, manufactured or grown here, & real estate Commands high prices, also luxuries that are scarce. Pine apples bring from 4 to $8—Good oranges 50 cts.—Potatoes 10 cts. ea., Onions 35 cts., & flour $7 per bbl. Of importations all goods not verry perishable in first hands sell at verry fair prices.

The City is humming with business & industry, the carpenter's hatchet & saw constantly fills the ear from the first dawn of day till dark, & reminds me of an immense copper & tin manufactory. The streets are filled with men, merchandise & wild looking Indians. There are not warehouses sufficient to hold half the goods & consequently enclosed lots are stacked full of barrels & boxes. Money here seems to be of little value, & every person has plenty, none complains of the high prices but the newcomer. A placer of Gold exists at the head of the streets, & it is washed down by the rain & cleaned by the wind. Scales can now be picked up in almost any of the streets (where there is a small drift of coarse sand or gravel) in limited quantities. From 3 to $5[.]oo worth can be easily gathered per day, but this will not pay the enterprizing gold hunter, & you will see but few gathering it, unless for curiosity as a specimen to send home. The Gov. gathered some, a part of which I enclosed in a letter & sent home to wife.[1] The city is infested with Gamblers, & they seem to be rapidly on the increase; about 30 of these creatures came up with us, & are already establishing themselves, having rented rooms & commenced operating. They succeed well, & many have already amassed immense sums of money & wisely retired. The heaviest rents in the City are paid by them.

Sunday, 17th. We arose early this morning, & were ready at the appointed hour for our departure, 8 oclock. Our boatmen disap-

---

[1]The presence of particles of gold in the streets of San Francisco is also mentioned in the San Francisco *Alta California,* May 16, 1849; Bayard Taylor, *Eldorado, or, Adventures on the Path of Empire* . . . (New York, 1850), I, 60-61; and Frank Soulé, John H. Gihon, and James Nisbet, *The Annals of San Francisco* . . . (New York, 1855), pp. 417-418. The consensus was that these were the leakings from miners' bags and the sweepings of stores and bars. Possibly to a very minor extent they were small nuggets from native earth. In 1850 gold was found in the sand brought up from deep wells sunk in San Francisco.

pointed us in making an early start. We did not get off untill 12. The wind at this hour was blowing verry considerably, & the bay was consequently verry rough for a craft so small as the whale boat. We put out in splendid style, & made rapid sailing, but by the time we were fairly out, the wind had much increased, & the bay became verry rough, & our situation quite dangerous. Our vessel leaked considerably, which with the regular dashing in of the waves, kept the Gov. constantly & laboriously engaged in bailing out the water. He was literally drenched with water. Our situation was so dangerous that we were compelled to sit & take it. It continued this way untill we entered the bay of [San Pablo] where we got along better. We arrived at the City of Benecia a little before sunset, distance 40 miles.

This is a beautiful location for a city, has an excellent landing, vessels of the largest class coming in boldly to the shore. It has also an excellent harbor. I think it will become a place of considerable importance. We here have a splendid view of Mount Diablo rearing his majestic peak high above the surrounding mountains. There are 3 boats in our company, & Barnett, not getting upon our boat, is behind us, the bay being so rough she has been unable to get along. We saw them land, & feel verry uneasy about their safety, knowing they would make another effort.

Monday, 18th. We waited until 9 oclock for the boat on which Barnett was, & they not coming, we again pulled out & were soon upon Suisson Bay. We see many seals swimming here. They look much like dogs swimming in the water, as they swim mostly with their heads out of the water. We had smooth water in crossing this Bay, & consequently had some comfort.

Wednesday, 20th. This evening we all landed at Sacramento City. A portion of us, leaving the boat at Webster, walked across the plain to Sutter's celebrated Fort, distance 7 miles. We found the passage here verry unpleasant on account of millions of mosquitoes that constantly kept us uneasy day & night.

Thursday, 21st. We remained here all day to determine what to do, & this afternoon a company of us concluded to buy a Whale boat & make for Yuba river. We paid for it $190—& start early in the morning.

Friday, 22d June. We arose early this morning, & find John [Harding] missing. He concluded I suppose he could do better.

Sunday, 24th. We arrived this afternoon at Capt. Sutter's Hock farm, where we found the Capt. He is a clever fellow & verry hospitable; his wine was most excellent.

Monday, 25th. We sold our Boat to the Capt. for $300—& contracted with him to haul us to the Yuba River, for $10 per hundred lbs.

Tuesday, 26th. This day brought us to the first Gold diggins. We are left upon the top of the mountain in full view of the river dashing along below us among the rocks. We all went down to see the Gold, but alas! we could find but little; returned & slept on the summit.

Wednesday, 27th. We commenced early this morning moving our plunder down the mountain, by cutting branches of trees & placing our goods upon them & hauling them down. By noon we completed the job & dined under a widespreading oak. We here find an Englishman, who hails from Chili, with a Company of Chilians, mining. His partner, a Chilian, is on the North fork near Foster's bar, with most of their company, & they all expect to move as soon as possible, considering the digging here exhausted. Our Company now consists of thc Gov., Barnett, Riva, a young Spaniard, Doct. Weeks & myself, & attached to us are Mr. C. Gilman & Son from Baltimore, the head of a Company of 37 coming around the Horn, Mr. Fisher also the head of another of [blank in MS] coming around, & a Mr. Dahl, an acquaintance of Fisher's.

We all went to work panning, & fixing up our machine. We gathered verry [little] gold this day, & conclude tomorrow to cross the river & try what can be done there, our neighbour offering us his rope to cross upon.

Thursday, June 28th. We have crossed the river & find more earth to work & conclude tomorrow to move all our goods across & pitch our tent. We have gathered verry little Gold.

Friday, 29th. To day we spent in moving & fixing up our tent, & gathered verry little of the Stuff.

Saturday, 30th. A portion of us concluded to go down the river to day to Foster's Bar, and see what chance would be for us there, & to see how they work, & how their diggins look. The distance by the river [is] 2 miles, but over the mountain near 5. I returned late nearly worn out with fatigue &c. but learned something of the manner of working. This place is considered verry rich, & has 10 or 15 tents, which entitles it to the name of the Town. The Gov. & Fisher remained to procure horses to make the northern exploration.

Sunday, July 1st. To day we kept quiet & laid about our tent.

Monday, 2d. We found a washing machine buried in the sand left by an Oregonian, whilst he made some explorations. We dug it up & commenced work with it, but got but little.[2]

Tuesday, 3d. Doct. Weeks & Dahl left us to day for good, disgusted with Gold digging. The Gov., Mr. Fisher & Gilman left to day, to explore the northern branches of this river.

Sunday, 8th. We used the machine some & panned some up to this time & gathered about 6 oz. We became satisfied we could do little without the machine, & to day the Oregonian came after it. He proposed to sell it & to take $100 for it rather than pack it up the river. He took a great fancy to a Gun of the Gov. which we sold him for $50 —& a pair of Horse pistols for $50—with which we paid for the machine.

Saturday, 14th. Our Company now consists of Barnett, Riva, a young Spaniard, & Young Gilman. During this week about 40 Chilians landed on the opposite side, & are busy at work. We washed out Gold enough the first day to pay for our machine. We have gathered this week—

[2]The "washing machine" was doubtless a "rocker" or "cradle" such as was introduced into the California mines in the summer of 1848. It consisted of a long box, without a top and open at one end, mounted on rockers. Cleats were nailed to the bottom and a sieve or hopper was attached to the head. Auriferous "dirt" was poured into the sieve, through which the sand and smaller stones went to the bottom of the rocker. Water was also bailed into the hopper, and this carried the dirt along the length of the box, the heavier gold being caught by the cleats, and the lighter sand being carried by the water out the open end. The contrivance was kept in motion on its rockers during the whole process in order to expedite the settling of the gold. See Rodman Wilson Paul, *California Gold: The Beginning of Mining in the Far West* (Cambridge, Mass., 1947), pp. 52-53.

R[iva], B[arnett] & I,	21 [oz.]	10 dwt.	08 gr.[3]
Gathered last week & before	04.	12.	16.

Saturday, 21st. The Gov. & party returned during the week & left again on Yesterday to visit Nye's ranch & to explore the Southern branches. Our place for working has given out & to day we have done no work.

We went up the river to drive off some Chilians & an Englishman & take their place as they claimed too much ground, but we considered it too poor to make a fuss about. To day I hired a couple of Sailors to work on the halves, named [blank in MS] Banks & Wm. Collins. John Simmons came on Sat. [blank in MS] last, & commenced working with us on Monday. We gathered this week—

R[iva], B[arnett], S[immons] & I on Mond. & Tuesd. Th. & F. 13.02.00
B[arnett], S[immons] & I—Wed.   3.15.00
                                                                        ──────
                                                                       16.17.00

Monday, 23d. Simmons left yesterday & took Dr. Weeks's plunder.

Saturday, 28th. The Gov. returned on Wednesday, & reported the lower rivers good but mostly filled up with miners. He returned alone, & reported having seen John Harding on Mormon Island, & that he was sick & verry anxious to return, saying he did not intend to leave us &c. & that he was now on his way here. He arrived on Friday, & truly in a bad condition, dirty, ragged & sick. We worked hard this week & got almost no gold. It seems the ground here is not worth working & to day we done nothing. We have reports of verry rich dry diggins about 3 leagues from here, & are determined to find them. A Chilian who has been there proposed to guide our neighbour chilian there, & the Gov. & Riva accompanies him. They left here this afternoon.

Sailor B[anks] & I this week—   7 oz.   1 dwt.   16 gr.

Sunday, 29th. To day we spent entirely in camp, discouraged & anxious for the report of dry diggins. This evening our Yankee neighbours came over to get their week's gatherings weighed, & it amounted to over 1 oz. per day for each man, there being 3 of them in Company.

---

[3]The measures of gold used by Osbun were: oz. (ounces), which consisted of 20 pennyweights or 430 grains; dwt. (pennyweights), which consisted of 24 grains; gr. (grains).

We found they had been digging on a bar on the opposite side about 1½ miles up the river. They tell us there is plenty of room for us if we wish to go up there. We have concluded to go up.

Monday, 30th. My Journal since I left San Francisco up to this time has been made up from memory, not having an opportunity at first to write, & afterward, busy & tired, & of course many incidents [are] left out that would be interesting, & that I should have desired to record.

To day the sailors, Barnett & self packed up our tools & cradle, crossed the river & moved for the rocky bar. We took also a kettle & some beans to boil for Dinner. We made a location, & went to work & soon found we had chosen a rich spot. The Gold glittered in every shovel full, which, by the bye, it does not do unless the spot is rich. We worked on in fine spirits, boiled our beans, & ate our dinner with a fine relish, having nothing else. Another Company of our neighbours finding out the luck, went up & located close beside us. There were 3 of them, & they with their cradle gathered only about 1 oz. The Co. below of 3 gathered about 1½ oz. In the Co. of our near neighbour is a Tailor who gave out & went to camp. He will soon be a candidate for San Francisco. Gathered 4 of us—8 oz. 10 dwt. S[immons], B[arnett] & [I].

Tuesday, 31st. Arose before day light, got our breakfasts & put off to our bar. We worked verry hard. My labour however being light, viz., panning & boiling the beans, I did not tire so much, but one of our Sailors, Banks, at noon gave out & hoisted sail for San Francisco, saying he could not stand the hot sun & the turning of the rocks. I left after dinner, went to camp, & settled with him & he put off in fine humor wishing us luck & fair winds. Banks being a Gunsmith, he concluded he would rather work at his trade. The other one, Collins, would not go, but remains with us. One of our Neighbours, a Ship builder, has also given out & goes with Banks. Yesterday 2 others left, sick of mining. Gathered 4 of us in forenoon 2 oz. in all during the day—2 oz. 18 dwts.

Wednesday, August 1st. We were all verry tired & did not get up so early as usual. John Harding is still sick. His disease proves to be ague, with a chill every other day; he is taking Quinine & has missed his chill to day.

35

12 new Chilians arrived last evening. The sun now beams down upon us verry hot, & were it not for a breeze that gets up every day, I do think we could not stand it. Every tent as far as I know up & down has more or less sickness, & all produced by this hot sun, working with feet & legs in the water & the sun striking down upon the head. We dined again to day on Beans, & burnt at that; they were hard to take. I left the diggins at noon expecting the Gov's return, it being our calculation to move from this place immediately after. But he did not arrive. I employed my time getting tea, & fixing up things for a move. This has been a poor day's work & we do not work with spirit, gathered 3 of us—1 oz. 18 dwts.

Thursday, 2d. John and I went to river this morning & washed out the dirty bags & dish cloths preparing for a move. I concluded not to mine to day, but to employ myself around the camp, thinking that the Gov. will certainly return during the day. Game here is very scarce; we have searched several times & killed nothing but one Hare; it was verry good. The mountains are covered with a species of Wolf that some nights ring with their howl.[4] We see their tracks every morning close to our tents. Poisonous Insects are scarce; I have seen but one Centipede. We have caught 3 scorpions in our tent among the cloathes; they are small & not worse in their sting than a Hornet. I have seen but few snakes, not as many as at home, & they were water & Garter snakes. I understand there are some Rattle snakes seen, but few however. Lizards of all sizes are verry numerous, but harmless. They are running around us & in our Tent & over the table all the time. We pay no more attention to them than to the flys. There is a verry large species of ground Squirrel here, about the size & the same appearance of our Grey Squirrel.

About 9 oclock the whole party returned, & reported the diggins much better above on this river, & that it would be better for us to move up as soon as possible. The dry diggins they went in search of all turned out a hoax.

They brot extravagant reports of the amt. gathered above, & we shall now think of nothing else than getting there as soon as possible. A Yankee by name Geo. Champlain joined work at the machine. He belonged to a party who came out 3 weeks [ago] & are now about dissolving, not being able to do any good together. Our Sailor came to

[4]Coyotes probably are the animals described.

tent this evening verry sick with a high fever. I gave him a dose of Calomel. Collected to day 4 oz. 2 dwt.

Friday, Aug. 3d. Our Sailor is verry sick this morning & unable to work. I went up & worked one half the day, & in the evening our neighbours the Yankees all left for Sacramento. The Gov. concluded to go with them, & to go on to San Francisco, & meet our men. We also concluded to hire a dozen Chilians & employed our neighbour Chilian to get them for us at Sacramento, where he will be in 2 or 3 days, & the conclusion arrived at is for the Gov. to buy provisions there & an extra horse if one can be had at fair price, & send them up by the Chilians & as soon as they arrive all to leave for diggins about 25 miles up.

The Gov. was not verry well when he left, & I feel verry uneasy about him. I feel this evening like having the blues, for the first since I left home. The Spaniard Riva has left & gone to packing.

Collected to day, having worked only one half day, Barnett & self, 2 oz. 18 dwt.

Saturday, 4th. Barnett & myself have to work alone; John considers himself too weak to work, & our Sailor is still verry sick. I gave him an emetic this evening, he having had a high fever all day. Being alone we did not work hard tho I am to night verry tired. We commence work about ½ past 5, & work to 11 or 12, & then rest to about 4, & work till near sundown. We collected 3 oz. 8 dwt.

Sunday, 5th. Our Sailor is some better this morning, & has continued to improve all day. John is also improving, & will soon be ready to work. We spent the day in camp resting ourselves.

Monday, 6th. Barnett & myself were up this [morning] in good time, got our breakfast early, & were off to work. We worked the machine alone & did verry well altho we could not keep it running but a portion of the time, having the digging & carrying of the dirt to do. We both narrowly escaped being either crushed or badly hurt by the slide & falling down of a large [rock] to just where we were working. I had been setting down, bailing out water from our hole, & had just risen up & taken 2 or 3 steps, when I was nearly knocked down by Barnett; the rock striking him, knocked him against me & aligh[t]ed

37

just where I was setting. Our day's work of gold was setting upon this rock, & it was spilled. We however collected nearly all again. We collected to day 4 oz. 13 dwt.

Tuesday, 7th. The wolves kept up last night a most tremendous howling all around us; a dead Horse has lodged in the river near us, which makes fine food for them. Barnett & I collected 5 oz. 2 dwt.

Wednesday, 8th. Having worked out our old places, & not being able to find a rich new one, we concluded this morning to move down to camp our tools &c. & spend our time in preparation to move, as our horses & provisions might arrive by tomorrow evening. And after they arrive we do not wish to be detained here one hour longer than necessary. Our machine is verry heavy, & rather too much for 2 to carry tho our Sailors carried it up. Barnett & I concluded to put it into the river & float it down, & when it arrived swim over with the rope, & haul it to the tent side.

I tied a long rope to it & undertook to hold to it, but the rapid current took it faster than I was able to run, & tore it from me, upset [it] & off it went. Such a race I never had before over the rocks; lower down, the current lessened, & I overtook it just in time to save it from passing over the falls at the camp, which if it had passed, it would have been lost. I hauled it ashore with a long pole & tied it up. We then returned & finished the move. This night we are both more than usually tired. Our neighbours consisting of 7 or 8 tents are all now preparing to leave, some [for] home & others for the diggins up the river. A good many are sick. I am giving medicine to 5, all chills & fever. John is now beginning to do some little turns & he eats like a horse. Our Sailor has missed his chill to day. We gathered before we moved this morning—11 dwts.

Thursday, 9th. We this day put in our time at the tent, Barnett at work at repairing up a cradle & I assisting a little.

Young Gilman & myself concluded to watch for wolves, & kill one. We sat up about ¾ hour, & concluded to quit it & go to bed, none making their appearance.

Friday, 10th. I spent one half this day in mending my pants & Boots. I find I can get along pretty well at it. Barnett has put in order

2 machines that I bought from the Yankees, for which I paid $5 each.

Saturday, 11th. Barnett & myself concluded it would not do to be altogether idle. Our men & Horses & provisions not arriving last evening as we confidently expected, we shouldered our cradle & worked a few hours & got as we considered poorly paid for our labour. The diggins here in the present stage of the water are entirely worked out at the present value of labor. We collected 15 dwt.

Sunday, 12th. Five of our neighbours, Yankees & Chilians, left on Friday evening for the up River. We spent the evening seeing them off. Poor fellows they had their own troubles with their packs & horses, getting up the mountain.

Our men, horses & provisions have not yet arrived, & we are getting verry impatient to be off. News from above is verry flattering, gathering from 2 to 5 oz. each daily, & we here doing what we consider nothing. This morning Barnett & I took a stroll up the ravine & killed a Hare. Young Gilman followed soon after, & seeing me sitting at a distance upon a rock, took me to be a Bear; he ran back with great speed, alarmed the camp, & armed with Guns, Pistols & knives he & Jno. Harding hastened back for an attack. They met us & told what he had seen. We went back to the spot & discovered his mistake. His faith was so strong in what he had seen that he would have fired his gun but was afraid to do it when alone.

To day our Sailors cooked up the Hare into a most excellent pot pye, & I believe I never relished a meal more. It made 5 of us 2 good meals.

Monday, 13th. We all concluded to work a little to day. Jno. & I took our pans & tried a while & gathered 5 dwts. Barnett & Collins the Sailor cradled out 1 oz. 17 dwts.

This evening we have been verry pleasantly entertained by a couple of young Indians; they speak a little Spanish, & we could thus understand them. They sang many songs for us & cut up many of their anticks. We gave them some bread & they gave us what Gold they had —$1 in value. I came across a Rattle snake to day, the first we have seen in this country, & I was verry near being bitten by it. I had my hands within 2 inches of his head, lifting away stone, several times before I discovered him. He moved slowly off & then coiled himself up for fight. Jno. & I soon despached him; he was spotted & had 7 rattles.

Tuesday, 14th. Our horses are not yet here, & we scarcely know what we ought to do. We promised to wait for their return, & they promised not to be absent longer than 6 days. We are here doing no good, whilst good diggins are unworked above us. Barnett suffers most; his impatience almost uses him up.

Jno. has worked alone & gathered—	07 dwts	— grs.
Barnett & sailor in forenoon	18	—
Barnett & Self in afternoon; sailor not well	04.	12.

Wednesday, 15th. Our men & provisions not arriving last night or today, our impatience overcame us & we this afternoon made an effort to get other Horses & leave tomorrow if possible. Young Gilman & my-self got an interpreter & went up the river about 2 miles to the camp of a Peruvian, & got the promise of 3 horses as soon as they were re-turned, being hired to a company that went from here last week. He looked for them hourly. We baked bread & fixed up, & are now ready to start at a moment's warning.

Barnett & the sailor gathered before breakfast, & then quit—

	1 dwt.
John hung on to it untill noon & got	5 dwts.

Thursday, 16th. Our Yankee neighbours returned at noon to day, with the horses; one of them having a verry sore back was pronounced unfit for use. I returned it & got another in its place, & tomorrow we expect to leave this place. We have agreed with 4 of our neighbours that they occupy ½ of 1 horse & go with us, 3 of them, 1 to return with the horses, so we get clear of that job. We pay $25 ea. for the horses for the trip.

Friday, 17th. Got up early, & labored hard to get off. About 11 oclock we brot up our Horses, packed on our loads, & such a time I never before experienced. Between kicking mares & bad loading, none of us having ever before loaded a pack horse, I thought we never would get up the mountain, & we had finally to pack a part of our Cargo on our own backs. After going a short distance we were compelled to leave a bag of rice & hulled wheat; we hung it up in the fork of a tree expecting to get it some time. After loading & unloading 3 or 4 times we succeeded in overcoming this mountain. We travelled this day from 8 to 10 miles & camped in a beautiful spot, along side of a most excellent spring. Here we found a dwarf species of wild Cherry, most excellent. We spread our blankets upon the ground & rested untill morning, being much disturbed during the night with the noise of wild animals. I slept but little, tho I arose much refreshed in the morning.

Saturday, 18th. Arose verry early & was off by sun up. We had another hard day with our horses. Two of them gave out & we were compelled to lay bye a part of the day. Barnett killed a hare, which we cooked for supper, & fared richly upon it. He also killed or wounded fatally a deer, but being far behind us he could not detain to get it, knowing also that our horses were unable to carry it.

We succeed in reaching the river about sun down. Bought a loaf of bread from an Oregon family located at the mouth of the creek, for which we paid $6.75—being 75 cts. per lb. Our horses were so tired that we did not leave here untill after dinner. We then packed up, after leaving a portion of our loading, for Wambos bar, & travelled 6 miles to a run where we camped for the night. One of our horses gave out entirely, & we were compelled to leave it on the road side & go on ourselves to water. This has been another severe afternoon's work for us all.

Monday, 20th. Four of us got up Early & went back for the worn out horse & baggage. After hunting her for some time we found her standing in the woods. Still verry weak, we carried about half her load & came back to tent & found all gone. We followed & arrived at the top of the hill near noon. We remained there untill evening & sent back our horses. This evening we loaded up ourselves & made the descent to the river, & such a descent I never before made, over stones & slate & sliding earth. In about 1 hour we reached the bottom. This I consider the greatest feat I ever performed in the way of descending a precipice. We carried each about 40 to 60 lbs. of baggage & provisions. We find our old yankee neighbours here doing well, gathering about 3 oz. ea. per day, panning.

Tuesday, 21st. We all started up the hill this morning for another load, & about half way up met 2 Chilians with letters from Mr. Shannon & Riva, & having brot up a horse & mule to us. This was provoking, & particularly as they led them both up without a load. Mr. Shannon requested me to have a letter by all means at Sacramento on his return, & Riva stated the company had arrived at San Francisco &

41

would be there in a few days. He gave no reason for detaining the Horses, but we understood from the Chilians that Mr. Luco was sick, & had sent up for all his men & intended to quit mining. We had now been deceived by Spaniards twice & much injured, & I think we will not be so again.

Knowing the Horse & mule would be needed to pack & also that Mr. Shannon would be verry anxious to see me, I at once concluded to start back immediately with them & meet him. We all took down our loads, & I returned in the evening to start & to get out far enough for grass & water. I travelled 3 miles & lay alone in the grass wrapped up in my blanket with my saddle for a pillow. The road from below here is through mountains, covered about half the way with heavy timber, Pine, Fir & Cedar, some of the finest timber I ever saw, but so located as to be useless. The road or trail cannot be complained much of except the mountains at the crossings of the river.

Wednesday, 22d. I eat no supper last night, & arose early, saddled my horse & started, & travelled 6 miles to the crossings & at the mouth of the creek got my breakfast at an Oregon tent, & bought some bread for my supper to night. To day the mule gave out, & I could not get it along. It proved to be verry worthless; Riva bought it for us, & we fear he has not done right by us. I stopped to night at the spring we lay at the first night going up. Having no ma[t]ches, I slept up a deep hollow without fire, & made my supper & dinner of Sweetened water & a little bread. I have had a hard day, getting along the broken down mule.

Thursday, 23d. I arose by the break of day, & started about 10 A.M. I arrivd at Rose's bar a few miles below our old place, & got my breakfast from another Oregon Lady & I eat it with great relish. It was a little extra: warm bread, molasses, tea, pepper sauce & pickles. A meal costs $1.50. I did expect to find the company here, as I saw a person a few miles back who saw them in Sacramento on Friday, & they stated they would leave in a day or two & in 3 or 4 days be at Rose's bar. Not being here & no feed for horses, I started on, & met them about half way on the road to Johnson's Ranch. There we had a happy meeting. None of them knew me. My beard had grown verry long, & my cloathes much worn & dirty, even ragged, a check shirt, & tin buckled around me. I suppose I did not look much like myself but they were equally changed in appearance being verry dirty & much tanned, with long beards. The company were not all here, having left Wm. Shannon at San Francisco, to look after the freight, & Huchinson at Sacramento, sick with dysentery & Johnson to attend him. Motte was behind, stopped to rest at Johnson's, his feet being verry sore. We travelled on & camped within a few miles of our old ground.

Friday, 24th. To day we concluded to go to the old camp & leave half of the men & Mr. Shannon there to work, & I to take on 7 to the slate bar & investigate it fully, & return the mules & report the propriety of all going up. We made it about noon. I here ascertained the Horses I hired had not yet been returned & the person who started back had not been heard from. What the result will be is now doubtfull as we are bound for their return.

Saturday, 25th. This forenoon our men tried their skill in washing gold & got along verry well. I went up to the rock bar & showed them the places I considered best to work, & after dinner we saddled 6 mules & 1 horse, loaded them with provisions &c. & about 4 oclock mounted the hill in fine style, o[u]r mules proving themselves to be fine packers. We got along with but little trouble. We travelled untill 9 oclock to make good grass & water. We travelled from 8 to 10 miles, it being to the same place we tented the first night on our first trip.

Sunday, 26th. We travelled until noon to day & then turned out our mules to pasture & remained untill morning. We stopped at a most delightful spot, where there was an excellent spring & plenty of grass, both difficult things to find here. We had a fine pot pie for dinner prepared from a Hare shot by Mulvaney. Stelle & myself took a stroll during the evening & found several springs & some grape vines with green grapes upon them, verry common.

Monday, 27th. We stopped at noon to day within 4 miles of camp several hours to give our animals an opportunity to fill themselves with grass, as none can be had there for them. We arrived at the top of the hill about sun down, tied up our horses & each took a load & made the descent. It was long after night when we came into camp & all in bed. Several of our men came near giving out in the descent & would have been verry willing to lie down on the path & slept untill morning. Several of them got off the road & wandered deep down into the valley & with much labor got back into the road again.

43

Tuesday, 28th. Our men brot down to day the provisions, & I employed myself in investigating the diggins above & below, & find that we can do nothing here. Every spot is occupied for a cradle, & the panning has been carried to such an extent that scarcely any is left. We are all much discouraged with the prospect here, & have determined to send back the mules in the morning, & inform the Gov. & tell him to hunt other diggins.

Wednesday, 29th. This morning Mulvany & Castle started back with the mules, & left the Horse to rest, he being much worn down, being on the run constantly since his purchase. About ½ oz. was collected today.

Thursday, 30th. To day Barnett & myself prospected up the river above the fork, having went up about 6 or seven miles & found nothing worth going up for. After my return I went up the hill to send out to a corrall the horse but could not find him, not going to the right place, so I had my trip for nothing & the poor horse has to do without water untill morning. This evening a poor old ox was killed, & we got some of him. I paid $2.50 for half the liver, & 50 cts. per lb. for the meat. All still discouraged, tho we try to be cheerfull. Got about as much as yesterday. We have here now, of our home company, Barnett, Steel, Lacey, Wheeler, Jelley, & Booker; also attached Harding, Collins & Beaumont, & man from Wisconsin, who joined our company yesterday for one year. There is also with us young Gilman, & the 2 Irishmen still staying & working on their own account.

Friday, 31st. Collins has had a return of ague & [has] not worked any for several days. Lacey is to day quite sick with dystentery, & confined to camp during the afternoon. I tramped up the hill again, found the Horse & sent him out to grass. We are still doing but little, & wish to leave.

Saturday, Sept. 1st. I took another tramp down the river, to hunt a place to work, but can find none better than the slate bar. Yesterday the men went up the river 1 mile & worked but to day are again upon the slate. Lacey is verry sick to day. Beaumont left this morning for the south fork to get his clothing, & to remain permanently. Lacey is much worse.

Tuesday, 4th. Got word to day to return to the old camp, that some of our men were sick.

Wednesday, 5th. Sent for my horse, & all concluded to return. I bought a yoke of Oxen & a waggon from a Mr. Brown, who joins our company. He & 2 of his brothers joins us, & adds a yoke of oxen to our team. It is our intention to bring the Company to the Oregon tent at the mouth of the creek, where provisions can be had at a cheaper rate, & there remain untill the train arrives to take us away.

Thursday, 6th. This morning we commenced early to pack up our baggage to the top of the mountain. By noon we have each taken up one load, averaging in weight about 40 lbs. We dined below, & immediately afterwards packed the balance on our backs & started; it takes about 1¼ hours to make the ascent. This has been for us all a verry hard day's work but by 3 oclock we had our two yoke of oxen hiched up & our baggage on the waggon, & ready for a start. Our company now consists of the 4 Wisconsonians, & 9 others beside myself with from 10 to 1200 lbs. baggage. The road has never been travelled by a waggon; we consequently will have the honor of making the first waggon road here, & which the Browns are fully capable of doing. Our horse is not to be found to day. I consequently must stay behind & assist hunting him. The Indian who herds him is out hunting for him, & if he does not bring him in, I must tomorrow assist. About 4 oclock all were on the road but myself.

Friday, 7th. This day I spent in hunting for the Horse, & travelled many miles over the mountains & across vallies in the neighbourhood of the corrall, but have not found him. The Indian got badly kicked by a mule to day & could not hunt much, so they think he might still be in the neighborhood. Tomorrow Mr. Goodyear, the proprietor of the corrall, promises to hunt himself with another Indian boy, & if he can be found to leave him with a Mr. Wright here or another friend, who will convey him to us, either at Johnson's Ranch or Rose's bar.

Saturday, 8th. I procured a mule, & started early this morning for the balance of the company, & found them all landed safe at the bar. They sold the oxen & waggon, & packed our baggage across the River. There I remained untill after dinner & put off for the lower diggins, Steele, Gilman, Booker, Collins, & Wheeler accompanying me. We travelled 6 miles & camped in the sweet spring valley, the same spot we camped at on going up, during the Sabbath. We found other companies here, also camping for the night, on their way up hunting for the upper diggins.

Sunday, 9th. We started early, & travelled with but few stoppings & soon after the middle of the day arrived at camp. And here we found our company engaged in the solemn service of burying one of our company. Young Gilleland took sick soon after I left, with dysentery, & grew regularly worse until he died. Poor fellow, he is perhaps only the *first* one from our company destined to leave his bones in this distant land, & hard to tell who will next follow him. He died last evening a little before 12 oclock.

I find Ibbotson & Jones both sick & confined to camp. Mr. Shannon & Mulvaney are both absent; they left here on Saturday week for Sacramento City, & are expected every hour. Poor Gilleland was buried on the left bank of the Iuba on an elevated flat of ground, a little above the grave of an old American who died & was buried here since our arrival. This spot is just below the rocky bar.[5]

[5]The following accounts, written in pencil on a flyleaf at the end of the book, may belong to about this time:

Copy of Settlement with C. Gilman

July 3d. 1849				
	31 days			
Aug. — 20		51	@ $2	102.00
"	11			
Sept. 9		20	$3	60.00
"		9	$2	18.00
		Pan		8.00
		Pick		4.00
		Horse hired		12.50
		Freight		8.00
				152.50
		off ft —		4.00
				148.50
Cr Ry Quinian [?]		40		40.00
6¾ oz & 50				

The following account appears in ink on the next page:

John Harding has gathered			oz. dwt.
August 28th Tuesday to this date			10.06
Tuesday 28th this day	2.16		4.04
	1.8		
	.18		
Wed. 29 " "	——		0.18
Th. 30			0.19
F. 31			0.16
Sept. 1			1.16
Sick	13.00		——
Sept. 5 Gathered	1.00.00		1.13.00	1.08.12.00
at Oregon tent			1.07.02

Wednesday, 12th. Ibbotson & Jones have gradually improved since my arrival. I found them greatly in need of medicine. About noon I recieved a letter from the Gov., directed to poor Gilleland (not knowing I was here), informing the Company here of the death of another of the Company, Huchison. He died in Sacramento, on the Saturday after they left, which would be on 25th. The letter was written by a Mr. Giffen, by the direction of Mr. Shannon; it informed us also that the Gov. & Mulvaney were both sick with chills & fever in Sacramento. This was sorrowful news indeed to us all. It spread quite a gloom over the Company. We continued all quite depressed untill evening, when to our great Joy the team arrived, & with it Wm. Shannon, Mr. Vandiver of N. York, & Mulvaney. They brot a letter to me giving me a full description of our future operations & intentions. The team has taken two loads to Specks at the mouth of Feather river, & deposited them there. The Gov., not being yet able to travel, will meet us all there as soon as we can make the trip. Our future operations are to collect the whole company immediately at the mouth of Feather river, & from there proceed without delay to the head water of [the] Sacramento, a distance of 200 miles, & to mine both on the Sacramento & the Trinity.[6]

Friday [*Thursday*], *13th*. About noon to day we started Booker & Thrasher with 5 mules to the upper camp for the balance of our Co. & tools. Ground for working on is getting scarce here, & we have concluded to commence moving tomorrow to the top of the Mountain, so as to be ready to start immediately on their arrival.

Friday, 14th. Early this morning we commenced our move, by packing up the mountain our goods on our backs. Ibbotson & Jones have continued to improve slowly, & by bringing a mule to the brink of the bank we have been enabled to get them to the top of the hill. By noon we had all things up & putting them on the waggon we pushed it about ¾ of a mile to the creek & there encamped on a delightful spot. We had just completed all our camp arrangements, & were preparing supper, when Barton came into camp carrying a fine Hare. He was hailed as soon as he came into sight with loud cheering, all expecting now a pot pye. He threw it down, & dryly informed us he had

---

[6]For the period from this point until January 1850 considerable additional data on the experiences of the Shannon Party are to be found in the letters beginning on p. 189.

killed either 2 or 3 Antelope, he did not know which. His manner was so free from excitement, he was scarcely believed; however a number of the Co. went out with him & in a short time returned with 2 fine deer; a buck & a doe, suspended under a pole on their shoulders. The hides were soon off, & a part of them in the pans for supper. Our sick men improved much to day, altho much fatigued by their trip.

Saturday, 15th. Our Camp to day presents quite a cheerful appearance, its location being delightfull, & under the spreading branches [of] a verry large Oak. On its limbs hang two fine deer, that make the mouths of the numerous passers by water. This place is becoming a popular route for emigrants, crossing the plains, & to day we have seen a great number of emigrants pass, & among them many females. They travel with Ox teams, many waggons having from 4 to 5 Yoke of them. About dark our men arrived from the upper Camp.

Sunday, 16th. This morning we arose before day, & were off before breakfast, our mules having but little to eat. We travelled only about 8 miles & camped on the plain where we had good grass.

Monday, 17th. We arrived at Johnson's ranch about 11 oclock. Purchased some provisions, & camped on Bear Creek about 4 miles below. We here came across David Hilligas, who was verry anxious to join our company. I proposed to him to come with us to Fremont, & when we would see the Gov., we could probably make some arrangement with us; he thereupon joined us. Barnett shot to day a verry fine half grown deer which we eat at one meal.

3

SACRAMENTO RIVER

◎

Tuesday, 18th [September]. We to day passed Nicholas ranch before noon & arrived at Fremont about the middle of the afternoon. The Gov. is not here; we find word sent us to remain untill he comes, that he has gone to San Francisco, & no time set for his arrival. We went up the Sacramento & camped about ¼ mile. News here is good of the diggins above & diggers are beginning to move in that direction rapidly. I find Dr. Weeks here practicing medicine & say he is doing verry well. I was called upon by Old Greenwood to day, who camped 3 miles above, for medicine for himself & one of his company. This Greenwood is an old mountain trapper, has been in this country & rocky mountains 43 years, & figured largely as a guide & interpreted among the Indians. He tells me he speaks 10 or 12 different languages, has had 6 Indian wives & verry many children. His last wife is dead, & [he] has 3 of his children with him, 2 verry small. The old man is nearly burnt out with liquor, & confesses freely his drinking propensity. He is verry anxious to get something to make him quit it. This man has ague for which I administred, & also gave the old man an emetic & some eye water. He presented us with a fine mess of fat veal which he had just killed & was jerking.

Wednesday, 19th. This morning several of our Company went down to Sacramento City to attend to different little matters for the Company. We here find the Gov. went to the Coast for his health. And I now feel my duties verry heavy upon my shoulders. This evening Barnett, Castle, Frazier, Motte, Hilligas & myself concluded to have an elk hunt. We brought in 3 mules, packed upon them our blankets, & started for the Tule Swamp, where we arrived sometime after night, it being 5 or 6 miles, & further than we expected. We tied down our mules, [spread] our Blankets, & lay down to sleep untill morning.

49

Thursday, 20th. Last night Barnett & myself lay together & we slept but little. The Elk discovered us, & serenaded us the whole night with the music of their bellowing. About 1 oclock one came verry near us through curiosity. We fired at him, being but 30 steps off, but must have missed as we discovered no blood in the morning. As day light approached we discovered by the sound of their bellowing, they were receding to the swamp. And as soon as we could see the sight upon our guns, we pursued after them. Castle shot a verry large one, a Buck, before he got in. Barnett & I followed the sound far into the swamp & must have killed [one, but did] not succeed in getting any. We must have seen at least 50, standing in & near a pool of water in the centre of the swamp. A large elk is a formidable looking animal; his large antlers reaching high & wide, look as [if] they are mooved about above the rushes like a travelling forest, & I felt almost afraid to shoot at them. Barnett & I pursued the wounded one by the blood for miles through the swamp, but hearing us behind they kept ahead untill we were completely exhausted. We all returned before noon with but one elk, tho much delighted with our hunt. It was not very fat, but eat well. We jerked one hind quarter & still found we had more than we could eat.

Friday, 21st. Ibbotson & Jones have both relapsed & are now quite sick again. Booker & a Mr. Perry, who is travelling up with us, returned this evening from Sacramento & reported our team of oxen on the road & would be here tomorrow. Our company is getting verry impatient at the delay, & are almost unmanageable. I hope the Gov. will soon recruit, & return to us.

Saturday, 22d. About noon to day the team arrived. I started Wm. Shannon this morning to Sacramento to recover the lost mule stolen by a Chilian. He returned about midnight being unable to make it out. Mr. Giffen came with him & reports that he & the Gov. have purchased the Reading ranch, & that he is now ready to pilot us up & conduct us to good diggins. This has given our company new life.

Sunday, 23d. This morning I sent Booker back on the emigrant trail to buy several yoke of Oxen; he returned in the evening having bought 6 yoke & a waggon for $325—but it would not be here untill [illegible word].

Monday, 24th. I bought this morning 2 yoke more of Oxen from J. Frazier which with the 3 brought up from Sacramento makes us have 11 Yoke in all. Some of them are verry poor & weak & we will no doubt have much trouble in getting them to the ranch. We went to work loading our waggons & by noon were ready for a march, having 2 ox teams of 5 Yoke & 1 of 6. Also a team of 6 mules. Our sick men we placed upon a covered waggon, & suppose they will be able to travel in that way without injury. We halted & camped for the night one mile below Knight's ranch on the bank of the river, under the shade of a beautiful grove of Oaks & in the midst of fine grass. About sundown we were all much surprised & delighted by the sudden appearance of the Gov. in our midst. He grew better soon after he left Sacramento, went on to San Francisco, & improved rapidly, soon became impatient to be with us, & travelled with all possible speed by hiring horses untill he came up to us. Now all is right, things will go on better at least with me, the sick will receive more of my attention. They are now however no better & considerably fatigued tho anxious to proceed. Just as the Gov. arrived, Barnett & several others came in with the fattest deer I ever saw, its kidneys being covered deep with fat, & a thick layer between the skin & muscle. It was a black tail. We also shot in camp several partridge.

Tuesday, 25th. To day our distance to travel to the lone tree was 14 miles, but we missed the road & went to Gordon's ranch where we are as far from it as when we started. We encamped beside a small lake, in which were several oxen belonging to travellers, swamped. Our sick men are very much exhausted, & think they can go no further.

Wednesday, 26th. We have to return some miles back upon the same road we travelled yesterday & then cross the plain to the lone tree, & no water on the road. Yesterday we suffered for water much but to day have supplied ourselves better. We found the march verry oppressive & particularly to the sick. Last night Hilligas had a shake of ague, & Castle & Harding are to day taken with Dysentery. We arrived before sundown at the tree. Several of our oxen having given out, from weakness & want of water, we were compelled to turn them out, & drive them on behind.

Thursday, 27th. Our sick men, Ibbotson & Jones, not improving, & Castle & Harding being quite ill, we have concluded to stop them here, untill they recruit. Consequently Nutting was selected with myself to remain. The two yoke of Oxen is also left. It is the intention to return to Fremont & get the cart & as soon as possible proceed on. Either take back a yoke from here or buy others down there. About 3 oclock the balance of the company put off, leaving us behind feeling verry lonesome. We have fixed up our Tent verry comfortable, having covered it with branches of the willow so that it is well shaded & cool even at midday.

Friday, 28th. Castle & Harding are both also verry sick with dysentery. Ibbotson & Jones are improving a little.

Saturday, 29th. Our sick are all improving a little. We find this to be a verry public place; many teams are here every night, it being the only watering place for 16 miles in either direction, & many arrive nearly exhausted for water. This evening Nutting returned to Fremont for our cart, & to purchase more oxen, & as soon as he returns we expect to leave this lonely spot. I am now here with 4 sick companions all depending upon me for food & medicine. I also have the Oxen to look after every morning & evening. This evening several sick persons are here who have called upon me for medicine.

Sunday, 30th. To day I took a walk far up the little valley to look after our oxen, & find it pretty well stocked with grass & they doing verry well, with one exception, he appearing to be verry sick & laying down. To day I had an application to recieve a sick man & take care of him. I thought my charge already heavy enough, & agreed to give him my medical attention, provided they remained to nurse [and that] they did not leave him. One of our neighbors who was out looking for their oxen came in this evening without them, but had the hind quarters of what they called a slow deer, meaning a wild cow. They gave us liberally of it, tho we needed but little. They also brot in an ox they caught among them, which they intend to put into their team, one of theirs having died a few nights ago. They also entered a narrow valley west of us about 8 miles, & found the remains of an old ranch, & saw there 6 verry superior wild horses, one of which, a Stallion, they pronounced the handsomest & best they ever saw.

Monday, October 1st, 1849. Lay about camp all day, excepting looking after the oxen. Castell is much worse, & also Harding. The others are no worse, a slight improvement only.

Tuesday, 2d. We have looked verry anxiously this evening for Nutting's return, but he came not. The sick all better.

Wednesday, 3d. We have walked out frequently & looked far out upon the plain to catch the first glimpse of our team returning, but as yet it has not come. We are getting verry impatient to be off, at least to the first watering place if no farther. Last night our poorest ox drowned in a narrow pool of water. He went in to drink, & could not turn around in the deep water for the rushes, so I found him dead, dead. Our clever neighbours brot in to day a 9 month calf & gave us bountifully of it. They hail from Coshocton, O. I shot a verry fine rabbit by moonlight last night, with which I made a pot [pie].[1]

[*Thursday, 25th.*] . . . but they failed there in getting them over, & had to send them to camp, to be taken below again. I went up to the diggins this evening on Rock Creek, & remained all night.

Friday, 26th. The mules & Horses were taken down 4 or 5 miles, & rode across by Indians, so this morning they all left the river in high spirits.

Thrasher becoming verry sick in the old camp, I had to return to it, at the mouth of Salt Creek, to attend him this evening. About 1 hour after dark Barnett came in quite exhausted & immediately threw himself down in the Tent. I knew instantly from his looks all was not right, & it was some time before I could get the history of his day's adventure. It seems after they left the river they all separated a short distance for the purpose of killing game, intending to be at no time more than 100 yards apart. After they had travelled about 8 or 10 miles, he got from the Company so far he could not find them; he soon became bewildered & did not know which way he should go. Three Indians came up to him naked & wanted his shirt & pants, then his Gun, watch &c. After some time parleying with them, they snached from him my Gold watch he had with him, & his powder horn, & ran off at full speed in different directions. Feeling mortified & angry to be thus robbed by naked savages, & not at all satisfied with seeing the fellow have possession & forever of the watch, he drew up

[1]There is apparently a page missing from the manuscript journal at this point. The entry for Oct. 3 breaks off at the bottom of a page, and another, evidently for Oct. 25, stands in part at the top of the next page. During this period of over three weeks, Osbun moved up the Sacramento River from the camp in the vicinity of the town of Colusa to Reading's Ranch, somewhat above the point where the town of Redding later grew up.

his rifle when about 60 yards off, & gave him its full contents in the back. He fell & with him the watch. He ran up, found the watch lying near, & the Indian struggling in death. He snatched up the watch & made off at full speed. Not knowing which direction to take to meet the company, he struck for the Coast range on this side, & came to the river below the bluffs 4 miles down, waded the riffle & arrived here as above. He states that the Gov. in passing through the brush on the bank of the river from the raft, upon his hands & knees, came suddenly upon a large Grisley Bear [snug] in his bed. Being mutually astonished at each other's presence, they silently agreed that each should take his own course in peace. The Bear walked off calmly to an oak tree in the neighbourhood, & took his mess of acorns, & the Gov. returned as quietly to his camp, where lay his Guns, provisions, bedding &c. dripping in water.

Thursday, Nov. 1st, 1848 [*1849*]. We have continued to work principally upon Rock Creek. Some are beginning to be discontented & talk of returning to Salt Creek.

Sunday, 11th. On last Saturday we concluded to leave the upper Sacramento. Our exploring party had returned a few days previous & had not been able to find Gold on the eastern side of the river. They travelled upon the base of the mountains & examined every creek & gulch to Pitt river, a branch of the Sacramento. They found the valleys & mountains covered with Indians, & all manifested a friendly disposition. They were generally met & escorted into their rancherias, as they approached, but they showed a disposition rather to get them to pass around. They always met them with provisions in abundance, such as Salmon, Baked acorn bread, &c.

At one place, they were addressed by a chief holding in his hand a 3 forked stick with 3 kinds of bread on it, which, when done speaking, he presented to them. They did not understand its meaning.

It commenced raining on Wednesday last, & rained constantly until yesterday; that was Nov. 7th.

Monday, 12th. The rains having fallen to such an extent it rendered the roads impassible, we have concluded to build canoes & a portion of the Co. at least with baggage go down in them. To day we felled two pine trees for the purpose. Nov. 6th we sold out our flour, bread, & every thing we could spare intending to start immediately, but the rains & bad roads prevented us.

Thursday, 15th. Our provisions here are now exhausted; expecting we would have been at least at the ranch before this, we are compelled to buy. We sold our flour at c30, & now we must pay 75. Pork also c75. We purchased $333.75 worth of provisions. My health continues bad, & my spirits are verry low. We live miserably, our tents leak, & the water runs in under us. I get regularly wet. It raining almost constantly, our fires being out, we have no chance to warm or dry ourselves. When our exploring [party] were out they had their goods constantly stolen from them by the Indians in spite of all their close watching. They are verry expert in it. At one of their Rancherias across the river from their own camp, they discovered a Horse & concluded, knowing he was stolen, to make them give him up to them. They had with them 2 Indians; they made them understand what they wanted, & ordered them to speak to them & tell them to bring him over. They first refused, as they intended soon to eat him. They are verry fond of Horse flesh. They were answered if they did not bring him over, our party would go over & destroy their whole camp; they then swam him over. He proved to be a most excellent Poney & was verry handsome. He was a dappled grey, tho some disfigured by having his tail cut off very short. He was brought into our camp, put up at public auction & sold; the proceeds were divided among the party to pay for losses by theft by the Indians. He brought $65, about half his value, the title being considered not verry good, & his back was verry sore.

Saturday, 17th. Two canoes were finished & launched to day. The river is verry high, & dashes past us with tremenduous velocity. We have concluded to make two more canoes.

Monday, 19th. It has rained but little to day. They commenced on the canoes to day.

Tuesday, Nov. 20th, 1849. To day the tent upon Rock Creek with all the tools &c. was moved down.

Wednesday, 21st. We had our mules brought up some time ago intending to have been off long ere this. We put them out in a valley among the hills south of us to graze, there being a little very poor grass. Yesterday we brought in 4 not being able to find the other two. Those brought in are so poor they can scarcely walk. How they can pull the empty wagon to the ranch I know not. One of them got down last night & entangled himself in his [lines?] & killed himself. So we now have but 3.

Thursday, 22d. Our canoes were finished yesterday & to day we have launched them. The sun rose clear this morning & a fine prospect of a pleasant day. We all went to work hard to get off. It was as much as I could do to walk down to the camp being verry weak. However by 11 oclock all matters were arranged, our goods all aboard, team geared up & started & we pushed out into the foaming river. We put all the tools & cloathing into canoes, & nothing in the waggon but the bedding of those [who went] by land. Our small pair of canoes had [blank in MS] men in it, viz. Barnett, Steele, Cady, [blank in MS]. Our large pair had [blank in MS] men, viz. Shannon, Cady, Johnson, myself, Wheeler [blank in MS]. We had a verry dangerous trip passing over some of the rapids; we were dashed forward with fearful rapidity, our canoes were hard to steer, & we would sometimes be cast against the banks with great force, whirl round & pass on stern foremost. Our canoes were fastened within 3 feet of each other by pieces of timber reaching across, so that they were not easily upset.

Our craft arrived at the ranch about 5 oclock.[2] The other one, being a better floater, were ahead of us about 1 hour. A few days ago a canoe was capsized on the way & a man drowned. This made our company ahead quite uneasy about us, fearing something similar had happened [to] us. They were quite rejoiced when we hove into sight, & found all safe. I consider we had some verry narrow escapes & I have concluded to go no further by water, being willing to undergo the hardships of the trip by land, rather than the dangers & ease by water.

I find here a Mr. Jno. H. St. Clair from Carrolton, Ohio, a young lawyer sick & dying, so far sunk when we arrived as to notice nothing. He died this evening. Tom Hill has also shot one of his Indians to day, in an attempt to run away from punishment for stealing.

Friday, 23d. We buried St. Clair today as decently as we could with such materials as we had, on the bank of the [river] north of the house about 500 yards, facing the river. We selected a fine spot for his resting place. I sent a Horse to the Gov., he coming on foot, which met

[2]Reading's Ranch.

him at Clear Creek, & he arrived here about 1 oclock. The team got in about dark. They had a hard time of it getting along, & came near loosing the waggon at Clear Creek, it being verry high & rapid.

Mr. Giffin has charge of the ranch & we all fare well. Mr. Redding was here a short time ago & liberated the Gov. from the purchase & employed Mr. Giffin to take charge.

Sunday, 25th. Yesterday we were busy all day arranging baggage, provisions, &c. for a start, & to day our oxen were driven up & not more than half was found to be among them. Tom Hill however made up our number, & about noon we were all under way.

We had 2 ox teams, one of 4 yoke and one of six with one odd ox. One mule team of 4 mules. The canoes started at the same time, having taken out a portion of the baggage & several of the men, it being considered it was too heavily loaded. Cotton Wood Creek was full, tho' we all got over safe, & pitched our tents in the valley a short distance above the crossing. The grass is here verry poor, & we leave the yokes upon our oxen to keep them together as much as possible.

Monday, 26th Nov. This day has nearly all been spent hunting oxen, & by the middle of the afternoon all were found but 4 yoke. We have concluded to start without them. We leave one waggon, & gave word to Giffen, to take care of all, should the oxen be found. We travelled untill 10 oclock in the night & camped in the valley 4 miles from the red Bluffs. We got along to day very well excepting had much trouble in crossing 3 sloughs at the head of the valley putting up from Cottonwood. We came verry near swamping.

Tuesday, 27th. It rained all night last night, & has rained all day to day. We have passed through the worst roads I ever saw. One continued mire hole for miles, were regularly obliged to stop & haul out either an ox or a mule every few rods, on certain portions of the road. I have walked all day in the rain, tho I got none wet, having good water proof boots, Gum Coat & umbrella. I however suffered much with fatigue, altho we went verry slow. We travelled on untill some time in the night & encamped in sight of Ide's ranch.

Wednesday, 28th. This morning opened up clear & beautiful. We yoked up, went down to the ranch , & found o[u]r canoes & men here. They came near all being lost on the trip, one set of the canoes having struck a rock in one of the rapids, upset & threw all overboard. They succeeded in saving a few of the goods & their lives. They are now over all the dangerous rapids. We provisioned them anew and all started ahead again. I got here a fine mess of good fresh light bread & butter & sweet milk. And I enjoyed it much.

We travelled to day with fair speed having much better roads, tho they were even yet bad. We encamped in a valley with fair grass.

Thursday, 29th. This has been a hard day upon our teams & ourselves; we have crossed several verry bad sloughs & had regular swamps at each place, having to pull out more or less oxen & mules at each one. One place we took out the teams & cast in the waggons headlong & hitched to the toungue by chains after driving over the teams & pulling out a portion of them.

Friday, 30th. We have gotten along pretty well [to] day, rather better than yesterday, & encamped on bank [of] river; grass fair.

Saturday, December 1st, 1849. To day we have passed Williams' ranch, & encamped 2 or 3 miles beyond it. We travelled untill some time after night.

Sunday, 2d. We have had a fair travel to day considering all things. We did not stop untill after night some time, & then encamped on the Sycamore Slough.

Monday, 3d. We travelled along the slough several miles untill we arrived at the old stopping place & the point where the old road from the lone tree strikes it, & here we find trouble ahead. Some 15 or 20 teams have stopped here, trying to bridge a swamp to get over on a plain. But in doing it they have failed completely. We undertook to find a new road down the slough & drove our teams past all, down several miles, but found we could not get through here. We camped with much suffering. The wind got up; blew verry cold & it blew & rained all night. Oh but we wished for better quarters. We were in a wet swamp, without wood except a little green bush or two, but had to take it.

Tuesday, Dec. 4th. This morning we all arose in a verry gloomy state of mind, got some breakfast & took the back track. We went back several miles, untill we found a point suitable on the slough to bridge. And here we camped & all hands went to work. The slough is near 100 feet wide. We cut down trees on both sides, to meet; cut off limbs and fixed up a fair foot crossing. Being detained, all parties [were] longer on the road than was expected, several companies run entirely out of provisions, & ours was getting very short. We concluded to kill the fattest ox in our teams. We did so, & many lived several days on nothing but his meat.

Wednesday, 5th. This morning we formed a line over our [logs] & passed over all our plunder. We also run our waggons in the slough, fastened to them from the other side, & drawed them over & on the bank. By noon all was over, & under way. We now have quite a long train of waggons & men looking almost like the moving of an army. After passing a few miles, we came across a small band of elk, which were started by a part of our company ahead looking out the way. They took a circle & ran along close to our train so that our men all had a fair chance to kill. They generally shot at them but only one was killed by the whole company, & that was by Barton [?]. He shot a fine young Doe, verry fat. We here came across a lot of Indians generally dressed & they piloted us for some distance down the river, & were of great benefit to us. We crossed a low wet place verry swampy & were compelled to take out all our loading. The Indians carried it all through upon their backs, & when done took up the Gov., two of them, & carried him over. I know not how we would have gotten through without them. We gave them the neck of the ox with which they felt much pleased & feasted with great jollification upon it. We encamped to night close to their village. They stole several articles from different [wagons?] on the train during the evening. They have a great sleight in hiding what they steal by covering it up, & they seldom take it with them, but leave it concealed untill the party is gone. Several Axes & hatchets were uncovered near the fires by the men in the morning before leaving. They carried all our water for us & waited well upon us whilst with us.

Thursday, 6th. We made an early start, 10 or 12 Indians following us. After travelling a few miles, the path or trail we were following led out into the plains & into swampy ground. The teams ahead got swamped, & we concluded to hunt a new road. I struck off to the left on a mule & travelled about 2 miles to the bank of the river & followed it along through briars & close low bushes in the midst of harbors of the grisly Bear, seeing their wallows & tracks just fresh, about 1 or [2] miles further, untill I became uneasy for my safety, knowing if I came across an old She bear with cubs, I could not get my mule out of the way & might be torn to pieces in the bushes. I retraced my steps, reported the practicability of the route & took about one half the company that way. The others determined, being lightly loadened, to try to work their way through rather than make a new road. In passing through, a Bear was seen, but he soon concealed himself in the thick bushes, so our men could not get a shot at him.

The Indians seemed to be much alarmed, & fled immediately for trees. We now soon came to the slough leading from the swamps over which the balance of the Company were trying to pass. Here we were compelled to unload again, & get our things packed over on the backs of the Indians. The slough was not deep but was steep banks. We got over safe, but one of our comp. waggons upset, & not having unloaded injured their baggage verry much. We encamped 1 or 2 miles below the slough on the bank of the river; plenty of fine grass & wood. Duck, Geese & Sand hill crane seem to cover almost the whole face of the country here. The ducks raise in such number from the ponds here as sometimes to darken the sun.

Friday, 7th. Dec. We have found excellent ground for a road since we left the trail, & to night we have fallen in again with the trail & camped with the whole comp. They say they got through but with great difficulty. Some of the men came near being swamped. They were compelled to haul out their oxen several times. We have encamped on the bank of the river; good grass & plenty wood.

Saturday, 8th. This morning two of our mules have strayed & cannot be found. Understanding two bad sloughs were ahead, we put out. The first we crossed with only our usual trouble; the second we find verry wide, deep & rapid. Here we find hunters with a whale boat, & have hired them to carry over our baggage & men for $16. The teams we crossed in our usual way, swimming, floating & pulling. This has been our most difficult slough to cross. Tho we got all over safely by night, part of the comp. did not get over until morning. We not finding that our mules come this way, sent back for them by Ibbotson; he found them 8 or 10 miles back but could not catch them, & returned without them. We have been on short allowance for flour for several day & to night we eat the last.

Sunday, 9th. This morning we sent back Castle & Hillegas for the mules. We find out we are now but 2 or 3 miles above Knight's Ranch, which puts us in spirits. We made an early start & reached Fremont a little before night. There being nothing here for our teams, we concluded to go ahead until they would come to good grass & wood & then camp, which they did. The Gov., myself & Booker concluded we would stay here & get a good night's lodging & some thing fresh to eat. We consequently gave the charge of our Gold bag to Ibbotson & Jones, with particular instructions how to take care of it. On their arrival at camping ground Barton refused them the bag, he having charge of it in his waggon. Wanting it, as he said, for a pillow, it was left in the waggon untill his time for bed which was late, when he placed [it] under his head. The next day one purse full was missing, containing between $500 & $1000. Booker changed his notion & about 8 or 9 oclock went alone to camp.

Monday, 10th. We arrived before night opposite the city of Sacramento & camped. Hillegas & Castle arrived with the mules.

Tuesday, Dec. 11th, 1849. A part of our company crossed over, & occupied the tents on the other side. We find [here] our Canoe men all safe & encamped on the bank of the slough. The Governor has fully determined now to dissolve the Company on the best terms he can. His spirits seem much depressed; the loss of the gold, with other losses, seems to be a stroke of bad luck following others, & he is satisfied the Co. will do no good. Many of the men have become verry contrary & are doing all they can to dissatisfy the Gov. so as to have it broken.

Saturday, 15th. It has been verry wet & windy & unpleasant for several days. The Gov. has made several propositions to the [company] to dissolve, none of which they would accept. He told them to day to propose themselves. They met & agreed to dissolve provided the Gove. would give them their dividend of the Gold, & give up their bonds. He with reluctance accepted. And he commenced settling. A few of the men however dissented & proposed paying him as soon as able $200 each to pay for expenses bringing them out. Jelley, Barton, Mulvaney gave their duebills for it. Some of the others promised it verbally. Now our business is to dispose of the stock as soon as possible.

Saturday, 22d. We have effected settlement with all the men & paid them their dividend; also have sold all the stock we can find. The Gov. would leave immediately for San Francisco but is detained waiting for a claim coming from Langley for goods sold by him on commission last summer. My health at times is verry bad; I think seriously of going home & unless it improves I will do so. I am now lodging at Mr. Knight's.

4

SACRAMENTO—SAN FRANCISCO

◎

Sacramento City, California,[1] *January 15th [13th], 1850.*

This morning in consequence of the high waters having completely flooded the city, leaving no dry spot on which to rest, the travelling through the streets being done altogether in vessels, I concluded, in consequence of the bad state of my health, to move my quarters to San Francisco.[2] I consequently put myself aboard the Steamer Senator, & at half past 7 oclock was under full headway to my place of destination. The whole country or valley as we passed down appeared to be one immense lake bounded on both sides by the mountains at a great distance.

Cattle were seen wading about in the shallow water, browsing upon the low underwood, nearly famished for food & exhausted for rest, having no place free enough from water on which to rest themselves by laying down. Game had all fled to the mountains, having insticts suited to the nature of the coun[try].

Thousands of cattle & Horses & mules have perished by this flood, which will much increase the value of these animals [in] the coming spring. The hills as we approached Suisson bay & Benecia presented a beautiful & inviting appearance, being clothed in robes of richest green & decked with flowers of most magnificent colour. Here & there in great numbers were seen elk & antelope in droves feeding upon the

[1]There is a break in the journal from Dec. 22, 1849, to Jan. 13, 1850. In view of subsequent entries, Osbun was apparently ill during this period. In its original form, there must have been a beginning of a new blank book here since the page is headed: "A. G. Osbun's Journal continued Vol. 2d."

[2]The winter of 1849-50 was a very wet one in California. Between Nov. 2 and Mar. 22, thirty-six inches of rain fell in Sacramento. Osbun was in Sacramento when the water was at its highest. The average rise of water at the town was four feet, and on the night of Jan. 9 four fifths of the town was under water.

tender grass, in common with immense herds of cattle belonging to the neighbouring Ranchos.

Nothing of particular interest occurred during the trip.

We arrived at Clark's Point, San Francisco, about 4 oclock, having run the distance of 150 miles in 8½ hours. We were much favored in our speed by the rapid current in the river.

Well, here I am back again, & again landed upon the same spot on which I made my first entree in this great land of Gold & humbuggery. I went on shore immediately & commenced my search for Mrs. Robinson's boarding house, where I expected to find Mr. Shannon. Being verry weak I found it verry difficult to make any headway. The mud & filth of the city had so accumulated in its lower part next the wharves that they were nearly impassible; in many places Horses & mules were regularly swamping. I find the changes in the city so great that I could scarce believe it was the same place; it is now really a dense city & of no mean extent. The main streets appear to be constantly crowded from morning till night & it is with difficulty that a person as weak & feeble as I am can get through. Broadway in N. York or Chestnut Street in Philad'a is not more crowded than the leading streets here. After some time I succeeded in finding Mrs. Robinson's, & the Gov. When I was here last, her house stood solitary & alone, no other habitation near her. Now I could scarce find her *for the houses*, the whole neighborhood being covered with fine buildings.

Monday, Jan. 14th. In the night I was seized with severe & rapid diarrhoea. I took some morphia to quiet down the irritation, but taking it in the dark I took too much, which took away nearly all my senses for the whole day. I arose early & took some breakfast, but soon went to bed again, & laid untill noon. I got up & walked out but soon found I had but little sense. I made my way to the Gov's office in the Ward house, where I became verry sick & vomited several times. Mrs. Robinson not having room for more boarders, I was compelled to look out for a place to stay. During the afternoon Mr. Adam Johnson, the Indian Agent, came in & advised me to go with him to his boarding house, which advice I gladly took for I wished to be at some house where I had an acquaintance. I went with him to the Alhambra & found the proprietors verry clever men.

Tuesday, 15th. Last night I put in hard. It rained all night in torrents & I was compelled to go out several times by diarrhoea, tho' this morning I feel some better.

To day I went again to the Gov.'s office, looking out for a good place to lodge, as they had not a suitable place at the Alhambra.

And whilst there an old acquaintance, Mr. Perry, who was with us in the mines, came in, and being informed by him that he was keeping a boarding house, I immediately made up my mind to go with him. I calculated upon kind attention, & upon more of the feelings of being at home than I could find in any other house in this city, all of which I fully realized.

Tuesday, 22d. I have been verry sick during the last week, a portion of the time so weak I could not leave my bed. Mr. Perry attended upon me closely. I called in a Physician, who prescribed liniment to my bowels & Dover's powder, but I find hot Brandy toddy does me more good than any other medicine.

Saturday, 26th. I find myself now improving as fast as I could expect, & am beginning to walk about out doors.

Perry & myself have also concluded to get a vessel & make a voyage to the Friendly Islands for a cargo of Live Hogs, they being verry plenty & also verry cheap on those Islands, the only difficulty in the matter being the want of cash to carry it out. We having between us but a verry few hundred dollars, we called upon the Gov. & requested his assistance in borrowing $3,000.

Wednesday, 30th. The Governor not being able to negotiate for us, we concluded to offer an interest in the profets of one fourth for a loan of $3000—which was quickly taken by a Messrs. May & Randall, and we immediately commenced a search for a suitable vessel to purchase for the voyage. We finally concluded to buy the Ship Huron for $3500.

But before we concluded the purchase, Messrs. May & Randall informed us they had met with disappointment in getting a sum of money intended for us, & that they would not be able to raise enough for us. Our spirits were high before this announcement; we had bragged a little to ourselves of our powers in finance & raising the wind, but now were flat enough upon our backs, not knowing that we could find another set of men willing to go in with us, on any thing like so favorable terms. Mr. Perry has a partner, a Mr. Cohn from N. York, a Dutch Jew, in principle & in character. His arrangement with him being to close at any time he desired & draw out his cash advanced & profits, he requested a settlement to day to close up so that he could have all his time to attend to our business. But the Jew denied his contract, & placed Perry under the necessity of suing for a settlement.

Saturday, February 2d, 1850. This morning Perry commenced his suit & closed up the house by the Sheriff, which has truly thrown the old Jew into a state of the most severe excitement. When the Sheriff arrived, all the cash on hands was not to be found. He [Perry's partner] from some cause suspected what was going on, Perry being out all morning, [and] had taken about $400 & concealed it, denying that he had it on hands. We all took up our board together at a Dutch house a few doors below, & at a cheaper rate than is customary here. Perry's charge for board & lodging was $18 per week, which was considered low, but here we pay but $13 & verry good board, as good as I wish.

Thursday, 7th. We have spent the last 4 days busily engaged in closing up with Cohn, & hunting some arrangement to carry out our voyage of Speculation. I succeeded in effecting a pretty satisfactory compromise between Perry & Cohn, which saved much trouble, expense & sacrifice in the sale of stock & fixtures. Cohn kept the stock & fixtures & gave to Perry his share in cash.

To day we have effected a contract with Capt. Haff, Master of the Brig Rodolph, by which we charter her for the trip, he furnishing all the necessary fixtures for transporting live stock, or other things, the crew & provisions. We to furnish goods & cash for purchasing & to purchase the Cargo. He to recieve for his pay therefor one half the nett profits after deducting the cost of Cargo. The prospect for a Speculation being good, I consider the contract a good one for both parties. The vessel to be gotten in readiness for sea as soon as possible, which the Capt. thinks can be done in one week, & all be off. By the contract we go aboard as soon as we desire & to be free of cost for board. We have concluded to go abard on Saturday evening.

Saturday, 9th Feb. This afternoon we have taken up our abode, abard of the Brig Rudolph & expect before we leave her to be verry tired of her. She is a vessel 95 feet long, 21 feet wide and ten feet deep, & will carry about two hundred Tons. She has a cabin upon deck with Eight berths in it, & 2 pantries, & would be verry comfortable if its story was a little higher, it being only about 5 feet 9 inches high. This forces us to stoop a little whilst walking in it.

Saturday, 16th. We have been busily engaged this week attending auction & buying goods, & have purchased about what we consider sufficient & have them aboard. Our officers seem verry slow in the motion, the vessel not being as yet near ready for sea. And we discover not the best kind of feelings between the crew & the Capt.; this no doubt has kept back business.

Wednesday, 20th. The Capt. & mate have had considerable sparring for several days, & 3 of the crew have given notice of their intention to leave the vessel & have demanded their wages. The Capt. has to day ordered them all ashore. They have consequently left the vessel. This evening the Capt. filled up his crew list with the intention of clearing the vessel tomorrow, & leaving in the evening, fearing that those who left if not paid soon would attach the vessel & thus prevent us from getting off, he finding that he could not here raise money enough to pay them off, they having claims amounting to about $1000. As we had not stores or water sufficient aboard to carry us the whole trip, he concluded to clear for the Sandwich Islands & their make up our supplies.

Thursday, 21st. We all went early this morning ashore to close up all our matters there, expecting it to be our last day here. He arranged to have 2 casks water & a few stores brought aboard just at dark. In consequence of not being acquainted with the custom here of clearances, we did not go to the office properly prepared to get cleared in time, so we failed in getting it. We however arranged to take the vessel to the mouth of the bay & the Capt. to return in the morning & get it. But we were saved all the trouble. When we went aboard in the evening we found an officer aboard having full charge of the vessel, they having attatched her for their wages. The mate was also gone, he having left immediately after we did, & went ashore, & no doubt hastened the service of the writ. He embarked on board the Senator at 4 oclock for Sacramento City to see the owner of the vessel & report how things were going on here. He from his prompt conduct must have been apprized of the Captain's intentions. At least he has most signally defeated them. Although the Capt. had been loud in his denunciations against the mate, & threatened lustily how he would punish him when he got him out to sea, he is now completely floored & the mate has showed himself to be entirely the best at management. And being the first to see the owner, I have no doubt he will succeed in depriving the

67

Capt. of his post, & he remain upon the vessel himself & was he only a seaman would no doubt get charge of her himself.

The mate assured me before he left that our voyage would be made, which, altho it produces delay, keeps me in spirits, as I do not wish to have difficulty with the vessel, neither hunt up new partners, as we are determined to make the voyage if any person can be found to join us.

Monday, 25th. This day the suit comes on between the seamen & the vessel for the recovery of their wages. The Gov. has the management of the case in behalf of the vessel. The only matter of dispute is that 2 of the men claim $150 per month, and the Capt. avers that no contract was made, & that they are only entitled to the wages of the port. The 3d one claims $100 per month per contract, which the Capt. says is correct. The trial came on, two witnesses for the vessel were heard proving that one of them who officiated as seaman was not a full & capable seaman, & the other, our Cook, was not an experienced or capable Cook. The wages of the port was also proven to average from $60 per month to $130.

Without further testimony the California Judge ordered judgment to be entered in favor of the plaintiffs at $100 per month ea.

"What!" says the plaintiff's Lawyer, "do you decide the case without hearing our testimony?" "Why my dear Sir!" says the Judge, "have I not passed judgment in your favor, what more do you want?" "Why Sir we wish to get $150 per month." "Oh! you do Sir, then I put off the trial untill 12 oclock to morrow, when I will hear your testimony." So the trial was put off. I was in court a few days ago & witnessed another of this Judge's decisions. A certain point in law was in dispute between the Attorneys. One arose & made his speech; at its conclusion the other got up. "You need not argue this point any farther," says the Judge, "my mind is already made up. I had occasion to examine this point some time ago in one of my own cases, & I know just exactly what is right & what is law." He seated the fellow & made his decision.

To day another attachment was laid upon the vessel by a merchant of little over $100.00. We are now living some better, since the new stores were brought abard the evening we expected to sail. Hams, flour, pickles, nutmegs & Harve[y] sauce have been added to our stock; previously we have lived entirely on Hard bread, tea & pickled pork. We are considerably vexed with fleas, & Bugs, & an occasional white 6 footer in the cabin, all of which we would soon rid ourselves of were we out at sea.

Tuesday, 26th. The suit with the seamen was this day decided in favor of the plaintiffs, the cook to recieve $125 per month & the 2 sailors $100. The mate & owner of the vessel have not arrived yct. I am now beginning to feel quite uneasy to get off. Our Captain has given up all his prospects of going on the voyage. He considers that the mate will succeed in having him discharged, & he now seems to be making his calculations to go to the mines. This evening Capt. Perry seems to be quite unwell & I fear is agoing to have a spell of sickness. My own health has gradually continued to improve since I came upon the vessel, so that now I am pretty nearly restored to my general health, tho' a slight transgression from plain & simple diet will bring on diarrhoea. It has been raining mostly through the night & showring slightly through the day, but the rainy season is considered over this year. We have had but a few occasional showers since the commencement of this month. The Brig, a few days before we came aboard, lost her small boat. She hired another untill our mate left us. He then returned it to the owner, & since that time, which was Thursday last, we have had no boat. I have been to shore but once since on account of the expense, it costing me $2.00 every visit, $1 out, & $1 in.

Wednesday, 27th. To day Capt. Perry has been verry unwell all day; his disease has turned out Pneumonia, & he has been expectorating considerable bloody mucus. His bowels being too loose for an emetic, I prescribed a dose of antibilious pills, which have operated pretty well & given him some relief. Nothing new to day. Our men with some others have worked pretty hard all day getting our anchors & chains free from entanglement with those of the Ship Panama lying along side of us, but as yet have not succeeded.

No word yet from Mr. Bayley, the owner of the Brig, or Krissam, the mate.

Thursday, 28th. I am now getting tired waiting. My mind runs homeward, & I wish to be with my wife & children at least for a time, tho' I do not feel like giving up my present undertaking or enterprize.

Capt. Perry is no better. We have our vessel set to rights again, after employing 5 more men.

Friday, March 1st, 1850. I have to day written a long letter to Eliza & Wm. Fry, & requested them to send it to my wife & let her read it. I would have written to her but I am holding on untill I can tell her either that I am going or not going. Capt. P. is easier to day. Still no word of our mate.

It is my intention if they do not come to night, to go ashore tomorrow & consult the Gov. what we had better do. The vessel is advertised to be sold on the 9th by the Sheriff, & unless a claim for damages is laid in by us soon, we may be preceded by others, & have trouble in getting justice done us. I have not been off the vessel since last Saturday, & it is just 20 days since we came aboard.

Saturday, March 2nd. This day has been verry unpleasant, damp, cool & occasional showers all day, so unpleasant that I remained close to the vessel; did not go into the city. I employed myself during the forenoon dressing up & waiting for it to quit raining. I put in the afternoon writing a long letter to Ross's boys. No Mr. Bailey yet. To day another notice was served upon our vessel, to repair damages done by her to the ship Panama, during the entanglement, or she would immediately sue for damages. So here is another difficulty. Our Capt. answered them to go ahead, and on Monday I suppose the Sheriff will be again aboard of us. Perry is still easier tho verry unwell yet, no blood discharged to day.

Sunday, March 3d. This has been a pleasant day, but I have not left the vessel. I have spent a good portion of it writing a letter to Brother Samuel. Perry is still improving.

Monday, March 4th. This day I have spent in the city, looking around, but saw nothing of unusual interest. I took my stand in the ranks at the post office to get letters, but unluckily there was none for me. I dined at the Alhambra on venison pie & roast pig, sweet potatoe & squash. I had been confined for some time to salt meat & hard bread or sad half baked biscuit, & this meal was a great luxury. I have just cheated the taylor out of a bill by cutting out & putting in a pair of new sleeve linings in my overcoat, & I have succeeded admirably. Perry is up to day.

Tuesday, March 5th. Our long looked for men, viz. Bayley & Kissam, have at length arrived, & we have had a long interview on the subject of our charter & of the voyage. Bayley I find to be a verry keen shrewd business man; he finds great fault with our charter, he thinks it altogether one sided, that it has but one leg, & declares his unwillingness to carry it out. He took it to his Lawyer who pronounced it not binding in law on him, & that he needs pay no attention to it. But inasmuch as we have been depending upon the voyage, & made considerable purchases of otherwise unsaleable goods than in this speculation, if we could give him a satisfactory reference that we were the right kind of men, & that the prospect of the speculation was a good one, he would make a new contract with us, one based upon equality, & still carry out the voyage. It being true that the contract on our side was a good one, & would bear clipping, we made no objections to his proposition, & referred him to Mr. Shannon, Col. Collier & Col. A. Johnson. He called upon the Gov. & went no further. He then informed me he was ready to meet all parties & to see if we could come to terms. We accordingly appointed a meeting at the Governor's office at 7 oclock this evening.

Kissam, Capt. Gunner, Perry, Mr. Bayley & myself all met at the hour, & after canvassing the voyage, conditions &c., came to a general agreement upon the terms of the voyage. Committed them to the Gov. for arrangement & for committal to paper by tomorrow forenoon, when we are to meet again & close the arrangement by our signatures.

We returned altogether to the vessel between 9 & 10 oclock.

Wednesday, March 6th. It has rained hard all night. Immediately after breakfast we repaired to the Gov's office to close our arrangement. We soon met Mr. Bayley, but judge our surprise when he informed us that in consequence of his inability to get an insurance upon the vessel he could not think of letting it go to sea. Here was a damper to all our present prospects. We had let slip other good opportunities, & the season being now far advanced & our acquaintances all fixed in business, we knew not what to do, or who to go to that would likely join us in the enterprise. We had spent much time waiting for these men to arrange their business, & all our means was locked up in it so that we really felt as if we were to have no luck in California. I commenced looking round in my mind to see what I could go at, but could settle down on nothing, unless it would be to go home, & probably that would be the best thing I could do. We also *talked* the matter over. Perry rather concluded he would get a birth on a vessel if possible & cast his lot again upon the wide ocean, preferring it to returning to the mines.

I cast my eyes homeward, & concluded that it would be better for me to direct my course there, start myself again in business & be with my wife & children. Mr. Bailey promised to reconsider & let us know his conclusion in the afternoon. We then met, & Mr. Bayley had concluded to risk his vessel, so we closed the arrangement, but not verry satisfactorily to us.

Thursday, 7th. It rained again last night. We this morning commenced anew & with much spirit to arrange for our departure. Perry went on shore to arrange some matters & I remained upon the vessel to repack & fix up our goods. About noon, in comes Mr. Bayley with another new proposition. He just had an offer to full freight the vessel to Stockton, which would amount to $5000—& he now asked the priviledge of making this trip before we went to sea. Here was indeed another stumper, & what to do I did not know. It will detain us from 3 to 4 weeks & be of no material advantage to us, tho to Mr. Bayley, who has lost heavily by the bad management of the Ship, it is a matter of considerable importance, as it will bring things up straight with him. He was not bound to make the voyage, tho to prevent our disappointment he agreed to make it. This reflection operated on my mind & induced me to accede to his proposition. I went on shore to see the Gov. & Perry. The Gov. advised me to accept. But I could not find Perry. After I had acceded to it & reflected upon what I had done I was much dissatisfied with myself, & believe if I had not acted from impulse, I would not have done it, & now if I had to do it over, I would not accede without having better terms. The Gov. sending me advice rather hushed up reflection. In the evening Perry returned & is much dissatisfied.

Friday, 8th. Perry has engaged to work up to Stockton at the rate of $150 per month. They promise me wages, but there is so little that I can do, I know not how I can employ myself. They have shipped 3 new hands & have thrown nearly all the ballast upon deck. I went ashore to hunt freight, intending, if I could find a load, either to charter a vessel or buy one, & Perry & I take it up. I got the promise of some if any was left. And it is supposed there will be a load. Bayley left at 4 last evening.

Saturday, 9th. I went ashore this morning & remained there all day. The prospect for freight sufficient to justify & to load a vessel is now verry slim. The vessel dropped down to near Clark's point & has taken in a portion of her Cargo, about 17000 feet of boards. I attended this afternoon a grand democratic meeting in the Plaza, which ended in a general row & fight.[3] It was the first pugillistic political meeting I was ever at. The Gov. presided at the meeting, & made quite a Speech on the occasion. Several others spoke also, the drift of their speeches being the right of democrats to govern this country, & insisting upon union in their ranks as their only means of success, disunion having already lost them two important offices. I left before the speeches were through, but returned whilst they were passing some resolutions, referring certain duties to a certain committee. It was about this resolution they quarrelled. The fighting commenced upon the stand among the leaders of the meeting, & extended from thence to the crowd. I had to leave before it was through. It being near night, & our vessel having changed her anchorage, I feared if I did not hunt her up before night, I could not find her amidst the vast number of vessels lying in the bay. It is indeed as much as I can do to find her amongst the vessels when she does not change her position. I dined to day on a cup of tea, bread & Butter, two dough nuts, & a piece of mince pie for 62½ cts.

Sunday, March 10th. The Capt., Mate, Mr. Perry & myself all went on shore to day & dined at the "Central House." We had an excellent dinner—game of all kinds & cooked in every variety & form, a good assortment of vegetables, with a full & well assorted desert. We paid for it $1.50. This has been one of the most pleasant days I have experienced in California. I saw Mr. May on shore yesterday; he still expresses a great desire to make the voyage with us. As we are both much dissatisfied with the present arrangements & position, we will join him if he can arrange at all. I promised to see him again.

Monday, 11th. It has rained & stormed all this day, & nothing has been done towards putting out. One load of boards from the lighter was recieved yesterday & put aboard last night; the hands commenced work about 10 oclock & worked all night. I went ashore, & remained untill night. I spent most of the day in the court house, listening to the administration of Justice. I saw Mr. May & engaged to meet him to-

[3]The meeting at the Plaza was called to hear a report on party organization presented by the Committee on Conference. The San Francisco *Alta California* (Mar. 11, 1850, p. 2, col. 1) reported that the proceedings were conducted with "a good deal of spirit" and that there was some little disturbance once or twice caused by the interference of "outsiders" and that one or two men were "plugged." In all it was said to have been the most formidable political demonstration in San Francisco since the election in the fall of 1849.

morrow to see if we cannot make arrangements together for the voyage.

Tuesday, 12th. I have spent all the day in the city; but Mr. May did not meet me as by his agreement, so I know not what he designs doing. I recieved a letter from my wife this day, dated Jany. 10th with a letter of I. Sharon's enclosed, all well. I also rec'd one from I. Castell, having sent my lost Sack, but it did not come to hand, so I fear I will still loose it; it is now out of his hands & with a stranger & has been here two days without finding me. There have been frequent showers to day, & the streets have become verry muddy & slippery. Heavy & extensive sales of town lots are daily made at the public auctions. Merchandise from first hands is all thrown into aucton & sold, & at this time most of it is sold at an immense sacrifice. It is put up and sold honestly at just what it will bring. Heavy rents & expenses are now breaking up many merchants. I hear of many & heavy fail[ure]s every day. Houses to rent are now getting more numerous than houses occupied. Consequently they can be bought as delivered by the ships mu[ch] cheaper than they can be brought here. Boards can be had planed pl[MS illegible] & grooved for $70 per thousand, which a short time ago would comm[and] $600. It is computed that at least 7000 persons have left here for the mines, which has made a serious impression upon certain portions of the citizens. There is no longer the throng of people that crowded the streets.

Wednesday, 13th. The weather is still showery. I went ashore again & remained all day; spent my time principally in the Gov.'s office. I saw Mr. May, who tells me he is forced again to give up the enterprise, at least for the present, so we must reconcile ourselves to our situation, at least untill we can do better. We recieved another load of lumber to day which completes our load. The Capt. now says we shall be off tomorrow.

Thursday, 14th. It has rained regularly in showers all night & all day. I went on shore & deposited my letters with the Gov. to have them mailed, & returned as soon as possible, expecting that we would be off. But I find as little business tact in our present Captain as there was in the old one; he suffers at least half the time to pass away doing nothing. I do know with proper energy & push we could have been off Tuesday evening. But so it is we are now placed at the mercy of the officers of the vessel, & must either quietly submit to it or leave. The Capt. has spent the whole day ashore, as he has done days & nights previously, with but verry little to do, among his Cronies. And we are still unable to proceed. Water & coal & a part of [our] stores are still to come aboard. One load of Liquors & one of Sto[res] is all that was put aboard to day, which need not have occupied [more] than two hours. I am getting out of all patience.

Friday, 15th. Matters were pushed this forenoon & every thing [is] on board. After dinner the Capt. came aboard & in a short time our anchors were raised, & the sails unfurled & we were off on our Voyage to Stockton.

5

VOYAGE TO STOCKTON—SAN FRANCISCO

◎

Friday, 15th. We left at half past two, & at 3 we were along side of Angel Island. The wind blowing a good breeze, has quite ruffled the waters of the bay, its surface being covered with white caps. Still our vessel recieves it with apparent exultation as she rides proudly upon its waves.

We sailed ahead with rapid speed, entered the straights of Carquines about dusk, & a little after dark anchored in Benecia bay a short distance below the town of Benecia.

Saturday, 16th. About sun rise this morning our sails were again spread to the wind, & we were off. We soon entered Suisoon Bay. We were however, when opposite Benecia, boarded by a revenue officer, & our papers or licence demanded, which caused some detention. We had not sailed far before we found we were wrong, having sailed too far North. We grounded & remained untill near night; we then got off, floated back with the tide untill near the entrance of the bay again. Here at dark we cast our anchor & were ready for a fresh start in the morning. We have lain all day just opposite the celebrated "Monte diablo." It appears verry near to us; its snow capt head towers high above the surrounding hills. The hills at its base & the valleys are covered with a rich & heavy coat of grass, producing quite a contrast with its cold & barren peaks. We were aground but twice.

Sunday, 17th. This morning our Brig was again put under way, but our destiny was not to go far untill yesterday's misfortunes were to be again upon us. We got quite out of the channel, too much to the left, & became badly grounded with an ebbing tide. Our anchor was cast a great distance behind us, & by the united force of crew & passengers we succeeded in pulling her off. We got into the channel & soon was caught up again. We cleared ourselves in the same manner, & soon made our exit from this bay of trouble. This Bay has been the source of much trouble to sailors in consequence of the general shallowness of its waters, & the crooked & narrow courses of its various channels. We passed New York at the mouth of the San Joaquin about one hour before sundown, & sailed up it about 10 miles, cast our anchor & remained for the night. Col. Stevenson has made quite an effort to build up & make a city of New York, but thus far it is quite a failure. There are 4 or 5 ships & a Brig or two lying here, & from 6 to 8 small Houses. Some steam boats have been built or put together here, & I see one small vessel now on the stocks. The bottom has at this place widened out & gives a fine space for building up a city.

Immense herds of cattle are grazing around the town & along the base of the hills.

Monday, March 18th. About 9 oclock a favorable wind arose & we put off. We find plenty of water, but the great difficulty here consists in finding our way among the many sloughs that are constantly putting in & out. It is altogether impossible to judge from appearances which is the right branch for us to take. We had not proceeded far before we took a wrong one & soon were laid up again for another 24 hours. We entered a slough & followed it up untill we found it closed up. I commenced making a map of the river this morning from our anchorage & intend to take the notes, as we return, for the lower part.

We have alarmed several flocks of Antelope by coming up here, as we see them running to & fro, with great apparent curiosity gazing upon us. This is no doubt the first vessel that has been here at least for some time. Several of our men went out to hunt them but they all fled beyond their reach. The country here is near altogether low flat Tule Swamp, intersected with sloughs running in all directions.

The wind to day has been fine, & could we have kept the right stream we would with ease have been to night half way up the river to the end of our journey. In consequence of the high wind it is thought useless to undertake to tow back our vessel. We are now waiting for it to fall. Our company consists of 4 passangers on deck. Members of the "Mechanics Own" Company.[1] They are verry companioble men. With 4 sailors, cook, Capt., Mate, Perry & myself.

---

[1] The American ship *Mechanic's Own,* Captain Malcom, arrived at San Francisco on Jan. 25, 1850, 165 days from New York, with 149 passengers.

Tuesday, 19th. This is a most delightful morning. All it wants to make it most enchanting is the music of birds, but not a single voice is heard save the croak of the Sand hill Crane, as he flies above us entirely out of sight, or the squall of the wild goose passing in large flocks southward.

All being calm & quiet, we made an early start by hauling ourselves back with a cord fastened to shore. But the winds being so much against us, we have not been able to retrace our steps verry far, not even back to the turning off place. We think one hour's work during the morning's calm will take us again to the main river, & when there I do hope we will be able to keep in it.

Wednesday, 20th. We this morning dropped down to the mouth of the slough, & made our grand entrance again within the bosom of the San Joaquin. We were all much delighted with the return, being absent about two days only. Whilst beating down we observed a flock of 14 Elk grazing at a distance, upon an elevated spot of ground in the valley. Several of us, feeling verry elkish, concluded we would visit them & let them know that we were about. We consequently rubbed up our guns, loaded them, had the small boat hauled up, & the Capt., myself & two others of the passenges jumped aboard, & were immediately put ashore, & were soon wending our way upon our errand of death. We travelled at the start with much vigor having some 2 or 3 miles to go. But soon our courage was cooled off. The swamp of tule deepened the farther we proceeded, so that at last the water came near the top of our boots. The expedition was given up as entirely impracticable, & the Messrs. Elks, whom we supposed were acting verry foolishly by exposing themselves on this high ground, we found were really the lords of the valley, & not to be approached by such creatures as we are. We turned our backs upon them after going about one half mile & returned to the vessel. There has been a great deal of firing from the vessel at Ducks, Dippers, Shags, Cranes &c. but nothing has been slain excepting a large Hawk, if it is indeed a Hawk. It measures four and one half feet from the tips of its wings, has quite large talons, is of a verry rich dark brown colour on its back & wings, but its belly & head is of beautiful snow white.[2] I have dressed him for the table tomorrow; having eaten a Hawk up the Sacramento, I know their flesh to be not inferior to chicken. I found his stomach filled with fish.

[2]This was possibly a bald eagle.

About the middle of the afternoon we were so unfortunate again as to run aground upon a bar, & the wind being high, we have to remain upon it untill morning, when we anticipate no trouble in getting off. We suppose we have sailed to day in the San Joaquin about 6 or 7 miles. This bar we have christened "Gunnings Bar."

Thursday, 21st. This morning we have been disappointed; we expected an early start, but no wind rising we lay after floating down from the shallows untill 4 oclock, when the wind getting up we got off. We sailed untill some time after dark, then getting into shallow water, & not being able to see our course well, we concluded to stop for the night.

The forenoon was spent by the Capt., Perry, myself & a passenger hunting along a Bayou. We found Duck, but was not successfull in killing any; they have become verry wild. I took notes of the Course of the Bayou for between 2 & 3 miles & have it entered upon my map. Its mouth is at the bar we stuck upon, & lay all night. In the afternoon a party crossed over & went up a Bayou on the other side to hunt, & found many Otter but killed none. We have no good hunters in our company. It has clouded up, & shows much sign of rain. We have sailed probably from 12 to 15 miles.

Friday, 22d. It commenced raining in the night, & continued untill between 10 & 11 oclock. We find this morning a slight breeze with a flowing tide, which we take advantage of. We sailed & floated untill between 10 & 11, when we were compelled to cast anchor. There being no more wind & the tide ebbing here, we have been compelled to remain during the balance of the day & night. All hands now went to work to chase up something to pass away time. Some went up the Bayous hunting, & others brought forth their fishing lines, & put in

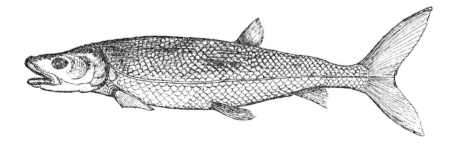

the day. The above is a drawing of the only kind of a Fish we could catch with a hook, & it was also the only kind we could take on the Yuba when there last summer. We caught sufficient to make all hands aboard a fine mess in the form of a Chowder. We find them excellent eating. The size of those we catch is from 12 to 20 inches in length. I have not as yet heard a name given to them.[3] The hunters as usual killed nothing. This river seems to be flooded with vessels. Several are almost constantly in view going up & down. And it seems we are doomed to be always at the tail end. To day a schooner passed down that passed us going up whilst we were in the sloughs. She has been up to Stockton & discharged her cargo & tomorrow will be in San Francisco. The face of the country is still the same tule swamp with no trees. Dwarf bushes & shrubs occasionally line the bank of the river, the sloughs & bayous. I am still going ahead with map. It is quite an amusement for me & helps to pass away the time. Sailed from 8 to 10 miles.

Saturday, March 23d. The tide still ebbing & no wind, we were forced to lay still & wait & hope; about 10 a gentle breeze arose & the tide changed & we put off tho at a slow pace. The river has now become verry crooked & many large sloughs put out from it, & were it not for the many vessels constantly in view we could not decide which to take. The borders of the river now begin to be covered with more bushes, which seems to invite the feathered tribes to inhabit them. To day we have been delightfully entertained by their music. The varieties seem to be new to me; they are small birds resembling our sparrows or reed birds. We occasionally see a blue Jay. And to day we have seen many Sand hill Cranes walking about on shore, but too far off to shoot, & being under full sail, could not loose the time to stop. About 2 oclock we came suddenly upon a great bend in the river, which brought the wind directly in front of us & stopped our further progress, by wind, untill we warped through. Here we were detained the balance of the day & then not through it. The wind being favorable to this point has been the cause of gathering many vessels here warping their way through. Our course in this bend is directly west. We have sailed to day about 10 miles.

[3]This was a Sacramento squawfish (*Ptychocheilus grandis*), a large and predaceous species of the minnow family, common through the streams of the Central Valley of California.

Sunday, 24th. I find my right ankle & leg within the last few days getting verry sore; it has been somewhat tender for several weeks. It has the appearance of scurvcy, but is exactly similar to a disease my Father had on his legs. It is oedematous & covered with fine red points & bloches & tender to the touch. I have also had for several weeks severe fits dyspepsia. We hoisted sail this morning about 10 oclock, when the tide commenced flowing & the wind to blow gently & were soon under way. We have sailed to day through a verry crooked river. The country is still the same continued flat of tule swamp, with occasional clumps of dwarf bushes on spots of ground a little more elevated than is general. We see large flocks of the Swamp Blackbird, and also sand hill Cranes in great abundance. One of our passenges discovered a Raccoon from the mast head running through the grass & tules, & went ashore & shot him. He has prepared him for the cook, & we will probably dine off him tomorrow.

We did not succeed in getting our Bird cooked untill to day. Some of our Company did not like it but I think it excellent. We have made a fine sail to day, the wind blowing a strong breeze all afternoon. And had we not have been so unfortunate as again to run upon another bar, we think from the speed we were going we would have made Stockton to night. We run aground about the middle of the afternoon, & did not get off untill sun down. Stockton is now in full view from where we lay, & will certainly make it tomorrow if our usual bad luck does not happen us. We have sailed to day about 25 miles.

Monday, 25th. This morning opened finely: the whole swamps around us seem to be alive with the swamp Blackbird, & their constant music for the whole day has kept the tules ringing with their perpetual song.

There are here no bushes or trees within a great distance; grass & tules, the latter almost entirely, seem to cover solitary & alone the whole face of the valley. About 10 oclock it commenced raining & rained untill 12. No wind rising, we are compelled to lay to & be as contented as possible. About 5 oclock a breeze struck up; we hoisted sail & off we went, but it did not last long. We cast anchor in less than an hour. Between 10 & 11, the wind getting up, we were aroused & soon under sail. We sailed rapidly a short distance untill we arrived at a verry sudden bend in the river, the entrance of what is called [Calaveras] River; here in spite of all our efforts we were cast upon the point, & were compelled to remain untill morning. We had our Coon roasted for supper this evening, & he, altho not fat, furnished a good meal for the cabin & passengers, making in all eight persons. We expect much trouble in the morning in getting out from our present situation.

The bend is so sudden & the currents making in from both rivers, & they narrow, with an eddy, & our vessel being long, will make it verry difficult, unless we have strong wind to force her through, to keep her from turning. We suppose we have sailed near 3 miles to day.

Tuesday, 26th March. This morning opened with rain. We also have considerable wind & have succeeded after about one hour's work towing &c. in making the bend. We were soon under full headway, but were doomed to run ashore again at the next bend. The view of the coast range from this point as the sun shines upon its slopes is truly most beautiful & magnificent. Immense beds of flowers seem to be their only production, giving to them the appearance of immense golden banks, & reminds me more of the extravagant tales of Aladdin than any thing I have ever seen. They are at a great distance from us, & have been so cloathed doubtless the whole way up, but were never so beautifully disclosed as by the reflection of this morning's sun. Many smaller vessels are now constantly passing us, & we are entirely satisfied that our vessel is too large for this river, the river for some distance having become verry crooked & narrow. We have had a verry hard day's work, warping & pulling off the shore & bars. The bends being so sudden, we got fast in turning almost every one. We run aground after dark this evening at the mouth of the slough leading to Stockton, & distance from there 3 miles.

Wednesday, 27th. This morning we find ourselves hard aground, & our men labored hard untill after the middle of the day before we got off. Then the wind blowing verry strong upon our side prevented us from sailing untill evening, when it slacked & we put out, & arrived at the anxiously looked for Town of Stockton, a little after dark, having been 12 days getting here, & we should have made it in 4 days, & would have done so if we only had procured a good pilot. By looking at the map it will be seen that the river is verry crooked, & in some places it was so narrow that we could not have turned our vessel in it, if we had desired to do so. The wind has generally been from the west, tho occasionally NW. & S. & SE. Hence the great difficulty in navigating such a stream with so large a vessel. During our stop to day, all hands went again to fishing & caught a fine lot of most excellent fish, & we had with them to night a most glorious supper for all hands. We had also several shots at seal but killed none. The Tule Swamps appear to be more covered & deeper with water for the last few days than they were below, & we have been regularly entertained during each night by the perpetual song of the Frog. They are verry numerous; the swamp appears to be full of them.

Thursday, 28th. This has been a verry warm day, entirely the warmest I have experienced this season. Our men went to work & erected a platform on which to carry out our freight, & by night they had our decks cleared, making about one third of our load. I have been verry lame this afternoon, so much so that I cannot walk but in great pain. My ankle is quite red & much swollen. The country around Stockton looks verry well; back of it, it is timbered land & yields fine grass. I observe here the first clover growing that I have seen in the country. It looks fine.

Friday, 29th. To day I have been confined closely to the cabin with my ankle & leg. I am verry lame & have suffered much. All hands have worked hard to day except the Capt. & he does nothing but prominade the streets & vessel. He is likely to have trouble with the freight, he not having transacted his business in rccieving it in a business like manner. I advised him & so did Mr. Perry how he should do it. But he knew too much to take our advice.

Saturday, March 30th. My leg is better to day & I have walked about some. The weather still continues verry hot. Having hired two hands both yesterday & to day, we have succeeded in unloading the vessel this evening. Wages $8 per day & found. We bought a hind quarter of about the fattest beef I ever saw on Thursday evening & have finished it this morning: it weighed 92 lbs. It was verry sweet, but too tender & soft to please me. It fattened itself entirely on acorns & grass. Cattle of all kinds in this country eat the acorn, & become verry fat upon them.

Sunday, 31st. This afternoon Perry & myself took a stroll through & around the town, and in my walk we collected a most beautiful bouquet of wild flowers. I believe I never saw so great a variety nor so handsome an assortment of spring flowers in so short a ramble. We

83

collected as beautiful 12 different kinds. A new variety of the Star of Bethlehem with its petals tipped with verry light straw.[4] Two varieties of flower similar to candy tuft, but a little larger & growing verry dense. One a snow white with a centre of brilliant yellow, the other a brilliant yellow with a centre of light straw, & pistils & stamen rich purple.[5] Also another flower of the same size & form of the white one but with bright orange petals marked with red & purple pistils.[6] A brilliant blue Larkspur.[7] Two new varieties of clover, one light and dark purple, the other a light straw, its petals 12 in number formed in tubes & terminating above similar to the dragons flower.[8] A verry pretty & sweet Hyacinth white & yellow. A verry gay white flower striped with purple of the size of an ordinary single pink, with three others.[9] All of which are remarkable for the beauty & clearness of their colours, & the richness of their perfume. We put them into mugs of water & thus handsomely decorated our cabin.

Monday, April 1st, 1850. This day all hands have been employed in measuring & piling up lumber, it having all to be measured & counted. And by night the job was nearly completed. Tomorrow our officers say we will sail. Time can only reveal its truth. I voted to day for the whole list of officers from Supreme Judge down, my first cast vote in California.[10]

One of our men shot a woodpecker yesterday, which differs much from ours: its back, tail, wings & the top of its head is a jet shining black colour, & has a white ring around its Neck, & extending a short distance down the breast. The balance of the breast, belly & sides is brilliant red & white intermixed; apparently every other fibre in each feather changes color, white & red, which gives a color of great rich-

---

[4]Probably star lily (*Zigadènus Fremontii*).

[5]*Linanthus androsàecus* and possibly a subspecies of the *Linanthus*.

[6]Possibly *Erysimum capitatum*.

[7]Probably larkspur (*Delphinium variegatum*).

[8]Probably owl's-clover (*Orthocarpus purpuráscens*) and *Orthocarpus attenàtus*.

[9]Possibly evening-snow (*Linanthus dichotomus*).

[10]Except for the clerk of the California State Supreme Court, this was an election for county officers. In Stockton the offices which were open for election were: district attorney, county clerk, county attorney, surveyor, sheriff, recorder, assessor, coroner, and treasurer. Osbun voted illegally, since the state Constitution required that a voter be not only a United States citizen but also a resident of California for six months and of the district in which he claimed his vote for thirty days.

ness; the side of the head around the eyes has its black feathers tipped with red & forms there a rich maroon colour. Take all in all, it is a beautiful bird. It is larger than ours, & lives on acorns, which it stores away in trees for winter's use. I dressed it, & eat it, & found it excellent.

Tuesday, 2d. As I expected, we did not get off to day, tho every thing is now ready I believe for a start. Wood & provisions have been laid in & the freights all settled. I have been much amused to day witnessing some Vaquaros lassoing calves & cattle on the Ranch here; they caught quite a number & take them when under full chase. They first catch them by the head & then the feet, when they throw them & tie them, & so leave them. I called this morning at the house of Mr. Weber, the owner of the ranch & proprietor of the town, & took a copy of the town plat with the sloughs &c. for my map.

Wednesday, 3d. This morning we made our exit from the town of Stockton a little after sun rise, with a favorable wind for a start. The town of Stockton, as will be seen by the map, is situated at the head of a slough, three miles from the river of San Joaquin. It was laid out last summer by Mr. Weber, & contains now a population of about [blank in MS].[11] During the winter her population is much more. Many come down from the mines to remain here during the season of rain. At this time but few are here excepting the regular citizens of the place. It is a regular stopping place for the miner. A great number of sail vessels & 4 or 5 small steamers now ply regularly between this place & San Francisco, well filled with passengers & merchandise.[12] Trains of mules & ox teams carry them off as fast as they arrive, so that but little delay is experienced here. Property here in certain locations rates verry high & in my opinion never will be higher. In a few years mining will be done by fewer persons, when the support for towns will

[11]The Census of 1850 gave the population of San Joaquin County, which included Stockton, as 3,647. There was no breakdown by political divisions within the county. In 1849 the permanent population of Stockton was estimated as 1,000, and in April 1850 some two to three thousand men were said to have landed there en route to the Southern Mines. *Seventh Census of the United States: 1850,* p. 969; Hubert Howe Bancroft, *History of California* (San Francisco, 1886-90), VI, 466.

[12]The steamer *Captain Sutter* was advertised as sailing from Stockton for San Francisco on Mondays and Thursdays at 7 A.M., and the steamer *Wm. Robinson* as sailing at 2 A.M. on Tuesdays and Fridays. *Stockton Times and Tualumne City Intelligencer,* May 18, 1850, [p. 6], col. 1.

be taken away considerably, & of course its property must depreciate. Its situation is indeed verry delightfull, being skirted on its back by timbered land, & in front by a full view of the Coast range with Monte Diable in the centre. But to me the association of sickness with the extensive swamps that lie in front & all along the valley, & the autumnal fevers that must cut down annually a goodly portion of the citizens, takes away all the charms of the location as a place to reside. It must forever remain a verry sickly place. There are not a great many business houses here, but there is still a great deal of business done. This summer it is expected many houses will be built. Our lumber was mostly for Mr. Weber, & with it was the frames for thirty houses, to be put up immediately.

The wind soon falling we were compelled to tow the vessel out of the slough; we then floated down the stream in fine style. The willows along the bank are putting forth their leaves rapidly, also the Black berries, whose blossoms are now in full bloom & leaves about half grown, a great many of which I see up here where the banks are a little elevated. We floated untill it became quite dark, when the Capt. ordered to weigh [sic] anchor, having floated at least 25 miles. And I think we could have safely went much farther.

Thursday, 4th. We again made an early start, but our progress has been verry slow. As usual many vessels have passed us to day, which is verry provoking. We caught a verry fine mess of our usual kind of Fish, & had a luxurious feast upon them, fried for supper. I ate of them verry heartily; they are the first kind of fish that I can say I ever really enjoyed myself in eating. Musquitoes are beginning to be verry bad, our vessel is to night verry full of them, & we anticipate but little sleep. Not expecting them so soon, none of us are provided with bars. We have to day filled our water casks, & wish we had them all here as it would save us some trouble at San Francisco. I have washed up most of my dirty cloathes to day & darned my socks, & intend to finish all before I leave the fresh water, preparatory to the voyage at sea. We floated to day about ten miles.

Friday, 5th March [April]. We have been much tormented to day with sand flies, a fly similar to our gnat. Our vessel became suddenly full of them. It showered occasionally through the day & this evening it fell in torrents for a short time. We have made but poor headway to day.

Saturday, 6th. We anchored last night about the same place we lay the first night after we entered the river. To day we have had verry high winds, & were compelled to beat our way. We in doing so ran aground several times, & finally at the foot of a small island above New York we ran upon a bar so hard we were compelled to wait for the tide to lift us off. In the night she floated off. Yesterday we all went to work, stripped the cabin of its contents, & with scalding water slew our thousands. To day has been a general wash day, and during the storm a pair of my drawers was blown overboard.

Sunday, 7th. This day we have made an early start, but as usual made but little headway. In passing down we took the wrong channel, & entered the Sacramento, instead of taking the slough by N. York, so that the distance was much increased, & as we desired to stop at New York, we were compelled to go back some distance, & were thus delayed. We stopped here & obtained 19 water casks for our outside voyage. We then hoisted sails, & were soon dashing through the waters of Suisson Bay. The wind being [a] head we were forced to tack, & in a verry short distance we were again upon high ground, & at high tide. So here we were good again for this night. The tide in falling turned up our vessel on its side so much that we could only with great difficulty walk on the deck. I went ashore at New York and collected another bouquet of most beautiful flowers, several new kinds. I took drawings of two of them.

Monday, 8th April. The tide arose & about 9 oclock last night we swung off. This morning we made an early start. The wind has been verry high, which has set old Suisson in great commotion, being covered with white caps & high rolling waves. It has rained occasional showers & also hailed during the day.

By the assistance of flag staffs placed upon Islands & Buoys, we have been enabled to pass through in fine style without a single stoppage. The wind has continued strong all day ahead, so it has been a day of constant tacking. We came to Anchor just as we entered the bay of San Pablo under the lee of an Island on the starboard side before sun set & remained untill morning.[13]

Tuesday, 9th. We made an early start & having a fair wind, we rode along in fine style, & by half past nine were moored off Clark's point

13This was probably Mare Island.

at San Francisco. We have been just 24 days making our voyage. And it could have been made in 12. We carried up a little over 89,000 feet of Boards at $50 per M. & 15 bbls. of Liquors, the freight amounting to a little over $4500.00. I went ashore after dinner, & was much struck with the changes that have taken place in the appearance of many parts of the city since I left, many large new houses having been put up & finished, & many old ones untenanted that were doing a heavy business & since failed. There has been within a few days extensive arrivals of vessels & immigrants, so that the city presents a bustling appearance. All busily employed making their purchases & arrangements for the mines. Merchants seem to be doing well. I did not see the Gov. untill late, he being absent on a visit to see his lots in pleasant valley. He tells me he has had a violent attack of fever & ague; his mouth & nose show the strong marks of it, being covered with fever sores. Neither Mr. May nor Mr. Bailey have been here. No letters from home. I eat ashore a piece of green grape pie, & 1 pint of milk for which I paid 50 cts.

Wednesday, 10th. Went ashore again & remained untill night. The Capt. & Mate have been busily engaged in settling up the business of the voyage to Stockton, so that nothing has as yet been done for the outside trip. There are many evening amusements advertised viz. Model Artists—Theatre—concert instrumental—& legerdemain, but I have not attended any of them, nor do I intend to.

Thursday, 11th. We have to day despatched Mr. Kissam to see Mr. Bayley to make new arrangements for our trip. We are not at all satisfied. He will be absent 3 or 4 days. So we can do but little untill he returns. My health has so improved my appearance & fattened me up that I am now scarcely known as the same person. Even the Gov. says he had to take the second look before he recognized me. I found my bag the evening I arrived here in the bar of the Bryant House. It was left there during my absence & the Gov. had not known it. So that all is now right; the first book of my Journal was in it, with some important records that I did not wish to loose.

Friday, April 12th. I enjoyed myself so poorly on shore yesterday I concluded to remain aboard to day. Consequently all hands went ashore, & left me alone. I put in the day verry well, writing, examining old papers and letters, & washing up some dirty cloathes.

88

Saturday, 13th. All hands went ashore, & I remained alone all day. I put in the day reading & washing cloathes. The ship Huron, which Mr. Perry & myself offered $3500 for, was sold at auction to day for $1300. Many are now sick here with dysentery, & it is quite fatal. I understand from 5 to 7 have been the daily interments for several days. The Capt. of the Huron is laying verry low with it.

Sunday, 14th. Perry & myself went on shore after breakfast & we took first quite a long walk past Rincon point & into the valley in which the Mission Dolores is located. We were much delighted with the great variety of flowers scattered on all sides of us; we collected a handsome bouquet each & left them in the Gov's office. We took dinners at a chinese house for which we paid ea. $1.00—& then took another ramble over the hills N. & NW. of the city. We were here shown the celebrated medicinal plant called Yerba Buena. I collected some with the intention of taking a drawing of it; it is a running plant of the species of mint, having a small heart shaped leaf the size of a 5 cent piece. We found also the California poppy, & a beautiful, large, deep orange coloured violet. The Steamer Tennessee arrived at 12 oclock to day having on board 551 passengers, besides the crew. I hope I may recieve letters from home. This is the largest number of passengers that have arrived in any one vessel.

Monday, 15th. I have remained aboard & alone all day. I spent it in reading, cooking, & drawing the Yerba Buena plant.

Tuesday, 16th. Mr. Kissam returned this morning. And succeeded in making the arrangements with Mr. Bayley as we desired. So we now go ahead in making our arrangements for a speedy departure. He brought a letter to the Governor authorising him to alter the charter paper & to make the parties consist of 4 instead of 5, striking out the name of Capt. Gunner. Mr. Perry now goes out as Capt. We all went on shore & remained untill night, looking around for men & provisions. We shipped one sailor, his wages to begin tomorrow. He went with us to Stockton & received upwards of $100 for his services. This sum he spent & was used up 2 or 3 days ago. Yesterday he earned $4 & it was burning in his pocket to day, so he could not commence untill it was gone. He came aboard this evening as full as a tick & as merry as a cricket. He is an old Man-of-Wars-Man: his name is William Austin.

We expect to get off on Saturday, & I think some of going out as cook.

Wednesday, 17th. This morning our cook was discharged, & I took up the reins of the galley to try how it would go. And my first day's experience is not verry favorable. We shipped two sailors to day, one a native of the Island of Otaheite, a large, stout & vigorous looking man. We pay him $60 per month; his name is Thomas Brown. The other is from New York; his name is Wm. Allen. We pay him $50 per month. The man we shipped yesterday begged off this morning & we let him go. Our men were employed to day partly in bringing aboard water casks & filling them, & arranging them below in their proper position.

Thursday, April 18th. This morning we moved our vessel up opposite Happy Valley & lashed to & alongside the Ship Splendid, for the purpose of taking aboard some provisions & boards. The wind being favorable we soon accomplished it. I find that I shall resign my office as cook verry soon. I am too green in that line to give satisfaction.

Friday, 19th. To day our men have been busy getting aboard the water casks & filling them with water for ballast, also boards & flour & meat & bread. The Steamer Tennesee leaves for Panama tomorrow; I sent home in her letters to wife & Daughter.

Saturday, 20th. Mr. Kissam has started this evening back again to Sacramento to see Mr. Bailey. He paid out all the money of the vessel, in paying her debts & some of Mr. Bailey's, before he was aware of it, & now has to call upon him to furnish us the promised funds. Our men have to day been busy in filling the water casks for ballast with salt water, & finished them. They also brought aboard a lot of stores from shore. We have to day taken aboard two men as hands, about noon one by name Noah Thayer as Cook. The other this evening, whose name is Richard Taylor, comes as a sailor. He is one of the four persons who went up the river to Stockton with us on his way to the mines. He went to near the Sinorian Camp & dug hard 10 days & collected but 3 dollars; he became disgusted with mining, left & pushed for us. He almost concluded at Stockton to come with us, but was persuaded to give them a trial.

Sunday, 21st. I took a walk over Rincon point & down to the valley south, & gathered a fine bunch of flowers. I saw on the Rocks where we landed a great number of Star fish from 4 to 6 inches across. They were verry beautiful & of different brilliant colours, Orange, blue &c. They have hundreds of small legs underneath, with which they attach themselves verry firmly to the rocks on the principle of sucktion. They are shaped like a Star with 4 projections.[14]

The wind being strong, we had to leave the Splendid this morning. As the tide was flowing, we unloosed our fastenings & dropped near & off from Rincon point. The Steamer did not get off until this morning. Taylor left us this evening; we suppose for higher wages.

Monday, 22d. I went on shore to day; took a copy of the Company's accounts & forwarded one to D. Peck Esqr. I walked up to Rincon point to hail the boat to take me aboard, & whilst there I saw many persons hunting for fish under the rocks laying along shore. It appears there is a variety of fish called here flat heads that look much like our cat fish.[15] They appear to live in holes under these rocks; the tide rising gives them fresh water regularly. They run sticks under these rocks, & if any are there they make a croaking noise when they put in a stick with a hook on its end & pull it out. I suppose they were left there accidentally by the ebbing tide; but one of the fishermen told me he frequently found them where the entrance to them would not permit them to pass out. I have taken a drawing to day of the limb or branch of a beautiful flowering shrub, growing among the rocks & in a thin dry sandy soil.[16] It seems to flourish here best on the steep hill sides. I found it also on the rocky bars of the Yuba.[17] It is a gummy shrub with beautiful bright orange flowers. I have not been able to find out its name. It grows from 3 to 4 feet high.

The Steamer Panama arrived here this morning with near 300 passengers aboard. The Gov. is sick again with ague; he is now verry sick; he had a chill on Saturday, & another to day.

Tuesday, April 23d. The climate here is now delightful. News continues to come in from the mines that the waters are still too high for

[14]This was almost surely the "sea bat" or web star (*Patiria miniata*), which varies spectacularly in color and is common in such habitats.

[15]This was obviously the northern midshipman (*Porichthys notatus*), the males of which hold nest territories under intertidal rocks in central California. It is a species of the toadfish family.

[16]This was the *Mimulus aurantiacus,* or *Diplacus aurantiacus.*

[17]This was the *Mimulus bifidus,* or *Diplacus grandiflorus.*

doing much, tho hundreds seem flocking to them daily. I have remained all day aboard; the Capt. ashore, trying to ship more men.

Wednesday, 24th. The Capt. & myself went ashore to clear the vessel & fill up the crew. We shipped a Mr. Pease as 2d Mate & succeeded after much trouble in clearing the vessel, having 7 men on our list. The Gov. is out to day for the first & looks verry bad.

I took my stand this afternoon in the ranks at the post office expecting we might possibly leave tomorrow. I was determined if any letters were there to get them to day. There were about 50 persons ahead of me on the line from I to T. It kept me 1½ hours only waiting & then got nothing.

Thursday, 25th. The Steamer Senator did not arrive last night & has not yet. Something must be wrong. Of course Kissam did not come as he expected to come in her. The Capt. went on shore & remained all day, looking for the arrival of the boat every moment. We are still in the same spot, but the Capt. says we will certainly move from here tomorrow for Stone ballast.

I took a drawing to day of another flower. My friend here, the cook, says it is a species of the Iris. It is a cluster of beautiful brilliant blue flowers, on the head of a foot stock 1 foot long. It has a bulbous root with long narrow leaves shooting directly from the root.[18] I made up my account with the mining Company in a small book to day together with the reciepts & expenditures of funds in my hands.

Friday, 26th. The Senator arrived last night, & brot Mr. Kissam. He & I went on shore & make some more purchases of goods, & to remain there untill the vessel would go to Angel Island & take in some stone for ballast. Immediately after we left her she started. We shipped another seaman this morning; his name is Charles Platt.

Saturday, 27th. Kissam & myself hunted around among the auction stores for goods such as we wanted, but none were offered of the kind we wanted. During the afternoon we made our purchases, at the regular houses. I to day recieved a letter from John Gill and answered it. I also yesterday recieved one from my wife & daughter & one from Hazen. I wrote to wife yesterday. The letters were brought by the

[18]Probably the *Iris longipétala.*

Companies from St. Clairsville neighborhood, & Flushing. I saw to day in the most public street of the city a house fitted up entirely for the purpose of cockfighting. They have up a regular sign, & have every thing arranged in the best manner for the purpose. The admission fee is $2.00. They told me a fight was expected to come off to night, on the result of which bets to the amount of $2000 are made.

Sunday, 28th. Kissam & I took a long walk along the beach to see if our vessel had made a moove to come in, but we saw her laying still at anchor off the Island. We returned about noon & dined at the Central house. I spent the afternoon at the Governor's Office. We expected the vessel to send for us certainly this evening, but she arrived off the point too late. So we must put in another night here.

6

VOYAGE TO FANNING ISLAND

©

Monday, 29th. This morning immediately after breakfast Perry came after us, which rejoiced us much. I cannot put in my time with any comfort on shore, having there nothing to do. We went aboard & at half past 2 oclock we commenced our voyage. The wind was ahead, which required us to make frequent tacks. It has blown quite a strong gale all afternoon. We came to Anchor in the left bend below the old fort, thinking it not prudent to attempt crossing the bar at the entrance of the Bay during low tide. The roaring of the surf here as it lashes the shore reminds me much of the romance described so vividly by novelists. The Lat. of the Fort is 37°48′30″. Long. 122°27′23″; of the Port 37°49′ & Long 122°14′.

Tuesday, 30th. Last night our vessel tossed about at a great rate. I awoke several times during the night & found myself quite sick. This morning immediately after breakfast we were under sail. I soon became verry sick & vomited several times during the day. We were out of sight of land long before night; the wind blowing a strong breeze from the West & NW. by W. made the sea verry rough. Several vessels were seen with their course directed towards San Francisco. Wind NW. by W. Av. 6 ms. per hor.

Wednesday, May 1st. Yesterday was denseley clouded all day so that no observations were taken. Today the sun could be seen occasionally. I have been verry sick & kept my berth all day. Our position at noon to day is in Lat. 35°38′. Longitude 125°08′ [penciled notation 124°28′]. Wind NW. 218 Ms. from San F.

Thursday, 2d. This day we have but little wind, & of course have not made much progress. I am quite well of my sea sickness & have en-

94

joyed & amused myself, with some slight exceptions, well upon deck. I fixed a hook & bated it for birds, & caught what the sailors call a Stinker, a large water bird about the size of our Goose with a web foot & of a grey colour. It has a large bill like the Gull or Albatross; its right name is [blank in MS].[1] I caught it by hooking it in the bill, from the water. We also dragged in a stock of Sea Kelp, it having been detached from rock. It was about 50 feet long, hollow, & covered with small sea worms, crabs & shells. I cut off the bottom with the roots, covered with shells, & am making an attempt to dry it altogether, to carry home. Wind NW. Our position at noon was in Lat. 33°54'— Long. 126°36'. Sailed S. 42, W. 136 ms.

Friday, 3d. It has been clouded all day, & this evening it commenced raining. We have had more wind to day than yesterday. Its general direction was from SW. & our course S. 14° E. At noon our Latitude was 33°22'. Longitude 126°28'. Our distance sailed the last 24 hours was 33 miles, & our whole distance from San Francisco 387 miles. Nothing of interest has occurred to day, & nothing worthy of notice seen. Perry had a shake of Ague about 3 oclock this afternoon.

Saturday, 4th. At noon to day our Lat. is 33°01'. Long. 128°10'. Course S. 78°45' W. Distance run 104½ miles. Whole distance 491 miles.

It rained for several hours this morning quite hard, but cleared up before noon & we had a pleasant afternoon with a fair sailing breeze. I put in my time after my professional duties studying the calculations & taking observations in Navigation. To day I have spent in calculating longitude by the chronometer. I succeeded but am not entirely satisfied with its "Modus operandi." I can I think make the observations & take them down correctly & also calculate latitudes. Wind SE. by E.

Sunday, 5th. At noon to day our Latitude is 31°04'. Long. 129°43' 30". Course S. 38°30' W. Dist. run 150 miles. Whole distance 641 miles.

This has been a pleasant day upon the Ocean. My leg & ancle pains me to day considerably; they are inflamed & swelled. I have listened to day to many marvellous tales told respecting whales & whalefishery

[1]Probably a black-footed albatross.

by our 2d Mate who is an old whaler. He tells me the carcass of one whale would fill our vessel.

A good portion of my time has been spent in making calculations. And also in thinking of my family. Oh how I would like to see my wife & dear children. I have also indulged the idea of spending a few years on sea, in trading from port to port, & from one country to another, but not without my whole family along. I have imagined I could teach & train them better than on shore. Wind NW. by W.

Monday, 6th May. At noon to day we find ourselves in Latitude 29°52′ N. & Longitude 131°02′ W. Our course to day or since noon yesterday has been S. 47°30′ W., distance run 107 miles, whole distance 748. The wind has been from NW. by W. I have spent all my leizure time to day studying the rules of Navigation & making calculations. I have made myself the calculations of the vessel correctly, altho I do not as yet consider myself master of them. Nothing has been seen or done to day worth noting.

Tuesday, 7th. Our Latitude is 28°47′. Longitude 132°09′. Our course S. 46° W. Dist. run 93 miles, whole dist. 841 miles. Wind NW. To day several droves of Porpoise were seen, & this evening it has clouded up & is raining.

Thursday, 9th. Yesterday being cloudy our observations were imperfect. To day at noon we are in Latitude 25°23′ N. & Longitude 135°51′ W. Our course S. 47°20′ W. & distance since the 7th being 2 days 303 miles, whole distance 1144 miles. Last night we entered the trade winds, being NE. by N. So to day we are going ahead with fine speed.

Friday, 10th. Our latitude is 23°20′ N. & Longitude 138°25′ W. Our course S. 51°30′ W. & distance run 198 miles: whole distance 1342 m. The wind has been steady & fine from E. & NE. This forenoon we have crossed the *Tropical line*, & are now within the *Tropics*. This line is the tropic of Cancer.

Saturday, 11th. Our Lat. is 21°35′ N. & Long. 140°27′. Our distance run 162 ms. Wind East by N. Course S. 49°30′ W. Whole distance run 1504 miles. Since crossing the Tropical line, it has appeared to grow warm & pleasant rapidly. The air is now soft & most refreshing.

This morning a pair of birds of a new variety came sailing around our vessel. Sailors call them Boatswains, or Tropics. They are a white bird, somewhat larger than a Pidgeon, having a red bill, straight & pointed. Its tail is its most remarkable peculiarity, having but 3 singularly formed feathers, about 15 inches long. I have only seen them at a distance flying & have this description from the sailors. The tail feathers run to a point, & its feet are webbed.[2] A flock of Stinkers are as yet always with us & we now occasionally see a few Petrel, or as the sailors call them Mother Carey's chickens, skimming along the surface of the waves. We also see an occasion[al] drove of Flying fish. One flew upon the deck just before I went to bed, about 6 inches long. I cut off two of his wings, a front & back one (they having 4 wings, 2 large & 2 small situated on their sides, & that answer both for flying & swimming) & placed them in the back of this book to dry. The capt. will cook him & eat him for his breakfast in the morning, he being yet on the sick list.

Sunday, 12th. Our Latitude is 19°54′ N. & Longitude 142°17′ W. Wind ENE. Course SW. by S. Distance run 149 ms., whole distance 1653.

Monday, 13th. Our Latitude is 17°56′ N. & Longitude 143°56′. Wind NE. by E. Dist. run 154, whole dist. 1807. We this morning passed under the present meridian of the sun; consequently we are now south of her. At noon we see here no shadows, & altho her rays fall perpendicularly upon us, it is still uncommonly pleasant; a fine breeze is constantly blowing, which feels as mellow & soft as the finest velvet or down upon the skin. It would indeed be revelling in nature's luxuries could one enjoy such an atmosphere the year round. This evening the sky in the west assumed a threatening aspect. All hands were busied preparing for a blow, the ropes & fixtures all examined & properly placed & replaced. But the storm passed around us. We experienced only a fine gale.

Tuesday, 14th. Our Latitude is 15°52′ N. Longitude 145°46′ W. & course since noon yesterday by Compass SW. by S. & wind NE. & changeable. Dist. run 167 ms., whole dist. 1974. I saw last evening for the first time during this voyage the Southern Cross. It was how-

2Probably a red-billed tropic bird.

97

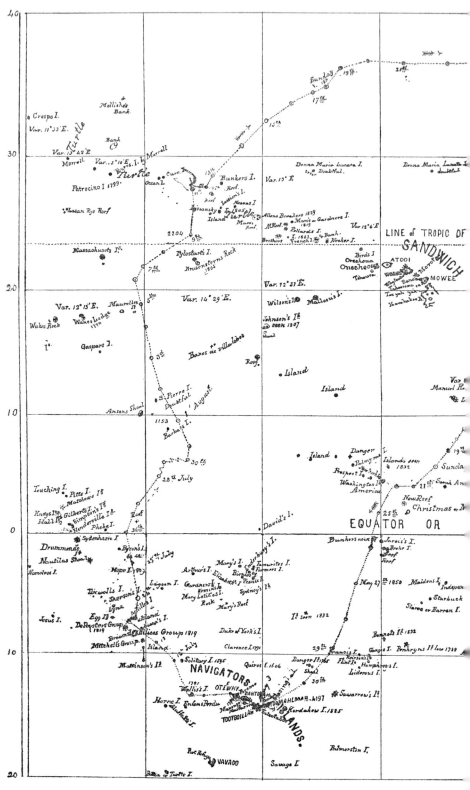

CHART OF THE PACIFIC OCE

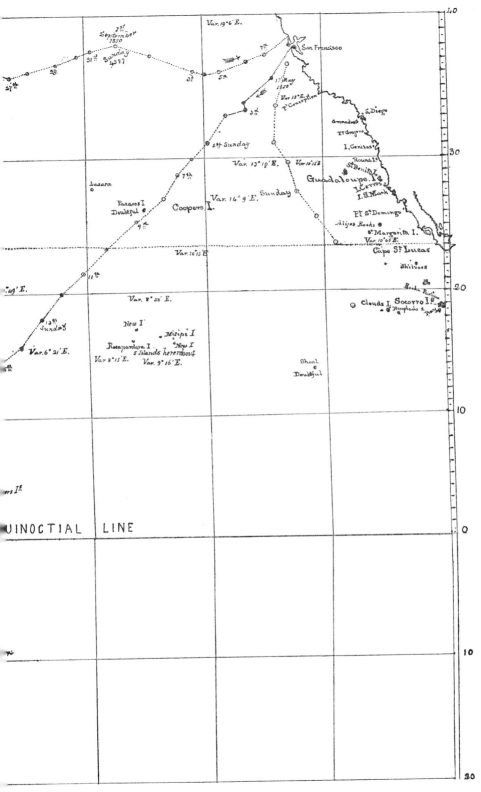

Var. 19°6' E.

1st
September
1850
31st Sunday
4587

28

27th

7th

San Francisco

1st May
1850
Var. 13°E. Pt. Conception

3rd

8th Sunday

S. Diego
Coronados
Pt. Grayro
I. Cenizas

Var. 13°19' E. Var. 10°55' Round I.
St. Benito I.
Guadaloupe I.
I. Cerros
I.S. Mark

7th Var. 14°9' E. Sunday

Lazara

Pararos I
Doubtful Coopers I.

9th

Pt. St. Domingo
Alijos Rocks
St. Margarith I.
Var. 10°65' E.

Var. 10°15' E. Cape St. Lucas

Shilvaes

11th Rocka Partida 20

Var. 8°50' E. Clouds I. Socorro I.
Neupiedo I.

ug' E.

3rd
Sunday

Var. 6°21' E. New I.

Misipi I.

Rosapardara I. New I.
5 Islands hereabout
Var. 8°15' E. Var. 9°16' E.

Shoal
Doubtful

rs I.

10

UINOCTIAL LINE 0

10

20

CRAWN BY ALBERT GALLATIN OSBUN

ever visible for a few evenings before, tho I did not see it. I have untill last evening generally spent my evenings in the Cabin reading & writing. I commenced a few days ago making a navigator's map of the Pacific Coast, Ocean & Islands, which has occupied a portion of my time. This, with making calculations & superintending the cooking department, occupies my whole time.

Wednesday, May 15th. To day our Latitude is 14°02′ N. & Longitude 148°10′ W. Our course by Compass SW. Wind E. by N. variable. Distance run 182 ms. Whole dist. 2156. It is still verry pleasant, with an occasional sprinkle or light shower of rain.

Thursday, 16th. Our Latitude to day is 11°32′ N & Longitude 150° 33′ W. Course SW. ½ S. Wind SE. by E. Dist. run 209 ms. Whole dist. 2365. We have made the last 24 hours our longest day's voyage, & we are fast approaching the Equator. I would not know that the heat of the sun was so great, on account of the breeze constantly blowing, were it not that but a few minutes' exposure of my skin to the rays of the sun burns me severely. My whole neck at this moment smarts severely, having been scorched through a thin chip hat whilst steering the vessel for a short time at midday. So regular has been our sailing that not a sail has been moved or meddled with for many days. We have 7 sails spread, Five to the foremast & 2 to the mainmast. Those on the foremast are called, beginning at the top: 1st Top gallant sail. 2d Top Sail. 3. Foresail. 4th Topmast Studding sail. 5. Lowermast studding sail. The two latter are placed along side the two lower centre sails. Those on the mainmast are called beginning below: 1st Mainsail. 2d Gaff-Topsail. This evening quite a large drove of Porpoise, having discovered us, came meeting us with tremendous speed. Long before they got to us we could see them leaping from the water, apparently looking for us, & making their course direct to us. They played around the vessel about one half hour & then left us. In playing they leap entirely from the water, & occasionally spring from 15 to 20 feet. They appear to be from 5 to 6 feet long, & are rather a fine looking fish. They bring forth their young, like the whale, alive, & suckle them. It has put us all quite in the notion of rigging up something to catch them, having no tool aboard for the purpose.

Friday, 17th. To day noon we are in Latitude 9°02′ N. & Long. 152°55′ W. Wind has been from ENE. & the weather quite squally.

Distance run 207 ms.—2572. It is now at times oppressively warm; last night between the heat & bed bugs I had but a poor night's rest. To day I overhauled my bed & committed many murders. Were it not for the constant breeze I suppose we would find it all the time uncomfortably hot. It commenced raining soon after dinner, & rained hard for several hours. We caught sufficient water to wash up all our cloathes. The wind fell off during the afternoon, so that our speed is considerably diminished. Nothing new is seen from day to day worthy of record; a continued sameness seems to pervade the whole voyage thus far. The interminable sheet of water spread all around us, disturbed & ruffled into constant swells by the wind, with an occasional sea bird skimming along its surface & the Brig ploughing up its track & dashing its foam right & left, occasionally scaring up shoals of flying fish, is about all that can be seen from day to day.

Saturday, May 18th. It has been clouded over all day, so that we have been unable to make our observations. We have however made but little progress in sailing, probably about one degree in Latitude & one in Long.

Sunday, 19th. Our Latitude is 7°13' N. & Longitude 154°23' W. Wind has been verry variable & light. We progress but slowly. Distance run 141 ms.—2713. We now begin to see more birds, which proves we are nearing land.

Monday, 20th. Latitude 5°43' N. Longitude 155°24'. Wind ENE. Dist. 109—2822. This morning we find our Cook sick with Lumbago; he has been sleeping for a few nights on deck & also got a wetting when in full perspiration on Friday, whilst assisting the men at the rigging. I took his place in the Galley & overheated myself, & drank considerable water which has made me verry unwell this evening. I have a verry severe headache, with a sour sick stomach. We have all felt the heat more to day than during any other day since we started. The sweat ran from me almost in a stream whilst employed in the galley, which was a good portion of the day. The Cook took his bed after breakfast & has not been out since.

Tuesday, 21st. Our Latitude is 4°01' N. & Longitude 157°18' W. Wind SSE. & squally. Dist. run 153—2975.
I have been verry unwell all night with severe pain in my head, &

slept in consequence but little. This morning I am better, my head & eyes only feeling verry sore. It has been verry warm again to day & I regret much that we have not a Thermometer to test its grade. This evening it is quite squally, clouded over & occasionally raining. Nothing new to be seen unless an increased number & variety of birds. This shows our proximity to islands, & tomorrow we expect to arrive at Fanning's Island where we will stop & go ashore for the purpose of seeing what can be done in trading. To day I assisted doing up the work, one of the men officiating as head cook. Our Cook is still in his bed & complains verry much.

Wednesday, May 22d. Latitude to day at noon is 4°04′ N. & Longitude 158°44′ W. Wind SE. by E. Dist. run 87 miles—3062 ms.

The position of Fanning's island as given in the Books is Lat. 3°44′ N. & Longitude 159°22′W. The chart gives it in Lat. 3°45′ N. & Long. 158°50′ W.[3] So that we do not know which is correct. We must be now too far west to make either locations with ease, with the present bearing of the winds. The wind is however shifting & we are enabled to steer SW.

Just as I was writing the above line the cry from the mast head came in "Land ho!" I ran out & discovered the land direct ahead, the trees in full view. Oh what a change this has produced upon my feelings. The prospect of getting my feet again upon land is indeed cheering to me, & the idea of stepping upon the Shore of an Island so remote from main land, so near the Earth's Equator, with all the productions of such a Latitude growing upon it, fills me with delight. It is now just 2 oclock. And all hands are already at work preparing to anchor. We are now approaching the Island from the NE., & sailed under a fine breeze untill we came quite near to it. It is covered with cocoa nut trees & smaller shrubs, is verry flat & seems to be considerably cut up with entrances of water & passages or lagoons running through it. We approached it at the mouth of one of those entrances, or bays as they look to be, the front of which seemed to be surrounded by breakers; they extend along eastward entirely around the point of the island.

[3]The position 3° 44′ N. latitude and 150° 22′ W. longitude for Fanning Island is given in Nathaniel Bowditch, *The New American Practical Navigator,* 17th edn. (New York, 1847), p. 375. Probably this was the book available aboard *Rodolph.* Charts of the Pacific by Aaron Arrowsmith, Frederick William Beechey, and John William Norie were all in print at the time. Also, the charts of the United States Exploring Expedition (commanded by Charles Wilkes) were in print, but it is doubtful that they were generally available.

We appear to be about one fourth of the distance across the island from its east point; & from its most easternly to its most westernly point as seen by us, we have calculated it to be about 20 miles. An elevated body like a high coral peak is visible standing out a short distance from the east point in the ocean. We know not yet what it is. This part of the Island we find not inhabited & no safe landing & have tacked ship to pass around along its eastern side & perhaps to its southern or southwestern. Eastward of us we can see the waves lashing the peaks of coral & rolling its foaming waves along & high up upon the shore. This warns us to keep off.

We have sailed since 4 oclock NE. in which direction we continued untill 8, when we tacked & took our course due South. The wind has abated verry much so that we have made but little progress.

Thursday, 23d. I arose before the sun this morning, went upon deck, & find that we are just about the same spot we were in when I went to my bed last night. That is about 4 or 5 miles from land & some short distance East of the inlet described above. There is quite a current here in the Sea rolling westward & there is scarcely wind enough to enable us to hold our own. From our observations at noon we find our Latitude is 3°52′ N. & Longitude 159°08′, taken at a point where the Eastern point of the Island bears SW. by W. & the distance to the nearest point of the island about 5 miles. A gentle breeze arose during the afternoon, & has carried us around the Island so that now at half past six we are on its SE. side & near down to the point, around which when we turn we will be on its south or SW. side. It is considered prudent to remain here untill morning, and we have just now tacked & are going SE. It is the intention to tack backwards & forwards all night, turn the point in the morning & make our landing. The shore all along the border of the island is a coral rock elevated several feet above the sea, & above the rolling of the surf. It looks to be verry regular in its formation, & of about the same elevation the whole way round thus far. The land appears to be but little elevated above the surface of the Ocean, & is covered with a luxuriant growth of vegetation. In looking at it with the glass I can only distinguish the cocoa nut; the other growths are generally underwood. Birds flock in from the sea in great numbers, from sun down untill late after dark. The last ones remind me of children when at play far from home; they frolic & play forgetting that night is close at hand & they a long distance yet to go before they are at home.

These birds spend their whole time skimming over the waves of the sea from morn untill night, catching fish.

Friday, 24th. I arose at day break this morning, & found we were upon the south side of the Island, & the most suitable side also for landing. We hurried up breakfast, & had it over by 7 oclock. We now percieved an inlet to the lagoon in the centre of the island & verry soon a flag hoisted around the point of this inlet on its east side & on the shore of the lagoon; it was an Otaheite flag. Verry soon were seen the inhabitants upon the beach & a whale boat upon the water making for our vessel. We had been preparing busily to make a landing but now we waited the arrival of the boat. Soon it arrived having a Yankee & 4 Natives in it. From the former we gathered all the information we desired respecting the Island, its productions &c., & then concluded to pay him a visit. The Capt. went out first & purchased from him some supplies, & returned with him got dinner. And afterwards the Capt., Kissam & myself went ashore & spent there the afternoon. This Yankee whose name is Delia Williston hails originally from Rhode Island, appears to be about 45 years of age & has been absent from home 20 years. He appears to be a verry clever man; at least we were well pleased with him from our short acquaintance. He has been residing upon the Island of Otaheite untill he was employed by a company of Englishmen to come to this Island & take charge of a lot of Kanackeys from the Chain Islands & work them in making Cocoa nut Oil. He has been here off & on he says 7 years. He has now been here 2 years. He has with him upwards of 70 of these people, old & young, Male & Female, & is married to one of them & has by her 2 children. She is a strapping big fat lazy looking wench. We found her sitting upon a mat on the floor suckling her child, with her breasts bare. He tells me he has two other wives on other islands & several children by each one. They have no bread or flour, nor have they had any for 6 months; they have been looking for their vessel for 6 months with provisions, but it has not yet arrived & the natives are becoming quite discontented. They live principally upon the Cocoa nut & fish. The latter they catch here in great abundance & of excellent quality. Our vessel is the only one they have seen for many months & they were verry glad to see us, but would have been more so had it been their own vessel. The term by contract having expired for laboring here with a good portion of the company makes them more discontented. They have filled all their vessels with Oil, & have had nothing to do the last 5 months but gather nuts & feed themselves, a few hogs & chickens. On the island are no wild animals, except rats, no snakes, occasionally a centipede is seen, a great many land crabs, & I saw some verry small ants. There are verry few birds except water fowls. I saw a verry beautiful variety of Paroquetts. Our host had several for pets. He has upon the island about 50 Hogs, some of them verry fine, similar to our Berkshire breed, 3 or 400 chickens, 4 or 5 dogs & a few cats. These all together about comprizes every thing that dwells upon this Coral island. He computes it to be about 14 or 15 miles long & 5 or 6 wide. It is covered almost entirely with Cocoa nut trees & at this time I suppose there are millions of them upon it, none having been used except for eating for 5 months. He tells me in making the Oil they gather about 150,000 nuts per month & scrape them & put them in vats to rot. They then gather the oil from the top, & then press the dregs. It yields about 1 Bbl. of Oil to every 1000 of nuts, & sells by the pound or ton. It brings $80 per ton at Otaheite, or about 4 cts. per lb. It is used in making soap & oiling machinery. The Hogs live entirely upon the nuts; the pigs are weaned too early in consequence of the milk drying up early, which requires them to be raised by hand, & gives much trouble. Many die in consequence of it, their bowels becoming affected with scowers. Potatoes cannot be raised in consequence of the great number of land crabs devouring them. Arrow root was found growing here, & is now cultivated to some extent; this & a few pumpkins are the only vegetables cultivated. We got from the island 200 Cocoa Nuts for $1.00, 8 chickens $1.50, 1 cord dry wood $5.00, some eggs &c. presents, & 2 verry fine fish.

We found the natives of this Isl[and] verry pleasant & attentive to us, & always ready to wait upon us. They are verry fond of Tobacco, & all became beggars for it & were willing to give any thing they had for it. A few of them have been on whale ships & can speak a little English. Several of them were verry anxious to come with us, & when we left in the evening ran out to the point & commenced undressing to swim to us, but the Capt. had promised their Overseer not to take any of them, & we bore out too much from shore for them to risk swimming to us, the surf being verry high & the Current Strong. I obtained here a pair of Shells of the Pearl Oyster, which the Overseer & his men found sticking to [blank in MS] of the Ship wrecked here about 5 years ago; this shell is consequently less than 5 years old.

The Ship is sunk deep in the water, & his men were diving & getting things from her. He tells me he has gotten from her about 2 tons of

Copper. This pair of Shells he presented to me, with a pair of Claws of a species of land crab living here upon the Island in holes. They catch them by putting a string down their hole, which they take hold of & hold on untill drawn out; they open & shut like a knife blade. Also the tail & fighting spears of the Diamond fish, or Devil fish as it is sometimes called. The tail is from 2 to 3 feet long, is slender like a riding switch & elastic; it appears to be of a cartilaginous formation & black. The fighting Spears are 4 in number & are attached to the base of the tail or extremity of the body passing off backwards within a small space of each other. They are verry hard, sharp at the point, & sharply serrated on their edges. One of the Kanackas presented me with an ornament, made for wearing above the ears; it is similar to a rose fastened upon the end of a small stick, & is made with beautifully coloured feathers, taken from birds of the island. They wear two, one above each ear, worn both by males & females. I visited their fish pond built up with stone laid loosely upon each other 20 or 30 yds. from shore in the lagoon, the water being about 2½ feet deep, the stone reaching 18 in. above water. In this pond they deposit their fish as soon as they catch them with their hook, & when they wish to use them, they take them with a spear.

In it they had about one dozen of the most beautiful fish I ever saw from 2 feet down to 1 foot in length. Their colors struck me more than any thing else about them. Some of them were brilliant red, others blue with bright yellow fins, some variegated & handsomely striped & spotted. I collected on the beach several verry handsome specimens of Coral balls, but was not able to obtain any of the branching variety, it being some distance to the reef on which it grows. This is no Island for shells or other curiosities; the only thing peculiar is the immense quantity of loose Coral stone of small sizes piled up all around the island by the surf, & it being a place where lime of superior quality could be made at the most trifling expense & in any quantity, the shore being also lined with good wood for the purpose. They have plenty of fresh water upon the island, which they obtain by digging a hole & sinking in it a barrel. There are no running springs. For drinking however they use the water in the green cocoa nut. Each nut contains, when green & about full grown, from 1 pint to one quart of water, which is verry pleasant to the taste, & of which I became verry fond. It is verry thin, slightly sweet & acidulated. When Mr. Williston first came out to us in his whale boat, he brought about 20 of them with him for us, knowing that all seamen were fond of them. I cared but little for it when I took my first few drinks but like the Tomatoe it grew upon me rapidly, so that by night I became verry fond of it. We feasted with our host & hostess during the afternoon upon this Cocoa water & the head of a large fish, cooked in excellent style after the Kanacka mode, which is by heating stones & placing them in the ground around [the] fish, covering all up untill done. It was indeed excellent. In their small village they have from 15 to 20 houses or sheds, in which [they] live. They are thatched verry neatly & ingeniously with cocoa nut leaves, & generally surrounded or weatherboarded with the same material, the structure being kept up by upright poles or posts. Most of their houses have their floors covered entirely over with a coarse matting made from the Cocoa leaf, which gives an air of comfort to their rustic dwellings. We parted from our verry generous Islander & his Kanackes late in the afternoon, & by sundown our usual number of sails were unfurled & we under full sail, bearing South by West, having a fine breeze to waft us speedily upon our Course, our direction now being to the Friendly Islands via the Navigators. Our Cook has this evening resumed his duties.

Saturday, 25th May. The entrance to the lagoon & harbor of this Island [Fanning] has been Set down by our Capt. from our observations made on 23d & those of other ship masters, who have left with Mr. Williston their different observations, as in Latitude 3°44′ N. & Longitude 159°24′ W. 45 ms. To day at noon we find we are in Latitude 1°56′ N. & Longitude 160°09′ W. We have had a fine breeze SSW. & our vessel travels through the waves in gallant style. Soon now we will cross the Equator & commence our descent towards the South pole. I care not how fast. I anxiously look for the period to arrive when I shall start for home, to rest the balance of my days in the bosom of my family. Sailed 117 miles.

Sunday, 26th. Our Latitude to day is 1°05′ S. & Longitude 160°57′ W. Wind strong SSE. Dist. sailed to day 187 miles, whole dist. 3411.
We have now crossed the Equator, & are in the Southern hemisphere. We crossed it this morning between 3 & 4 oclock. The distance from San Francisco to the point where we crossed it in a strait line is about 3241 miles & averaging our daily sailing at about 130 miles per day. Our winds now are strong & we are sailing rapidly. The sea in consequence is quite rough & our vessel is tossed about to such an extent as to make it quite uncomfortable to move about in her. Our

dishes are with much difficulty kept steady long enough to eat our meals. We have side boards upon our table, but notwithstanding they are occasionally dashed over them & broken. The evenings are in consequence of the strong winds quite cool, & we are under the necessity of putting on our Coats.

Monday, 27th. Our Latitude is 4°05′ [S.] & Longitude 162°07′ W. Wind is still fresh & E. by S. & our headway good. Dist. sailed 193 miles—3604.

Tuesday, 28th. Latitude to day 7°00′ S. & Longitude 163°05′ W. Wind still strong. Our average sailing in 24 hours is about 180 miles. We have seen many birds during the night & this morning East of us which we consider evidences islands at no great distance in that direction. I understand there are many islands near our present position not on the charts, so that the hands are required during their watches, particularly at night, to keep a good lookout for them. We had for dinner yesterday Stewed Chicken & it was quite a relish. The day before we had feasted on fried pork & eggs. Our living generally is fair enough. We have excellent pickled pork & Beef in abundance, & always have it boiled & sliced on the table. Twice each week we have pea Soup made from peas dried & cut in halves; they are verry rich. Also occasionally Bean Soup & twice in each week Baked beans. These, with duff or Plum pudding twice a week, make up our dinners. We occasionally have a bread pudding, rice, Gingerbread & Sweet Cake. Also every other day boiled Mackarel & occasionally Potato stew or skouse, & bread Stew, & Scotch toast. Our meals are all eaten at certain regular hours, without variation, to suit the different watches. Viz. half past 7 A.M., 12 & 6 oclock. We sailed to day 184 miles—3788.

Wednesday, May 29th. Our Latitude is 9°52′ S. & Long. 164°12′ W. Wind variable from SSE. to ESE. Sailed 184 miles this day—3972.

We last evening let loose our chickens, 3 males & 1 female. They are verry tame being now all of them beside me in the cabin. Some of them setting down, others singing, they give variety & life to the vessel, & are good company, being good crowers & singers. They are now in fine health & spirits, but during the first day or two were verry sea sick. We feed them upon Cocoa Nuts principally, with bread & offal from the table.

7

SAMOAN ISLANDS

◎

Thursday, 30th. Our Latitude is 12°22' S. & Long. 166°32' W. Winds variable about SSE. Sailed 205 miles the last 24 hours—4177.

We now expect, the present winds keeping up, by tomorrow evening to have a view of the Navigator Islands, where we intend to land, & see what can be done. We were entirely disappointed at Fanning's Island, not finding any thing there to suit us, & I hope we will not be so disappointed at the Navigator or other islands we may visit. I have been loosing confidence in our Capt. for some time, & I have much feared & do now fear I will find all his representations false. I fear with our means our inability to purchase a cargo, even if we find plenty. He, having represented to us their exceeding cheapness, prevented us from bringing more. The ocean has been verry rough & our vessel unsteady. We are scarcely able to walk about in consequence of her rolling & pitching.

Friday, 31st. About half past 8 oclock this morning we suddenly came in full view of an Island, raising its peaks high up in the clouds. The whole morning had been squally, & considerable rain falling we were almost upon it before we were aware of it. In one hour we were sailing boldly along its NE. shore. It is called Toomalooah on the maps, but the natives call it Toomanooah. It is the largest of a group of 3 islands, laying most easternly of the main Navigator Islands. They reach SE. & NW. We came up on its SE. end & sailed down its NE. side in the direction of NW. to its NW. Extremity. The island at its SE. end I should judge is about [blank in MS] miles wide, & the side along which we sailed about [blank in MS] miles long. As we sailed along we saw a village of Kanackas about midway of the island & in its centre quite a large missionary church as white as snow, being built partly in American or English style, having a door in the centre & 4 windows on each side, & one story high.[1] The roof ran up high & is covered with Cocoa leaf in Kanacka style. We find at its NW. end a pretty fair harbor & another village, with its missionary & central church but not so large or fine. We also saw a number of streams pitching headlong down the steep sides of the mountain at least 500 feet: wet weather streams, as I was informed, they having made in their passage no impression upon the rock.

The island rises on this side suddenly from the sea shore to a high mountain & is covered with a rich & luxuriant growth of vegetation, among which I discovered many Cocoa nut trees. There was but one narrow strip of low flat land, & that was where the village was located. It appeared to be a beautiful grove of Cocoa nut trees.

At half past 10 we, having hauled to, were boarded by 3 Kanackas, One of them bearing a certificate of character &c. from the Capt. of a ship, as a good interpreter, honest &c. He has been on ships & to the States & is originally from the Island of Rottomah. He has been here several years. His name is Sam Henry. He tells us they have plenty of Hogs & Cocoa nuts, also Yams, Tara & Breadfruit, Bananas, Pine apples & chickens, these being the only things produced upon the Island. The Capt. & myself, after giving them something to eat & drink, went with them ashore in our boat. One of the 3 was a young man, the Son of the Chief. His name is Osheah, his wife Filuh. His father the chief's name is Osoowh. He conducted us to the chief's house, where we were introduced to him & his family. Mats were immediately spread for us on their already covered floors, & we were invited by our smiling hosts to be seated. His daughter was present, a very pleasant open countenance & smiling squaw, & did up in good style the duties of the female in spreading the mats &c.

It was now near noon & we were immediately asked what we would have for dinner, through the interpreter, whether Pig, chicken or fish. We told them not to put themselves to trouble to day, but that we would eat with them on another day. The Capt. returned to the vessel after finding a suitable place to anchor, to bring her in near shore & anchor her. He took out with him the chief, & gave him his dinner. I

[1]This sentence originally read: "As we sailed along we saw a village of Kanackas about midway of the island & in its centre quite a large church, of the missionary, a Kanacka, as white as snow, being built partly in American or English style. . . ." Later Osbun canceled "of the missionary" and substituted "missionary" between "large" and "church." This left the phrase reading "in its centre quite a large missionary church, a Kanacka, as white as snow." In the present version "a Kanacka" has been omitted, since Osbun certainly did not mean that he saw an albino native.

remained on shore & was singularly & pleasantly entertained untill sun down. We were met at the landing by a great number of the natives, probably among them 40 or 50 small boys & girls all naked except the loins. They are a fine looking race of people, quick & active in their motions & verry kind & hospitable. During the day or afternoon I took frequent walks along the beach & back through their groves of Cocoa nuts, Bread fruit trees &c., & was always attended by a crowd, some of them grasping my hands & leading me along, & in crossing their stone fences were ready with outstreached hands to raise me up & help me down. I was invited into every house I passed, to be seated & to eat something. I happened to pass near the house of their missionary, a Kanacka. He came out a short distance & met me & invited me verry cordially to go with him to his house. I did not know who he was, but he looked quite intelligent, tho only dressed around the loins. I presumed him a common man. I entered his house, it having two apartments in it, & went with him to his own room. There he invited me to be seated on his bed, & spread out his books. I found them to be tracts & the different books of the bible & Testament, & a prayer book, printed in the Kanacka language, & read them out to him, which pleased him much, he occasionally correcting me when I pronounced words wrong. I suspected him then to be their preacher & asked him if he was a missionary & he answered me yes. He could read & write fluently. I gave him card case & pencil & asked him to write his name, which he did. It is Moa Fituita. He spread upon a mat a roasted Tara, two small fish & some Cabbage dressed in Cocoa butter. The Tara eat pretty well, particularly when covered with the Cabbage, it having a rich spicy or minted taste. The fish were of a fine kind, but being roasted just as they were taken from the water without cleaning, scaling or any other dressing, & also having no salt upon them, I with difficulty eat any of them. I left him & proceeded up the village & in passing the chief's house was met & hailed & entreated to go in, & as I thought they were somewhat excited, I at first hesitated, afterwards concluded to go in. I found they had killed a chicken & dressed it for me in their best style, having baked it with their hot stones in the earth, & also prepared Tara &c. & fully expected me to dine with them. I saw them catch the chicken, & promised to dine with them, but did not understand what I promised. They knew I was eating in the parson's house, & supposed their labor was all for nothing, but when I entered, they produced & spread before me in mats the dinner. I went to work & ate what I could. As I finished, the crowd around devoured what I left without ceremony, tearing the fowl in pieces with their hands & teeth & dividing it among them. In this they acted like savages. They use no salt in their cooking.

I walked about during the afternoon to see the productions & curiosities of the island. I saw the bread fruit (oo'loo), the cocoa nut (ne'uh), mummy apple (Ase) & Banana (Fi) all growing most luxuriantly. I also saw bats flying near as large as chickens. Near night a native called me & asked me to go to his house & see yams &c. I asked him where he lived. He pointed down town. I followed him untill through the village & to where the road commenced ascending the mountain. I then found he lived in the town on the other side of the island, & refused to go further. He urged me hard to go, & offered to carry me; when I turned back his face showed a strong picture of disappointment. I returned about sundown to the vessel, leaving the Capt. ashore. It has been showery this afternoon. The Chief was verry anxious to kill a hog this afternoon & roast him & make a feast for our benefit. He accepted an invitation to come aboard & lodge with us, & came down to our boat with us to go aboard. But the Missionary complained, & sent after him a request not to go. Tomorrow being their Sunday, he thought he ought not to be absent even in the morning. He obeyed the request. His son & 5 others went aboard & lodged with us. After supper they proposed having worship but we did not understand them; they, however, prayed most fervently & solemnly & sang a hymn verry sweetly, & verry correctly carrying on two parts. They have excellent voices. I now have concluded that the Missionaries have accomplished more than I have been willing to acknowledge.

Saturday, June 1st, 1850. This day being Sunday upon the Island, & being almost as near it at home as it is to Saturday, we have concluded to keep it as such & go ashore & attend church.[2] After breakfast & worship was over in the morning, several of us went ashore & attended two sermons, one in the forenoon at 10 oclock & the other after dinner. We had a verry solemn service, the discourses being given by natives, one a native of this village, the other of a neighboring one. The Capt. went in the afternoon to the neighboring village with the

[2]Osbun's Saturday may have been the Sunday of the natives because of the use of east longitude dates. The London Missionary Society had its chief connections to the westward with New Zealand and Australia and with England via the Cape of Good Hope.

chief to attend church & found the same preacher there we had in the morning. I have been verry much interested with my visit ashore to day. I find the Sabbath even more strictly kept here than at home. No work of any kind is done; they even cook none. They are summoned to church by pounding upon a trough made from hard wood. They preach after the same manner of our churches, & conduct themselves with great propriety, solemnity & order. Their tunes are new to me but good & simple; they sing well & verry loud, making the Cocoa groves ring with their music. They all dress in their best on this day. By observation taken to day in this harbor we are in Lat. 14°09′ S. & Longitude 169°26′ W. 205—4382 from S. F.

Sunday, 2d. This morning we took ashore a lot of goods to try the trade. We took them to the house of the King or Chief, & spread them out much to the gratification of the natives. We found more beggars & traders for trifles, or with trifles, than anything else. Shells, cocoa oil refined for greasing the skin & hair, eggs, chickens, cloth made from bark of a species of Mulberry by pounding, Cocoa nuts & mummy apples were the principal things offered, a few pigs & hogs, & a few Baskets of Tara & Yams were brought; they asked too much for them. They asked from 15 to 20 yds. cloth for a Hog weighing about 125 lbs. & a pig from 4 to 6 Yds. weighing about 25 lbs. For tarah & yams they asked 2 yds. for a basket holding about 15 to 20 or 65 lbs. We soon found we could not deal with them & about noon we packed up our goods, after buying a pig for 4 yds. cloth & a few baskets of Tara & Yams for ship's use. We also bought, after we went aboard, a few unripe pine apples, some mummy apples, &c. with broken pipes, tobacco & fish hooks.

We dined with the chief at his private residence. He roasted a small pig, in good style, which with roasted Tara, Cabbage dressed with Cocoa butter, & roasted fish, made up our meal. I would have relished it verry [much] if we had had salt, but still I made a hearty meal. The provisions were brought in lapped in leaves in baskets, & spread out in the leaves on mats on the floor, which is matted. Other mats were spread for us to sit upon. We eat alone; we invited the Chief to join us but he would not. It appears to be their custom not to eat untill after their guests are done. He sat near us & waited upon us, untill we finished. We were not furnished any thing like knives or forks. After dinner water in a wood basin was furnished & a cloth with which to wash our hands. Capt. Perry went to the adjoining town to see how trade was there, & found that he could trade there to better advantage but still not satisfactorily. He returned in the evening, & we concluded to leave in the morning. The Chief wished us to remain with him to night, & we concluded to remain. We supped upon what was left from dinner. Our drink at meals was Cocoa water, drank from the nut, in its green state. Before going to bed, the family was called together, & worship performed. Mats were afterwards spread for our beds, & for us a roll of their cloth laid down for our heads; for a cover they gave us a roll of their cloth made heavy. They use for their heads during sleep a piece of rattan about as thick as the wrist, raised on 4 feet 3 or 4 inches high. These people manufacture but little. Paper Cloth, Mats, fish baskets, & fish hooks made from pearl shell, & turtle makes up about their list of manufactures. They roof their houses verry well & verry ingeniously, using the cocoa leaf plaited together & tied to a regular framed work of Bambo, & other arched wood, with strings plaited with 3 strands from cocoa thread. Their houses do not leak, & are kept verry clean, & well suited to the climate. The land is here all owned & marked off. The fences built of stone seem of great age. The present inhabitants are unable to tell when their ancestors first settled upon it. The King or Chief inherits his office, & all the landed estate of his ancestor. The island is divided into several governments, & the divisions marked by a stone wall. Nothing indicates that the island has been settled long except the appearance of the stone walls. Their tara & yams are raised among the bushes & grass, & but little labor or attention paid to their cultivation. These people are a strictly virtuous & well intending race.

Monday, 3d June. This morning we were aroused by the sound produced by beating on the trough, a summons to worship at the church, I supposed. We arose & washed, had worship, & called our boat to take us off. The Chief caught a chicken & wished to cook it for us, but we declined waiting. We went aboard, took the chief & his 2 girls with us, got breakfast, & were soon ready for sea. Our vessel was thronged with the natives from the time we made our appearance among them, but now it was doubly so; the sea around us was alive with them, both swimming & in Canoes, all begging "tobac. or pipe" or wanting to trade. We were compelled to drive them off the vessel. By 10 oclock we were under full sail. We passed down between Too-manoo'ah the first island & Olosinghah the 2d & then took our course near due West. We soon came in sight of Tootooilla Island.

Shortly after we got under way the wind caught our main sail, & drove it from larboard side around to starboard with tremenduous force & broke in two pieces the main boom. This crippled much our speed. We sailed past the Island during the night; it was verry squally with rain.

Tuesday, 4th. This morning the island of Oahtooah or Upolu, as it is now called, was in sight. We soon came up to it on our right or starboard side, & sailed along down its shore untill opposite its centre; here we observed a number of villages & concluded to lay to untill we mended up our main boom. Verry soon a crowd of canoes were around our vessel & its deck filled with Kanackas. Among them we find a colored man from N. York, a smart intelligent & good looking fellow, who speaks the English language well. He was with the King or Chief of a tribe & the principal chief or, as he styles him, the head Chief of this island & of the whole group. The Chief is accompanied also by his brother, & a few servants. The name of this cold. man is Wm. Henry. The Chief's name is Tuannah & his brother Samuell. We were boarded about 8 oclock A.M. & from the verry fair representations of Wm. of trade ashore the Capt. concluded to go out & try them; he started about 10 oclock & took with him a few samples of goods, & remained there untill night. He then came aboard with the Chief, Bill & 4 Kanackas that he hired to work the boat on tomorrow. He reports a good prospect for purchasing as many Yams as we wish, paying for them one fathom of cloth for a basket, that is 2 yds. for 20 Yams, which will weigh about 80 lbs. A few Hogs can be had here, but they say there are many on the Island. The chief's brother & servant did not go ashore.

Wednesday, 5th June. It rained & stormed with heavy thunder & lightning last night, & this morning we find ourselves 10 miles from shore, with verry light wind blowing from shore. By 12 oclock we were in full sight again of Tootooilla, by observation were in Latitude 14° 15' S. & continued beating off in the same direction untill 3 oclock. When we finished our main boom & hoisted the main sail, a breeze getting [up], we were soon under way to the island of Oahtooah again. Our distinguished guests were much pleased at the change. Wm. Henry tells me he came out from New Bedford in a whale ship, got his discharge from it & settled on this island about 5 months ago. Soon after he settled he married into the royal family & is now a great man among them. They are now all preparing for war, & want Guns & ammunition. They are fighting with a tribe on the same island; the quarrel has its origin in a love affair. A chief's daughter ran off & married against the consent of her parents into the royal family of a tribe upon the Island of Manonoo. She was refused the usual property or household articles given at marriage, & hence the war. We amused them much by showing them our guns, revolver &c. during the day; the Old King was much pleased with my gun, it being a U.S. rifled carbine that is loaded in the breach. He has a verry favorite & only daughter [whom] he offered me for a wife, for the rifle.

As I did not accept his proposition, I do not know how he will consider it, he being in good earnest in making the offer. During the afternoon, our guests all together concluded of their own accord to amuse us by giving us a specimen of their singing & dancing, which they performed in real Indian style. It is verry similar to the style of our Indians. Their modes & motions & attitudes & gesticulations were of the most grotesque character, their music monotonous & accompanied with slapping of the hands for time. After dark some time we arrived nearly opposite the landing of their town, & several of them concluded to go ashore with the Capt. Wm. the cold. man & 4 of the rowers left. And we still have on board the two chiefs & their two servants. It has rained again during the evening.

Thursday, 6th. This morning the boat came off to the vessel, manned by 4 Kanackas, the Capt. having hired them to boat off all our produce. I immediately went ashore & took along a stock of Goods for trade. I found a Scotchman there, engaged to assist in trading, the Negro not being master of the language. They were trading calico & muslin for Yams, giving 1 fathom, or as much as will reach from thumb to thumb, the arms outstretched, which was about 2 Yards, for 20 Yams; we suppose they will weigh from 80 to 100 lbs. We traded for about [blank in MS] & sent them aboard. The Capt. & myself remained ashore for the trade of the morning, it being the only principal time for doing business in trade. I find the natives here about as at the other Islands, great beggars for Tobacco; every one you meet asks for it. I supped & lodge with the Negro. We had for supper a Muscovy Duck roasted in good style, & some cold roasted pig with roasted Tara. The Capt. had taken salt & vinegar ashore, & I enjoyed the meals much; their mode of cooking makes the victuals verry sweet.

Mats were spread as usual on the floor both to sit on & eat from. On the centre mats are spread Banana leaves, & the victuals on them. The Queen of this tribe came in & spent the evening with us. She is quite a Lady, possesses good feelings, is verry kind & full of fun & joke. She brought her mats, & curtains for us to sleep on & under. She has her maids who wait upon her, & carried down the mats.

The royal family do no work; they have their waiters & cooks, & take any thing they want from their people. I observed every here & there cocoa trees with bands of leaves tied around them; these I was informed were the property of the King, & no one dared to touch the fruit growing upon them.

During the evening, Cav'ah, a favorite drink, was prepared for us, but I could not relish it. It is prepared from the root of the Cah-vah plant, by young girls, virgins. They chew it up verry fine & put it in a wooden bowl, add water to it, & rub it up well together with the hands. It is then served up, by wringing it from a rag into a cocoa shell, & then handed around by one of the girls. The females here seem to exert almost a controlling influence over the island, and do only a fair portion of household labor.

English Missionaries have been upon the island many years, & many of the natives appear verry pious, keeping up regularly family worship.[3]

I find here but few curiosities, & nothing new. Shells are held at high prices. I procured a few, also some Coral, coarse mats, & a stick of Cocoa wood from which to make some canes. I find here some cattle, Hogs, Turkeys, Muscovy ducks, & chicken, but in no great abundance. They manufacture paper cloth, & quite a variety of mats, some fine & handsome. It is still showery.

Friday, 7th June. This morning but a few baskets of Yams were brought in for trade & we concluded to leave. Consequently after breakfast I took the goods & went aboard, with what we had. The Capt. went down the beach westward 6 or 8 miles to see how the trade would be, & [we] were to send out the boat to him, he raising a signal at the point he wished us to land.

I sold my rifle to the King, who is still aboard, soon after I got aboard, for 6 large Hogs, & he sent the men ashore to get them a few miles below our trading post & before we could see the capt's signal.

---

[3]The London Missionary Society began its work actively on Upolu in 1835.

But the boat has not returned, & we have been unable to see the signal, & consequently do not know where either the Capt. or boat is. A canoe came to us with 4 of the Hogs, the balance yet to come.

Saturday, 8th. Our boat staid at shore last night & this morning the Capt. came in it aboard; & we came to anchor near a small island about one oclock, the Capt. having found considerable trade in Yams. This day being their Sunday no business can be done. We concluded however to go ashore & spend the balance of the day with the Natives. We anchored at some risk, our vessel being at one time within 5 or 6 feet of the reef. Our boat being hauled behind us dry over the reef, the vessel was held off by poles.

The Capt. & myself went ashore & remained all night. We found the people nearly all engaged at worship. They keep the Sabbath here verry strict, we being scarcely able to get a drink of cocoa water. They will not even pull a nut on this day. I asked several times for one & was answered, "Missionary" meaning it was Sunday. It is a custom on all the Pacific islands, when a stranger lands, for some one of the natives to call on you & offer himself to you to be your friend. If you accept his offer, he will be to you a friend indeed. While you remain he will furnish you daily with food as much as you can eat, either at his own house or in the vessel, & also any thing else you may want; only mention it to him, & he is at your service. Soon after we landed a friend offered himself, & I accepted; his name is "Simone Peter," a young man with a family. He insisted on my lodging with him, & I accepted his offer, the Chief's house being verry full.

I slept with him under a screen, upon mats. I also supped with him on Tara roasted, & cabbage made from Cocoa butter & Tara leaves cooked soft. I supped with much relish, being hungry. Before going to bed, we had worship, & at the same time the whole town rang with the sound of prayer & praise, every hut seeming to be occupied by professors of religion.

Sunday, 9th. This day we went aboard early, before breakfast, & took ashore with us some goods, & traded briskly for some time. We soon loaded our boat, it returned, & we sent out a second load. We then moved a short distance eastward to the next town, & opened up a brisk trade. Kissam came ashore during the afternoon, & we all remained during the night.

Monday, 10th June. We all went aboard to day after doing some trade, & again returned, & traded, & came aboard in the evening & took with us the goods, intending to do no more trading on shore.

Tuesday, 11th. This day I remained aboard; we traded some, but were crowded on the vessel the whole day. Many things are stolen from us & we find we cannot prevent it unless we drive them off; this we have been compelled to do several times. Several Chiefs are aboard to prevent it but still it is done. This evening an attempt was made late to take off some things, but we failed through the cunning of the native to detect him.

Kissam, being on watch, was advised by one of our men to search a certain native; he believed he had something stolen about him. He started aft to do it, the native going there ahead of him, & was urged & hurried on by the young son of a chief. The fellow was wrapped up in Kissam's oiled coat. He threw it off before he got back & as soon as he got there, he sprang overboard, & got into a canoe. He did so before Kissam got up to him. Kissam jumped immediately into our boat, & having hold on his canoe rope, commenced hauling him to him. He jumped out & whilst in the water took off his breach cloth, & let loose whatever he had in it. I heard the noise when he jumped into the water & immediately arose & went on deck. We made the fellow come aboard. The chief's son explained it away by saying he was sending him ashore in the small canoe to get a large one to take him & several others ashore. Not finding any thing on the fellow we were prevented from punishing him altho we were satisfied he had something concealed.

Wednesday, 12th. Our Cook has not been able to give satisfaction, & on Monday we shipped John Wilson, a Spaniard living here on the Island & married to a native, as Cook & Stewart. He has been living here some [blank in MS].

We have had a merry time of it on board to day. A great many have visited us, & most of them females. They are a people verry fond of fun & Jokes, of singing & of dancing, & they have given us specimens of their performances of every kind in great perfection & much to our gratification. We dealt out Tobacco to them in small quantities, & for it they will perform all the time if we wished it. I visited the small island near our vessel & procured 2 or 3 ordinary shells, & a cane from a tree called by the natives "Faw'sah"; it is taken from the root growing above ground, it being a tree whose roots unite to the trunk from 3 to 6 feet above the ground.[4] I was taken out by 4 natives in a canoe. Our men are now employed getting wood & water. We have paid an old musket for 6 loads of wood, about 4 cords, and included in it the harbor charge for anchorage. The[y] have also charged us for water 10 yds. cloth. We did not intend to pay for it, but they have concealed one of our casks & we are forced to do it. We get it from a large stream, by floating our casks into it during high tide. I have been called upon frequently for medicine, & dosed out to several patients. I find pneumonic diseases verry common. Bronchitis, from what I can find out, carries off more of the people than all other diseases. I see also a good many crooked spines from spinal disease. There is a disease common to all the Islands called Fayfay which is quite common here; it is a disease of the legs & feet, hands & arms.[5] They swell up, get hard & remain so for life. It occasionally disables them from going about, & is always a great impediment to their walking. One of the chiefs where we lay is quite bad with it, & is verry anxious for me to stay with him & cure him. I plugged a tooth this day for another of the chiefs, with which he is much pleased. Several others have since called upon me, but I could not attend to them. During the evening we were again richly entertained by songs & dancing.

Thursday, 13th. This morning a young Queen, a widow, came aboard. She is called the Lady of the island, and appears to be quite a Lady, altho she has the manners of the native. She possesses quite an open fine countenance, is verry hospitable, & a good friend to foreigners. Altho she is verry corpulent & large, her appearance is still interesting. Her name is Asuena as we pronounce it. Above is her name as written by herself in her own mode of writing & sounding of letters [omitted here]. The nobility use a powder for the skin which appears to be Chrome Yellow. The common people pay great respect to the nobility or royal family. She is cloathed only with a cloth wrapped around her hips & body, her breast being bare, & no shoes, being barefoot & bareheaded. In coming up she sprained her knee & is now not able to walk. One object in visiting the vessel in her lame condition was to get medicine & medical advice.

A young chief came aboard this afternoon, to beg tobacco, from

[4]Probably Pandanus.

[5]This disease is almost certainly elephantiasis, which is very common in the Samoan Islands.

another part of the island; he was dressed in fine native style, with white tappa cloth tied around his head & a white fringed mat around his hips. He was refused a present, & was told that our men were refused water on shore to drink to day, & that we had also to pay for our water for ship use. He became verry angry & left us. He came aboard while we were at supper & sent in to know if he could come in & eat; our table was full, & we did not invite him in. We have been bored to day until our patience has been almost exhausted for presents of tobacco. If we give to a female of the noble family, any one of the common people can take it from her. Or a chief can do it. If we give to a chief, any man [can] take it. I have been frequently vexed to day at seeing this custom. Kissam, in attempting to be polite to the Queen or Lady, committed quite a blunder. He desired to give her a drink. Supposing her to be sick, he asked her if she was. "Mi" is the native word for sick, & he used the word "me," which means to make water. She was much tickled at his mistake, knowing it to be only a mistake. No mock modesty was exhibited by her. She appears a child of nature.

We have been again entertained by native songs & dances in new forms. A great variety of fish are brought to us to trade, of most beautiful colors, & form, & of excellent quality. I have put some of the small ones in Brandy for preservation. We this evening miss several mats from below that have been stolen from us during the day. We now learn the females take as much watching as the males, we not allowing any males aboard but the chiefs. Others come aboard, trade & leave, & to those leaving they convey stolen goods. These people are all lice eaters; I see the women occasionally looking for them & eating them. This custom is so revolting to my feelings, I can scarcely treat them with even savage civility. A female belonging to the upper ranks, & a member of the house of the chief where we traded, requested me to write for her a letter to her husband, a white man, now in California, which I promised to do. To day she came aboard, & I wrote through an interpreter the following letter. I insert it to show the feelings of the natives & their mode of thinking, it being short, concise, & to the point.

Va'ou'va'e, Island of Oahtooah, June 12th, 1850.

Dear Husband. I send you this letter to tell you to send me some property, if a ship comes here. I do not know that we will ever see each other again, but I send my love to you. I want you to send me some of your hair, if you never come back. If you think any thing

121

of me, I want you to write me a letter, & to tell me whether you ever intend to come again to these islands.

Your wife,

Mary Oa Norton

To Charles Norton, San Francisco, California.

She appears to be a woman of good common sense, & if she had been educated would have been considered above the ordinary class of minds in any community.

Friday, 14th June. This forenoon we have been but little troubled with visiters, a few of the Chiefs only visiting us, & they sure to come about meal time. They are all extremely fond of our salted meat, particularly Pork, which they call Pooah. Beef they call Pulumatau. They always eat all the meat we put on the table & all the sugar. If they cannot eat it themselves they give it away to others of their people around. We have learned the lesson to put no more on the table than we think sufficient. We had a row this evening with the chiefs, in setting off for wood & anchorage. They agreed to furnish us with 6 loads of wood & the anchorage for a gun & 10 fathoms of cloth, & when we proposed paying them, a native claimed pay for part of it, saying it belonged it to him, and they all demanded 2 fathoms for each load. Perry at this demand became so much enraged that he acted like a madman; he seems to have no control over his feelings. I expected from his conduct we certainly would have trouble. He refused to give them their supper, & ordered them out of the cabin & to go ashore. They showed more tact in the matter than he did. They yielded their demand & took the cloth, but stuck to the vessel untill they recieved their suppers. They then all went ashore. They demanded pay also for water yesterday; the Capt. raved also about it, but they carried off one of the casks left there to fill, & refused to give it up untill the water was paid for. And he was compelled to accede to their demands. He gave them 5 fathoms of cloth for what we wanted.

Saturday, June 15th. This morning we took aboard the last of our water about noon, and immediately went to work preparing for our departure. We took up our anchor, & were driven around almost on the reef. We worked away untill night to keep her off & finally succeeded, & again anchored to remain until morning. This day being the

Sabbath of the natives, we were but little troubled with them. A few came aboard, & we were forced to drive them off. An American whaler, a barque ship, came in view this afternoon sailing eastward. She was boarded by Kanackas, who tell us she will anchor on the other side of this island. They could not tell us her name.

Sunday, 16th. This morning we went to work early & by 8 oclock were completely outside the reef & under full headway, the wind being fair. This island is girt around some distance from shore by a coral reef, with here & there a passage where vessels can enter & anchor on their inside. We have traded here for 19 pigs & Hogs, eight Ducks, [blank in MS] chickens & 100 Baskets of Yams. We also traded for Bananas, Tara, Sweet potatoes & fresh fish & Lobsters (Crawfish) sufficient for our own use. One old chief has acted in particular the gentleman with us; he was quite dissatisfied with the conduct of the others. He last evening, seeing us in trouble with our vessel, sent off a man to know what was the matter & if any thi[ng] was wrong with our vessel, & he soon after, before the return of his man, came aboard himself. This morning he came aboard, & remained with us untill we were under full sail. We sailed along the island a short distance from the beach, the natives coming out occasionally with Yams &c. in their Canoes to trade for Tobacco. A hurricane passed over the Island about the 1st April last, which destroyed all their tobacco & much of their fruit & trees, & which makes the demand for tobacco great. We, after we passed the lower end of this island, sailed up near & abreast of the small Island called *"Manonoo."* We then struck for the Southern point of Oteewhy called by the natives Savaii. It clouded up & rained all night upon us here. We tacked backwards & forward all night. Several small rocky barren looking islands, with lofty peaks, are situated near the last islands.

Monday, 17th. This morning at day break we find ourselves near shore on the south side of the island. During the night we had again the misfortune to get our main boom broken in a new place, & we must now get a new one. We soon passed around the SW. point of the island & sailed up along its western shore, & before dinner & about third way up we came to a point for anchoring. The Capt. went ashore & ascertained where the best anchorage was to be had, & at about 2 oclock we anchored opposite to a village called Salailua & also opposite the church & residence of a German missionary.

Several natives came aboard immediately to trade. They had ducks, Turkeys, Bananas, fish, Oranges, Cocoa nuts & pigs. I bought 2 pigs, weighing each about 100 lbs., one for 5 fathoms of cloth & the other for 2 shirts—also some cocoa nuts. The Capt. & Mate went ashore to select a suitable tree to make a new main boom & found a cocoa nut tree which they considered would answer the purpose, for which we have to pay 10 fathoms of cloth. It has rained almost constantly the whole day. We have an invitation to take tea with the missionary & his wife & we have extended to them one to take dinner with us tomorrow. The mate when ashore purchased a cat for 1 Yd. calico, so now Mr. rats & mice look out.

Tuesday, 18th June. The missionary could not dine with us to day in consequence of having a couple of the natives to marry. The Capt. promised to dine with him tomorrow & also to bring myself & mate with him. We traded on the vessel for several Hogs, & about 40 baskets of Yams, at usual rates. The Capt. & several of the men spent the day ashore working at the main boom.

Wednesday, 19th. I went ashore immediately after an early breakfast & proceeded to the house of the missionary with the Capt. & got an introduction to him & his wife. I then with the Capt. went to the place of working at the boom where I remained untill the missionary called upon me & took me to his house.

His name is *C. W. E. Schmidt*; he is a Prussian, & is supported here by the London Missionary Society. He has been here about 2 years, but tells me that missionaries have been here about 13 years.[6] I find both he & his wife a verry interresting & clever couple & obtained from them much information respecting the people upon these Islands. I have concluded that he is much respected by the natives & has great influence over them. His house is situated about 100 yds. back of the church upon a spot of ground elevated 6 or 8 feet above the surrounding land, by the hands of the natives, & the elevated portion is covered with stone. The natives consider such prepared spots as holy ground, & proper for the residence of good men or a missionary. His grounds consisting of probably 1½ acres of land is surrounded by a stone wall piled up by natives, & covered with cocoa nut, Banana, Breadfruit,

---

[6]John Williams and Charles Barff began the work of the London Missionary Society on Savaii Island in 1830. The first European missionaries sent by the society to be resident on the island came in 1836.

Orange, Lemon & Mummy apple trees. He also has growing finely the peach, plum & pomegranite trees, a few grape vines, & many pine apple plants. His house is a frame filled in, plastered & whitewashed inside & out, with floor of the same material, is one story high, & consists of 3 houses placed side by side of each other, each house having in it 2 rooms. It has also on 3 sides, extending around, a porch, which adds much to the comfort of the house. I was much pleased with the appearance of things in & around his residence. Every thing was clean, neat & bright in & about the house, & upon the grounds every thing grew most luxuriantly. But little of the fruit was ripe. But the trees all hung full, & promised a rich harvest for our worthy host. We dined most sumptuously upon a small roast pig & a duck & had also salt pork, preserved here by themselves, with baked Tara & Mummy apple, light bread & cakes. For drink we drank Cocoa water green, & from the shell. For dessert, a rich rice & goat milk pudding. We considered it the nicest & richest dinner we had eaten for many, many months, & we did it full Justice. The Capt. & men worked all day at the boom, & took it aboard this evening. I remained all night with the excellent missionary & enjoyed myself much in his and his interresting wife's company.

Thursday, 20th. This morning a native came early to me & informed me that the chiefs had at a meeting removed the *taboo* from the hogs, & that they desired us to bring our goods ashore & trade for them to day & tomorrow also, & trade for yams. The hogs had been tabooed or forbidden to be sold in consequence of the war. The same message was conveyed to the ship, & early this morning the Capt. came ashore with goods. Mr. Schmidt & his wife went aboard with me about 12 oclock & dined with us. He presented us with 2 copys of several of the Epistles of the New Testament, printed in the native language, also a bundle of tracts, some newspapers &c. Mrs. Schmidt also gave us 2 of the largest & finest pine apples I ever saw. They returned a short time before sundown. The Capt. remained ashore all day & traded for a goodly number Hogs & Cocoa nuts, & a few Yams. A piece of Tobacco a little smaller than the finger pays for 10 cocoa nuts. Last night one of our largest Hogs died. We were informed it was a wild hog & was hurt badly in catching. The people of this island are but little under the influence of their chiefs, they being merely their law makers when assembled in a body & are the magistrates to see the laws executed. I was much pleased this morning with a plan of Mr.

Schmidt's to enlist the children in his cause. I heard quite a loud noise, as of singing, in the direction of the church. We looked out and saw a long train of children coming in a regular line of march, each bearing upon his shoulder a large long bamboo stick, & all united in singing a song. I was informed it was the children of the village coming to pay their contributions to the church in cocoa oil which they were carrying in the bamboos. They marched on untill they arrived near us, where stood a large iron tank in which they deposited their oil. He has several servants to cook & do his labor, & they are generally the sons & daughters of chiefs. His schools, which are open daily, are kept by native teachers, he having a general superintendance over all of them. I find many of the natives can read & write.

Friday, 21st. This day I remained aboard trading untill evening. I then went ashore & found Kissam trading & surrounded by a horde of natives & in trouble. They became verry saucy, were stealing cocoas & selling them again to him, crowding upon him & giving him much trouble & uneasiness. An old chief, to whom he had sold a pipe, demanded an exchange after he had used it, it having a small piece broken from the cup. Kissam refused to exchange; he continued his demand, was pushed off. Both became very angry, & with clenched fists stood in an attitude for fight; the natives gathered around in numbers sufficient to demolish us both in an instant. Kissam, altho raving with passion, acted the wise part by giving him another, & thus ending the threatened fight. They still crowded upon us & we stopped trade, and might have still got into trouble, had it not been for another old chief, who came & made quite a speech & at its conclusion took up a switch & made at the crowd & in an instant scattered them. We gave him for his service a pipe & plug of tobacco which made him very attentive the balance of the evening. Rev'd. Schmidt proposed preaching to us & crew in English either on the vessel or shore, as we might prefer or think best. After deliberation we concluded to go ashore; fearing he might get sea sick, we concluded to go ashore all hands. We were untill late in the evening engaged in taking aboard our pigs & nuts. We have bought to day a great many nuts, paying about 1 lb. Tobacco for upwards of 400. The name of the town we are now trading in is *Salailua*, the population about 200.

Saturday, 22d. The whole crew but two went ashore to day at 9 oclock, & heard a sermon first in the native language & immediately afterwards a discourse & service in English. He preached from the text "Thy kingdom come" & gave us an interesting discourse. Four of us afterwards dined with him on an excellent cold dinner, no cooking being done here on this day. I was furnished with a couple of glasses of Goat's milk, which I relished much. We had a small roast pig, with several native vegetable dishes cooked & served up in good taste by our accomplished hostess. During the afternoon we were catechised upon the sermon but were not able to give such an account of it as even satisfied ourselves. I visited with him, & prescribed to several patients. The natives are verry fond of taking medicine, & think highly of a Doctor or Fomi as they call him.

Sunday, 23d. We have continued trade to day, and taken in a good many Yams, cocoa nuts, & pigs. The Capt. traded ashore, Kissam went several miles westward with an Englishman, & got between 3 & 400 Yams, & I remained aboard. I had a noisy day of it, & was kept verry busy between trading & watching. I kept the cabin closed most of the time. We have concluded to leave tomorrow early, & have invited Rev'd. Schmidt & wife & servants to go with us to Falealupo, he intending to move there tomorrow, which invitation he has pleasantly accepted.

Monday, June 24th. This morning we commenced preparing for our departure. The Capt. & men went in the boat at day break with the Englishman for another load of Yams, but they not having them ready he returned about noon with about 100. Rev'd. Schmidt, wife, servants, teachers & chiefs came aboard in their boat (which they took along) & luggage, & by 12 oclock we were under sail. The wind being favorable we had a fine sail, & by the middle of the afternoon we anchored off & near *Falealupo.* Our passengers all left us before supper. We have as usual been visited by a throng of natives in canoes. The natives here we find are more saucy & insolent than on the other islands we have visited.

Tuesday, 25th. This morning Perry took ashore some goods to try the trade, & in the course of the day bought 3 loads of nuts & 40 or 50 baskets of Yams. No pigs offered. I brought aboard a good many cocoas. Our vessel has been thronged all day with natives. This evening we supped & fed neither chief nor kanaka, at which the chiefs were much displeased. At sundown we ordered all ashore; a young chief

127

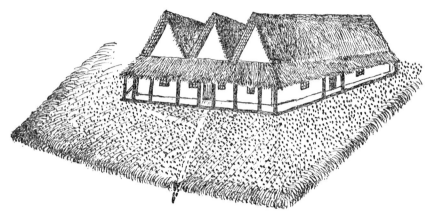

RESIDENCE OF THE REVD. MR. SCHMIDT, MISSIONARY ON THE
ISLAND OF SAVAII AND VILLAGE OF SALAILUA.

begged hard to stay with us, but we made him leave, having already
submitted to too much imposition. A number intending to stay had
sent ashore their canoes, but we ordered them to send for them, which
they did, & all left but one; he begged us to have pity on him, & let
him stay as he could not get ashore, the canoes being full. We permitted him to stay, but not to leave the vessel untill we arose in the
morning. A pompous young chief who had his canoe with him requested us to take him ashore in our boat, which of course we refused.

Wednesday, 26th. No trade coming aboard, I went ashore a little
before noon & spent the balance of the day there. Noah & myself
walked down the village some distance, & went into a hut & asked for
something to eat. The woman of the house quickly brought us some
cold Taro, & another one some baked bananas; a boy climbed a cocoa
tree & procured for us some green nuts for drink. We ate a hearty meal
& distributed tobacco among them for pay. We returned slowly exam-
ing every thing we saw, untill we arrived at the house of our old
friends, the Missionaries. We still find them as clever as ever; they
immediately spread their table with dinner, & no excuse would be
taken, we must eat. We did so, & could not get away untill after supper. I find them here in a large unfinished stone house, built by one of
their predecessors. It has 6 rooms, & large ones, in it. This house they

pay a rent of 5 pounds per annum, & if they occupy it at this rent for 10 years it becomes their property. There are several acres of land attached to it but much of its surface is a bare lava rock. On it are many Orange, bannana, Cocoa nut, bread fruit & mummy apple trees, also many pine apple plants. They requested me to furnish them with a draft of their house, which I took. The Capt. traded ashore & bought near 3000 cocoa nuts & but a few baskets of Yams.

Thursday, 27th June. I remained aboard all this day, but no trade was brought to us here excepting a few green cocoas. The capt. was ashore all day & traded for almost nothing, only 3 or 4 baskets of Yams, & a dog pup. We fastened a ferrule on a shot gun for a native for which we received a 4 fathom pig. The Capt. missed his razor this morning, & as no person but Noah was here during the time when it was missed, he & myself having used his box yesterday, we immediately suspected him. He went ashore this morning, & Kissam & myself examined his cloaths & found it among them. After he returned, we examined his cloathes by his permission & took it, he pretending not to know it was there. I have considered him not in his sound mind from the first day he came aboard. His own razor & part of his cloathes he says have been stolen by the natives. This is an unfortunate affair for the poor old fellow. I have had compassion on him knowing his infirmity, & been his only friend aboard. The balance of the Crew & particularly the Capt., who thinks he knows every thing, & is never wrong when his mind is made up, has been verry severe with him, & looked upon him as actuated by a devilish spirit. When acting as cook he was careless, negligent, wasteful, & verry absent minded, often not knowing what he was doing. The Capt., when he returned this evening, was verry anxious to flog him & would have done it, had not Kissam & myself frowned upon it.

Friday, 28th. The Capt. went ashore early for trading, supposing it would be a fine day for the purpose. The native men being all from home yesterday, it was supposed they were in the bush digging yams. But to day has proved that they have concluded to deal none with us; the cause we could not ascertain. We have at this place kept ourselves at a distance both from the chiefs & the natives, permitting none to sleep aboard or even to eat with us, & a portion of the time not even allowing a single one to come aboard. It has been supposed that our cloth was too narrow to please them & that they would not deal with us for it. But I incline to the opinion that it proceeded from our conduct towards the chiefs. Their power it is true is verry limited, but is still sufficient to bring about such a result. We traded for but a single basket of Yams & no person came near our trading post. He returned about noon bringing with him the goods, & an invitation from the Rev'd Schmidt, that we must dine with him & no refusal.

The Capt., Kissam & myself went ashore & dined with them at about half past two oclock. They had prepared in great haste a fine dinner for us; we now having concluded to sail immediately, they would not consent for us to leave untill we eat with them, which sudden conclusion to leave had forced them to prepare their dinner in much haste, but still we had a most excellent meal. It consisted of Roasted turkey, stewed chicken, cold boiled homemade pickled pork, Baked taro, mummy apple, & Banana, Bread &c. with a dessert of Rice & milk. After dinner our verry worthy missionaries wished to read a portion of Scriptures & to pray with us & for us before we parted from each other, so we all united in this exercise, & then left for our vessel. They made us many presents of fruits & a Turkey, also a portion of the Scriptures in the native language. They also required us to bring ashore our cloathes & have them washed. They came down with us to the beach & we parted after much expression of sorrow & friendly feeling. I am much pleased with these people, & think they are well calculated for their calling, & are doing much good. We were soon aboard & by 4 oclock our anchor was raised & soon we were under full sail with a fine breeze blowing from the SE. Our course was for Wallas's Island S. 79° W., or W. ½ S.

⑧

WALLIS ISLANDS

◎

Saturday, June 29th. We have to day made good headway, so that at 10 oclock this evening we came in full view & close to Wallas's island, or as the natives call it Uvea or Uva'ah. I have been verry sick again all day with seasickness, & laid a good portion of the day in my berth. My stomach was in bad order when I left Savaii which was the cause of it. At noon to day we find ourselves in Lat. [blank in MS].

Sunday, 30th. This morning we are close to the island having laid off & on during the night. We sailed along its south east side around a small island upon the reef & entered a harbor from the south & passed up between two reef islands, & anchored some distance from shore. We were soon as usual thronged with natives, our deck literally covered with them. This day as well as yesterday is kept by the people here as Sabbath, they observing two Sabbaths each week. The reason of their so doing I have not been able to get explained by them as yet.[1] They have brought aboard shells & cloth for trade. I obtained from them several verry pretty shells. Their cloth & mats are superior to any I have yet seen. One fellow is verry anxious to become my friend & tells me he has some verry fine mats at his house, also tortoise shell combs of his own make, & any thing I see there, if I will visit him, shall be mine as a present if I want it. He wishes me to come ashore & sleep at his house. I am informed he has verry fine mats & cloth. Before he left he urged me to accept a present of a beautifully painted piece of their cloth, made for a breech cloth or *lavalava*, as

---

[1]Although the Wallis Islands lie in 176° 10' W. longitude, they are near enough to the international date line that persons coming from east and west might well have continued to use the chronology of the region from which they came. The natives may quite properly have taken advantage of this and thus had two Sundays each week.

they call it. He is dressed with a straw or leaf plaited hat quite neat, of their own make, & plaited & sewed after our style, a red flannel shirt, wearing it loose & a pair of white clean linen pants & barefooted; he is the best dressed man I have seen here. I told him I had a pair of red pants, meaning my drawers, which I told him I might make him a present of, and he is much pleased with the idea of getting them. He says he has several pair of white ones at home but he does not like them; he wants a red pair that will keep him warm. The Capt. went ashore, became acquainted with the Catholic Bishop, & King John, & reports no Yams or Pigs here in any quantity, & a good many sweet potatoes.[2]

Monday, July 1st. The Capt. & myself went ashore this morning for trading & took with us goods, but not having made arrangements yesterday with King John nothing can be done to day. It appears that the King has the whole control of trade; no one dares to take the priviledge without his consent, & without his order. He establishes the terms of trade & all assent to it. He now says his men are all in the bush & cannot get their trade ready untill morrow. He is rather a fine look-ing man of middle age, with large long whiskers & fairly develloped head. His government is despotic, & all his subjects fear him much & implicitly obey his commands. He a few months ago murdered his wife, it is said in a fit of jealousy, & his people now fear to even talk about it, if they think their conversation will reach his ears. He rules one half the island & is now at war with the other, it being governed by two Kings. In consequence all his people live in a fort, & keep up their night guards regularly every night. It is supposed their whole number of souls large & small is about 3000. There are among them 3 white men & 1 negro, all married & have children. One from the States, one from Ireland & one from Scotland; all have been sailors. Some of them have quite interresting children. I took up board & lodging with the old Irishman, & find him full of blarney. He has all the duties of the kitchen to perform; it is considered here an everlasting disgrace for the [female] sex to perform the duties of cook. The male must provide all provisions & cook them; the female makes the tappa & mats. His wife, about the ugliest & most Satanic looking female I ever saw, sat upon her mat whilst he cooked the meals. She is a small broken backed lady, with a prominent mouth & nose & hair from 12 to 18

---

[2]Aubert Bouillon was Bishop and Vicar Apostolic of Central Oceania.

inches long, black & as curley as a negroe's, & sticks straight from the head in all directions. She has three children by her present husband, all little boys & verry fine looking children. Also a daughter before marriage, who is now a young woman, & quite good looking for a native. These people are more strictly moral & honest than any we have been amongst. As yet we have seen no disposition to steal, nor have we missed any thing. I have walked out this evening through their grounds & fort & seen some beautiful patches of Taro. Also groves of cocoa nut, Breadfruit & Bananas, mummy apple & a large tree yielding in great abundance large nuts similar to flattened buckeyes but larger, the kernal of which they roast & is verry good, tasting something similar to chesnuts. I found Noah in the fort with an immense crowd of astonished natives around him. He has an upper set of artificial teeth set upon a gold plate which he takes out & exhibits to them, at which they show much wonder & astonishment. When he commences taking them out they are crowded close around him & as he pulls them down, they apparantly spring involuntarily away as though he was performing a great & painful operation, their eyes fixed firmly on his mouth & staring in wonder. Nothing seems to be talked about but the man who can take out his jaw & clean his teeth. I have visited with my friend the native [in] his house & seen his mats. I also went with him around to verry many houses to see their mats, wishing to purchase one to take home. And it was quite amusing to see with what pride each female took down & exhibited her mats. It seemed to delight them much to exhibit them, & I invariably praised them, which seemed to give them much satisfaction altho I did not buy any. Their mats are deserving of praise, & how they make them so large & so neat by hand I cannot conceive. The priests here seem to have verry considerable influence over the people. I observe many of them crossing themselves, & always before they eat. They assemble night & morning regularly in the church & go through their service. They have several fine & large church bells, & a verry large church.

Tuesday, July 2d. I slept poorly last night on account of the musquitoes; they awoke me several times, & I frequently during the night found my old Irish friend awake fanning off the musquitoes from me. He was up early but was late getting breakfast; his table was spread upon the floor with a green Banana leaf for a cloth & spread with pancakes, sea buiscuit, boiled bananas, Yams, pared mummy apple & fried chicken. I ate verry heartily. Our boat came ashore before I had finished; I sent down the key of our chest to the Capt., & soon followed myself. I found already upon the ground a great many baskets of Yams, sweet potatoes, & ofelay's, a vegetable root, much resembling sweet potatoes, & also many chickens. King John was there in the midst, dressed up in a fashionable linnen coat & pants & shirt, with no hat or shoes. We now had to arrange with him, & employ him to deal for us. He demanded one cent for each yam he bought & would get us besides for each fathom of cloth 10 yams. This we would not consent to do. He then fell to ½ cent. We finally agreed to give $2.00 for this day's trade, & try it. We now commenced giving one fathom of cloth for each basket of Yams containing 10, & the same for each basket of potatoes containing about ⅓ of a bushel. At this rate our cloth was soon gone, & so also will all we have on board the ship, & then we will not have one half a load. Perry appears willing to continue this trade & now says we cannot do better. If so we will scarcely pay expenses. I now find my friend Perry has hoaxed us completely, & the result of the expedition rests in much doubt & uncertainty. I went aboard before dinner & sent off nearly 2 kegs of Tobacco, & a lot of goods, which he traded away verry rapidly, & bought from 4 to 5 loads of yams & potatoes. Our prospect now is to finish our trading here & put for home as soon as possible. We lay several miles from shore & get our trade aboard slowly, only 2 loads to day.

July 3d. There has not been a single native aboard to day, & my time has been spent rather lonesome. I put it in in redding up my trunks, eating pineapples, oranges &c. & in fishing. I caught several verry singular fish, about 2 feet long, slim & a skin hard & tough similar to the shark. Its great curiosity consists in a sucker formed on the top of its head about 4 inches long & 2 wide, formed with ribs running across & cells between; with it, it attaches itself to whales, rocks, or ships, so firmly that they with difficulty are pulled off; in pulling them from the water they sometimes sieze hold the side of the vessel & cling verry fast.[3] The Capt. & mate returned before dark having sold out all our goods & 2 kegs of Tobacco but about 30 lbs. Four plugs of the 5s & 1 of the lb. instead of one fathom of cloth. The bay has been so rough to day we could get nothing from shore. A strong wind blows from the SE. Our anchorage is within the reef, & were it

[3]The reference is to one of the remoras (*Echeneididae*). The large species (*Remilegia australis*) is the whalesucker, but it is very unlikely that it was one of these which Osbun described.

not so, it would be rough indeed. A reef extends all around the island, several miles from it, which forms a fine inland sea, & a delightful harbor for vessels. Our intention now is to finish trade on this Island, & leave for home as soon as possible. Having heard a good report of the Island of Vaitupu, or Tracy island, for Hogs, situated in Lat. 7°29' & Long. 178°35' E., we have concluded to go by it & stop, & have reserved some trade for the purpose.

July 4th, 1850. This being our anniversary day we ordered our cook to kill a Turkey & give us a good dinner. We all went ashore & traded untill our goods were gone, & after midday returned to the vessel & eat a most excellent dinner.

Our Capt. says (we having requested from him a speech) he would give us one if he only had time to think a little & prepare one. We are all of us verry sorry time is so scarce with him, for he doubtless would give us such a rhetorical display as these waters & Islands have seldom listened to. He is a man well versed in all the tropes & figures of Rhetoric. He can dissect with logical skill the most abstruse syllogism, & detect the true from the false. Not a word or syllable misplaced can escape his critical observation. In fine, besides being master of the art & science of sailing, he is also a complete master of the sailor's lingo, which few of our great men can boast of. And being always careful in making up his mind in all matters, not only in opinions upon all subjects, for no subject or science or profession has escaped his investigation, but also in the proper use of language, he is always right & never wrong. Consequently we have this day been deprived of no ordinary treat—a real feast for the soul. We commenced with a good hearty drink, by all hands aboard, of egg nog. And ended with the body feast upon poor old Mr. Turkey.

Friday, 5th. It has rained much during the night, & it still continues. About noon it ceased, & the wind falling we conclu[d]ed to lift our anchor, & drop in nearer to the shore, our position now being 3 or 4 miles off. Consequently we dropped in & anchored within & close to a small island about one mile from our landing place. We succeeded in getting aboard 2 full boat loads, & a part of a load of Yams & potatoes, leaving yet behind several loads.

Saturday, 6th. There has been much high wind to day, still we have succeeded in getting aboard 4 loads, about 300 Baskets. I remained aboard all day. During the afternoon it rained considerably. Wind still SE.

Sunday, 7th. We all concluded to go to church today. This village or fort being altogether Catholic, we concluded to go across to the Protestant fort, & spend the day there. Consequently after breakfast we all went ashore but 3, & walked across the country about 4 miles & arrived there between 10 & 11 oclock. We find it is their Monday; consequently they have no preaching. The country across is verry level & verry fertile; it has evidently been at one time thickly settled, but now is a dense forest. A good portion of the road is fenced with a verry ancient looking stone wall, with here & there partitions, & also roads walled in passing from the main road. Large orchards of cocoas & bananas regularly planted out extend at regular intervals along the road, mixed with bread fruit & mummy apple. I cut a verry handsome walking stick from a lemon bush as I walked along. We saw the fighting ground of a battle between the forts, & see the cocoa trees cut up considerably with musket balls. As we approached the fort, we found, as we were apprized of, holes dug in the ground, filled with sharp sticks & slightly covered over, made for the purpose of catching their enemies in. We opened one & examined it & found it filled both in the bottom & sides with sharp spikes made from verry hard wood. We have understood that even some of their men have been caught in them, & badly hurt. A Priest, in passing to the upper fort, fell into one & was badly hurt. This fort is most beautifully situated, & things around it look much finer than the one we left. It is in the midst of a large grove of fruit trees extending for a great distance from & around it, with here & there verry extensive patches of Taro & Yams & Sweet potatoes. Verry few pigs are seen at either place on account of the war, they having been either killed to eat from necessity, or to prevent their enemies from taking them. This appears to be the custom on all the islands where war exists.

We entered the fort & were conducted to the head chief's, & heir apparant to the crown of the island's, house where we were entertained whilst we remained. I visited & prescribed as usual to several sick persons, amongst whom was one old Chief suffering from the effects of a shot from a musket ball near the knee joint. I was invited into many of their houses & offered Kava to drink in all, but I could not drink with them. We dined at the Chief's on roasted chicken, shell fish, bread fruit & Yams, in our usual manner upon mats. I was presented with a handsome native comb by a female resident of the chief's house & in return I gave her a horn one I had in my pocket. I returned immediately after a late dinner alone & night had commenced coming in before I got to the fort, & was too dark to hail the crew to come for me, so I was compelled to lodge again with my Irish friend. The Capt., Mate & 2 of the crew remained all night at the upper fort. The wind has continued to blow all day & night quite a strong breeze.

Monday, 8th July. I arose this morning more refreshed by sleep than when I slept here last, the musquitoes being all driven away by the wind. The last thing last evening, before going to bed, & the first this morning in this family is the chewing of & preparing Kava & drinking it. Our boat came after us before breakfast, & we all went aboard, our whole company having came down this morning. The wind has continued high all day, & we have taken aboard 3 Boat loads, about 250 baskets.

Tuesday, 9th. This morning King John came aboard & has remained with us all day. He is a man of verry good common sense & understands managing & governing his people well. Night before last, 2 of his men came aboard & remained untill late, after all hands had gone to bed & were asleep but the Capt., who was on watch. In the morning some clothing & other things were missing, and of course they are blamed for it. The Capt. sent word to John of the fact, & wished him to get them back. He called them before him & accused them of it, but they continued to deny it in a most solemn manner so that John was disposed to think they might be innocent. To day the Capt. brought up the subject, & raved considerably about it. John spoke calmly about it, & said he would punish them most severely if he had any evidence of their guilt. He asked the Capt. if he or any of our men had seen them take them, or if they had seen them in their possession. The Capt. answered, "No," but he knew they had taken them from the circumstance of their going ashore when they did. One of the men being now aboard, as one of John's rowers, the Capt. insisted upon taking pistols, & threatning to blow his brains out if he did not confess. John told him he might do so, but he thought it no good plan. "The man," he said, "would be scared, & might say yes in fear, no good way; be quiet, look out, & after while see something if he guilty. No good plan to strike a man unless sure he be guilty & good proof." The Capt. took down a pistol & was about to proceed

137

forward to execute his noble plan. Kissam and myself talked it over, & concluded to stop his cowardly course if we could. So he [Kissam] spoke out & gave the opinion that it was an imprudent course. He then desisted, put up his pistol, to please him, tho unchanged in his opinion.

About noon the Capt. & Mate went in the boat to the Protestant fort, & took with them some cloth to trade. They remained there all night. John remained aboard untill after supper. I have been quite entertained by his company, & have been also surprised at his knowledge of human nature, & his common sense.

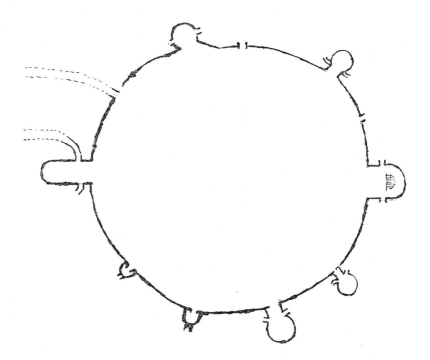

The above is the plan of John's fort or, as the natives call it, *Mooa*. The Catholicks call it St. Joseph. It is made by throwing up the earth about 10 feet high & surmounted by a fence of wicker work 6 feet high all around. The openings left are the entrances, & the offsets for watch houses. It is somewhat irregular in its form, being built, as I was informed, to suit the ground. I have taken the form for the purpose of comparing it with the ancient fortifications of America.

Wednesday, 10th July. I went ashore early to get some mats to take home but could find none that I considered worth taking. John offered me my pick from his stock of tappa, but I could see nothing among his worth getting under obligations to him for. After dinner the Capt. & Co. returned, bringing from 40 to 50 baskets of sweet potatoes. The wind this day since early in the morning has been from the East & quite favorable for our leaving, but the Capt. not being here, nothing was done untill afternoon. One anchor has been raised, & all getting ready for an early start tomorrow. Noah & myself hired some natives after dinner to take us out upon the reef at the small island south of us. We spent the afternoon there & on the island verry pleasantly. I saw here a large Porcupine fish & some Sea eggs, for the first time. My friend has a house here & a farm. We found him out upon the reef hunting shells for me; he took us to his house, & gave a meal of bread fruit & cocoa milk, & some of the fish. I relished it much. We returned late to the vessel completely wet. He gave me several good shells.

Thursday, 11th. My friend came aboard & brought me a large piece of verry pretty tappa early this morning. He now expects a present from me. I gave him a red bandana hdk. & some other small notions, but could not satisfy him. I had told him I would give him a pair of red flannel drawers I had, for a fine mat, which he said he had, but having no mat that pleased me I did not give it to him. He now insists upon getting it, & says he is a verry poor man. I find all the natives here from John down full of rich promises which are verry seldom performed. Our vessel is now crowded with natives, having potatoes &c. for trade, but all our trade for such things being gone, they had to take them away. We commenced early, raising our anchor, & after a late breakfast we were under full sail outside the reef. The wind blowing quite a fresh breeze from E. & SE. we have sailed well. I have been quite unwell this afternoon, head ache, sore throat & sick stomack.

Friday, 12th July. This day I have been verry sick, & confined to my berth. Fever, pain in the head, constant nausea, & inflamation of tonsils, my throat is so sore & so much swelled I can with difficulty swallow. This has all been produced by my getting wet on the reef & returning to the vessel.

Nothing has occurred to day new: at noon we were in Latitude 10°58′ S. & Longitude 177°32′ W. Prevailing wind E. by S. fresh.

Saturday, 13th. I am still verry unwell, & am compelled to keep my berth; no better. Observation at noon places us in Latitude 9°4′ S. and Longitude 179°05′ W. Wind from S. to E. Changeable.

Sunday, 14th. I have been better all day. It has been a verry unpleasant day. Storms & calms, rain, thunder & lightning. We could make no observations at noon, & consequently from the irregularity of the winds & calms we do not know our position. At 2 oclock we discovered land ahead, but were uncertain what island it might be. By sundown we were close to it, & the sun setting clear we were enabled to get an observation, from which we satisfied ourselves it was Achilles island, the one to which we were bound. We concluded to lay off & on untill morning & then round to the lee side, & see what we can do.

Monday, 15th. This morning at daylight we were near its SW. point, or rather its south point or end. We soon after passed around & after frequent tacks we came to an anchoring position, & anchored about 2 oclock close to the reef opposite or rather between t[w]o villages, & about ⅓ the length of the island from its S. end. Our anchorage we consider not good. The Capt. & Mate went ashore but could not learn with any amount of certainty what we can do. Nothing can be bought here but Hogs & cocoa nuts, nothing else being produced.

Tuesday, 16th. The Capt. & myself took some goods & went ashore early this morning to try what we could do in trade. But it proved an entire failure. It seems they have formed a project to hire us to go to an Island 40 miles off, called by them *Ufetou* & by us DePeysters Is., & bring home to this island their old king & several others, thrown there & their canoe destroyed about 15 months [ago], & have not since been able to get back. Two natives came across a few months ago to give information of them, & to get a ship to come after them.

It now seems they will take nothing from us, for any thing they have, but will give us any thing we want, if we will serve them. We asked them to give us 200 hogs, & 20,000 cocoa nuts, which they immediately agreed to. We then demanded one half down & the balance when we returned. This they said they could not do. They must wait for the return of the king to get his command, but that we should have all. The present King pro tem intended to go with us but at the meeting of their chiefs his going was tabooed. About 1 oclock we bundled up our goods & started for our boat. The old king arose & said he would go with us to the vessel, & walked with us a few rods from his house, when he turned suddenly & told us we must stop & go back with him, or, as it was expressed to us, he now taboo'd us from going untill some ceremony was ended. We saw a verry ugly old dried up squaw, coming in great haste towards his house, her mats & lava lava flying & fluttering in the wind, as she bustled along at the heighth of her best walking gate. The old man knew perhaps from her dress or something else her errand. Now it appears there is to be an assembling of the chiefs & speakers of the tribe, & the object to taboo the old man's visit to the ship. Our interpreter being a verry poor one, I could get a verry poor account of the object of the meeting, or of what was said, or the meaning of the ceremonies.

In a few minutes there were some dozen chiefs & this old woman seated around the house, it being verry large like a barn, with no enclosure, only the roof & the posts on which it rested. The old lady occupied the centre [of] one whole side, seated with her back to the king. In the centre was spread by the king two mats, which remained unoccupied for some time, & the meaning of which I could not understand, supposing however they were the seats of the absent chiefs, & out of respect to them they had spread them to show by their vacancy their absence. All sat silent & in their most dignified matter [sic] about ½ hour but the king. He kept up a constant talk, a part of which was in a verry low tone, & about one word every minute, which was not apparently directed to any person. Again his voice would be raised, & he would look around as tho he was addressing his assembly. At the end of about ½ hour from the commencement of this flummery, the old woman arose & advanced to one of the mats & seated herself, her side being towards the king. In a few minutes she commenced a speech, & spoke in most vehement noisy manner for some time, shaking her head & body most violently all the time, pitching backward & forward all the time with her body holding on to the mat with her hands. He occasionally during her speech spoke to her with much dignity of manner, seemingly in answer to her objections, making no impression. He then threw to her a mat, & was followed by all the chiefs, each throwing her one also. This was offered as a present to overcome her objections & quiet her, but it did not do it. She ceased a little, when a disagreeable looking fellow arose, advanced & took the other vacant mat. He began in a verry loud squealing voice, & unnatural, twisting his head, eyes, mouth & all the muscles of his ugly face in all directions, pulling & hauling at the mat with his hands & heaving at the breast, as tho' performing some great labor.

The king also answered him but without effect. He pulled off his own mat, & threw it to him; none else were offered him, & he finally arose in the midst of most violent gesticulations & left, his feelings being unaltered. They then dispersed. We went to our boat; he being ta-booed staid behind. We gave them to understand we would go after their people, & would start verry early in the morning. They then sent us aboard several canoe loads of cocoa nuts, green & ripe, to use on the journey. The old lady, I understood, was the wife of a deceased chief or speaker, which no doubt was the cause of her influence.

Wednesday, 17th April [*July*]. This morning early all hands were at work, & before breakfast we were under way to the Island of Ufetou. We have with us two persons from the island, a son of the absent king, & a native of Otaheite who lives on the island. Two other persons desired to go along, friends of those with us, but our captain drove them from the vessel & made them swim some distance before they reached canoes. This, together with some other imprudence, I fear will injure us in obtaining full pay for the trip. Our contract being with savages, our pay when not receiving it or a part of it before hand is extremely uncertain. We made sail directly for the island, & at a little past noon were up to it. Not knowing where their town was, there being a great many small islands, we scarcely knew how to find them. We sailed along down its eastern side, some 10 or 15 miles, & saw no person. We then rounded its southern point, & sailed several miles along the reef & in view of several islands, & finally percieved on a central island many natives running about on shore. Soon 2 ca-noes were seen rounding the point of the island & coming towards us. We hauled to, & were soon boarded by them. They were of the party we were after & had come off in haste to employ us to take them away. We were informed they were suffering for food & that they numbered about 20 persons & would give 3 hogs for each person. We now un-furled our sails & passed around the Western point of the island, when we came in view of their island.

A storm coming up, we were prevented from getting to our an-chorage untill after dark, when we anchored near the reef in 6 fathoms water.

There was great rejoicing when they found out we had come for them. Ben, the King's son who is with us, has not seen his father or brothers here many years, he having been on a ship whaling, & re-turned a few months ago. He was quite a small boy when he left home

& is now grown up. One of his brothers being in the canoe recognized him, & seemed to be overwhelmed with joy, & such a noise & confusion & striking each other on their backs with open hands, & other demonstrations of natural & savage feeling, I never before witnessed. Wind ESE. o[u]r course South.

Thursday, April [July] 18th. This morning the Capt. & myself went ashore to have an interview with our passengers & to get them aboard as soon as possible.

We found the King an old man 80 years at least of age, verry feeble & tottering, setting at his breakfast on roasted fish & Taro. He stopped instantly, embraced us affectionately with tears running down his cheeks & talked, but we could not understand him. Their embrace consists in hugging & pressing & rubbing noses together. All his higher officers & [men] of the island embraced us in this manner; others rubbed their noses on the back of our hands. He stopped eating & offered us his meal & would recieve no denial; we were forced to eat some. We told him that we desired them to get ready as soon as possible, that we wished to sail. He then called together his people outside the house to show us their number, & there were about 20 men, women & children. Then following it was an assembly of the King & Chief of this island to give their presents, to make speeches & bid farewell. This took up some time. There were several white headed grave looking men among them; they spoke fluently & were answered by our party. What was said I could not ascertain. The presents consists in cloth, shells & mats, which were all spread out before him. The whole value of the presents was not more than from 5 to 10 dollars. One shell of a beautiful orange colour I have taken a fancy to, & will trade for if I can. We hurried them up & by 10 oclock had them, with their luggage of mats & provisions, all aboard. But instead of 20 persons, I counted upwards of 70 & suppose there were about 80 persons, men, women & children, aboard, & such a noisy set of passengers I never expect again to see. They soon became sea sick & were lying in all directions vomiting up cocoa nuts, &c. This island is verry poor, producing naturally little but cocoa nuts, & the natives are too lazy to raise such vegetables as might be produced with little labor. At their meals cocoas either scraped raw or roasted with some fish constitutes their eatables. These islands produce immense quantities of cocoa nuts. Soon we got under way, & by 12 oclock we were outside the reef & all the islands. We steered NE. ½ N. but the wind blowing strong

143

& also a strong current making west, we did not make the island, being at dark some miles to leeward. We tacked & lay off & on untill morning. The wind has been from ESE.

Friday, 19th. This morning we find ourselves near & to the windward a few miles of the island of *Ufetou* again. And our passengers all much delighted at the sight of their homes. We soon rounded the point, & a short time after sun up came to anchor in 15 fathoms water, close to our last anchorage here. Canoes were soon off to us; & after an early breakfast, the King & suite left the vessel in our boat, the Capt. & mate accompanying them. Soon all were gone, & the vessel once more enjoying its peaceful calm. This day I understand was spent in great rejoicing & rubbing of noses ashore during the forenoon. Capt. & mate returned soon & immediately after early dinner Capt. & self went ashore to ascertain when our Hogs will be forthcoming. Soon after their dinner & about 2 oclock they all assembled, male & female, before the King's house, dressed in every fantastic manner imaginable with such things as they had to use. No two being fixed up alike, some covered with wreaths of flowers verry handsomly arranged. Others, strings of white shells around the neck hanging down upon the breast, & large white ones tied around the arms, strings of them also around the hips outside their mats or lava lavas, faces painted in different figures generally using white, black & red colours. Natural vines twined their heads, neck & bodies, &c. &c. A band as singers seated themselves on the ground or rough coral & commenced a song in which I could see no music, accompanied by a constant clapping of the hands keeping time. The dancers all approached them dancing or rather jumping to the time & singing & clapping hands, every now & then looking upwards, screwing & twisting the muscles of face & of all the body, hallooing at the top of their voice, "Huhoo, huhoo." In this dance were engaged many verry old people. Male & female appeared to join & mingle in it indiscriminately. The old king & his chiefs all sat in a line upon their mats & seemed to enjoy it much, by their constant attention & frequent exclamations of approval.

A perpetual smile sat upon the countenance of every one, & each dance terminated in loud fits of laughter. The presents from the other island were spread out before the King, & remained there during the whole performance, which lasted untill near sundown. The people of this island have always refused & still refuse to have missionaries among them. What their religious notions are I have as yet been unable to ascertain, our interpreters being too dumb to give explanations.

I see graveyards with houses close to them, but nothing in them. Many of the graves are covered with mats to keep off the rain, but generally are surrounded with stone, with high head & feet stone cut in steps, & covered with pebbles of white coral. They look verry pretty, being all elevated above the earth from 1 to 2 feet. I observe many graves in the houses, husbands having buried their wives there & sleeping along side of them, or children their parents. This idea I have been much pleased with, & shows a good feeling in such people. It has given me more confidence in them than I otherwise would have had. They have stolen from me to day all the tobacco I had in my pockets, & are verry expert at it. I consider them greater thieves than any we have been among. And if they get hold of any thing, knife, hdk., coat, &c., it is apt to be the last of it. If you give your consent, in showing any thing, for them to take it into their hands, they will not give it back willingly but seem to consider it theirs. I started aboard about sundown, the Capt. & mate remaining ashore all night. They promise that tomorrow the pigs will be forthcoming.

Saturday, 20th July. This morning the Capt. & 2 Mates went ashore early & returned about dark, no pigs having been delivered to day. They said they were still engaged in their rejoicings & in their dances. They brought with them Ben, who says that tomorrow the pigs will come. I must acknowledge that I fear we will never get but verry few pigs. Altho they appear verry grateful, still I have but little confidence in their faith, & think the sooner we close up the matter the better. If we are to have a row, the sooner the better & let us be off.

Sunday, 21st. This day the natives have brought off to us 2 medium sized hogs & 17 little pigs. Also 633 cocoa nuts. The Capt. & mate have been ashore all day, & report that these are all the hogs the party we brought up have & that the others are unwilling to give any. They have continued their dance.

Monday, 22d. To day we have concluded to kill a pig & invite the ex-king aboard to dine, or some of the other natives, & after dinner raise our anchore & lay off and on, untill we were paid, & not permitting our guests to leave us unless we were paid. Consequently the Capt. & mate went ashore early & brought off the ex-king & his little daughter, but reported that the people ashore had turned so much against him that they believed they would not be displeased if we took him off. We then concluded to go ashore & propose to take 25 large hogs & go off satisfied, but if they would not do it, to threaten them with vengeance, either through an American man of war or by ourselves on our return. The Capt. & myself went ashore immediately after dinner, and found them all engaged as usual in the dance. After they had finished they held a council concerning our pay, the old King asking more, but the people refused. We then communicated our designs, & told them we would leave this night. The old King seemed in much trouble, & shed tears, after hearing our determination, but [it] seems that nothing more can be had from them unless by force. We have not one pound of powder aboard with which to claim our rights. And it is now evident that that is the only way we can get justice done us. I believe 10 men armed can take the whole island in a verry short time, burn up all their houses, & carry away all their Hogs. And this we have now promised to do. We ordered them to send us aboard some green cocoa nuts & some men to assist us in raising our anchor, which they did, but concluded to lay untill morning & they staid aboard. These people are not warlike; they have no warclubs or instruments of warfare of their own make, we having seen 2 or 3 old muskets out of order, the only tools for warfare on the whole island. They are great thieves, & when they get possession of any article, either by our consent or otherwise, they seem to consider it their own. And if called upon for it, it is with great difficulty we can obtain it back. They hang upon us & fondle upon us ashore all the time there & steal from our pockets every thing they contain. This they do verry expertly, & succeed even when we are closely watching them. They are verry lazy & live poorly, their food being principally cocoa nuts, either raw or roasted, or green. They eat green cocoa nuts rind & all, excepting the thin outside green bark. They have a small quantity of wild Taro they occasionally use with it on particular occasions. They are small eaters. Their amusements are solely dancing, of which they are verry fond. I understand it is a daily habit with them to assemble before the King's house & dance before him. The balance of their time is spent in sleeping. They are verry fond of fish, but altho they are verry plenty here, they are too lazy to catch them. They manufacture nothing but coarse mats for wearing around their bodies & sleeping on. None of them have cloth of any kind. Boys & girls go entirely naked untill about 12 years of age, when they get tattooed, & commence to use the lava lava. The population of the whole Island will not reach 500 including every soul.

Tuesday, 23rd July. This morning early we commenced raising our anchor, having aboard an English Sydney man, Heite Bill, Ben, & some natives to assist. This young English Sydney fellow we brought from Ufetou, where he was living, & we thought he had prevented the natives from paying us, as far as he could influence them. The Capt., to get him out of the way, yesterday sent him aboard to work, & thus to help pay his passage up also. After our anchor was raised, the Capt. ordered [him] off the vessel as quick as possible, telling him our opinion of his conduct, & of his character, & that if we found him here when we returned what he might expect from us. He seemed alarmed, & conscious of the truth of what was told him. Bill also we lectured, telling him, he being our interpreter, that we blamed him also for not carrying out his promises, & for assisting to get us into the disappointment. Poor Ben seemed in trouble. He says he told his Father if they did not pay us, he would leave the island in the first ship that would come. We made Bill & Ben some trifling presents & told them to tell the people to be on the lookout; they would certainly be visited & punished. My opinion is that the whole of them are dishonest & need punishment. The party we brought up, being however more disposed to do justice than the other, as evidenced not only by their professions but by their conduct & continued kindness & friendly disposition. The others appearing unwilling to do us the least favor. In my opinion several errors were committed in our treatment of the home party, by which we got their ill will, & which contributed much to prevent them from carrying out their contract. No pains whatever was taken to please any of them, but the most rigid rules enforced & strictness observed in trifles. Bill desired verry much the two natives to go with us that were driven overboard, & he was much displeased. Ben, not acting right, was also ordered back, tho I think he was in the end reconciled by a little attention & kindness. He is a verry weak minded fellow, having either little sense or energy. Bill possesses an opposite character, is cunning & two faced, & has ability enough to manage the natives & carry out his designs.

Before we got fairly under way, quite a storm arose & continued for about one half hour. It has continued to storm occasionally all day & also to rain considerably. Before the middle of the day we were entirely out of sight of the island. The wind being from the East, our course has been generally N. by E. At noon we were in Latitude 7°09′ S. & Longitude 179° 10′ E.—having sailed towards home 29 miles.

9

VOYAGE TO PEARL AND HERMES REEF— RETURN TO SAN FRANCISCO

©

Wednesday, 24th July. Last night we had several heavy blows, but no damage done. The ocean being rough has made our sailing verry unpleasant to day. I have felt verry unpleasant about my stomach ever since we got under way. The wind has been N. of E. all day & we have sailed as near to it as we could, our course varying to & from N. Our Latitude at noon as near as we could get it was 5°26′ S. & Longitude 179°22′ E. Our observation for Latitude was poor & not to be relied on. Sailed 104 ms.—133.

Thursday, 25th. Wind still ranges NE. by E. & our course N. by W. At noon we find ourselves in Latitude 2°34′ S. & Longitude 178°40′ E. Our sailing is still unpleasant & my stomach keeps me uneasy all the time. The Capt. examined our Potatoes & Yams to day & reports all in fine keeping condition. Our pigs are now, with the exception of 2 recieved at the last island, all doing well. They have recovered from their seasickness & are improving in flesh fast. Some of our chickens have been verry sick, heads down & slime running from their mouths, but they are now better. But one chicken & 1 Duck has as yet died, & they were weak & trodden upon. We have now aboard 85 Hogs & 25 small pigs—33 chickens and 12 Ducks & 1 Turkey. One dog & 1 cat. Sailed 177 ms.—in all 310 ms.

Friday, 26th. We have been enabled to steer to day from one to 1½ points E. of N., the wind a little more from E. than yesterday. At noon our Latitude is 0°00′ being on the line & Longitude 178°30′. Our observation at noon was not good. It has been verry squally with showers of rain all day. This morning after breakfast we discovered a vessel ahead of us, & in a few hours caught up to her. A short time before we came up to her, she hoisted her colors, showing a British flag, & took up part of her sail showing a desire to speak to us, & to wait untill we came up. We were soon along side, our vessel being able to sail with double the speed of her. She proved to be a whaling Barque from Sidney, New South Wales, out 2 months with 60 or 80 bbls. of Oil. Her Capt's name was Elliott but her name not being on the vessel I could not get it. They requested our Capt. to come aboard of her, & proposed to send their boat for him; he accepted the offer & went aboard & dined with him. He collected some facts interresting to us, such as that Yams & Uphelas can be kept many months at sea, say from 4, 6, 8, to 10 months in good order, if kept dry, & that salt water does not hurt them. Sweet potatoes he knows nothing about. She passed in sight of us on Saturday morning whilst we lay at anchor at Witaboo, & has been sailing as fast as she could ever since on this course. We did not leave until 2 days afterwards. After our Capt. came aboard, in a few hours we left her so far she could not be seen. Sailed 155 ms.—465 ms.

Saturday, 27th. Our observations are not to be relied on to day. We have had a fine breeze all day & last night from E. by N. & ESE., so that our course has been generally NNE. We put down our Latitude 2°30' N. & Longitude 179°30' E. One small Wytebu pig thrown overboard dead. Sailed 162 ms.—627.

Sunday, 28th. Our observations to day are good & to be relied on. We find at noon our position in Latitude 4°44' N. & Longitude 178° 47' W. Wind has been light, & from a little S. of E. One chicken & one large Witabu pig thrown overboard this morning, dead. We find for several days a current here running to the East, which is unusual; it is reported as always running west. Its velocity is supposed to be about 1 mile per hour. Sailed 131 ms.—758 miles.

Monday, 29th. The winds have been verry variable to day: moving from N. to E. & verry light, with occasional calms. Our course has consequently been verry crooked, sailing to all points from W. to E. Our object now is to get out of this belt of calms & variable winds as soon as possible, by making northings as fast as possible. Eastings or westings made here is of no use to us. A few degrees further North places us again in the regular trade winds from NE. & E. At noon to day we are in Latitude 5°52' & Longitude 178°17' W. Sailed 74 ms.— 832.

Tuesday, 30th July. Latitude this day is 6°08′ N. & Longitude 176° 23′ W. We this morning passed through a drove or school of sperm whales, worth if we had them many thousand dollars, & had we only the right kind of a boat & harpoon we doubtless could have taken 3 or 4000 dollars worth, without detaining us but a short time. We have men aboard well trained to whaling & who have spent many years at it. It was exciting to see how the excitement ran through them as we passed by them. During the night many porpoises were playing around us. Sailed to day 115 miles, whole distance 947 miles.

Wednesday, 31st. Our Latitude to day is 7°14′ N. & Longitude 176° 21′ W. Winds are still variable, with calms. Our course has averaged about North, steering at all times as near the wind as possible.

We have overhauled our vegetables to day, & find the Yams & Uphelas growing some, but not verry much, & in good condition, being dry, & the bruised ones all dried where broken with a thin shell & doing well. The sweet potatoes are growing verry much. We concluded not to disturb the 2 former, but think it better perhaps to bruise the sprouts on the potatoes, & not break them off.

I now put in a few hours of my time every day at the wheel steering, to permit all hands to work at cleaning decks & feeding the Hogs. This is all the labor I perform; the balance of my time I pass in reading, making calculations & feeding a pet dove I purchased at the Island of Upolu. It is a beautiful creature, & amuses us frequently with its song. Our hogs generally continue to thrive & do well, & few of them will yet most probably die. We lost 2 to day of the small Witabu pigs. We find that it takes but a little over one cocoa nut per day to feed each hog. John Wilson our cook has been off duty for some time. He was seized before we left Witabu with a fit of *Fayfa* but continued to work several days. He has had several chills & considerable fever, with increased swelling of his left leg. One of the lymphatics in his left groin has swelled up & is full of pus. I intend opening it in the morning. Sailed 66 ms.—1013.

Thursday, August 1st, 1850. Winds are now settled down into the regular trade from NE. & NE. by E. Our latitude is 9°27′ N. and Longitude 177°10′ W. Wind being now good, we are making good headway. Our sweet potatoes are already rotting fast, 8 or 10 baskets being to day thrown overboard, supposed to be those wet with salt water & not washed off, & that were purchased just as we left Wallace's

Island from the Protestant fort people. I occasionally become now verry home sick. I long to be with my dear wife & children, & spend much of my time thinking over my future course of life, & the many happy moments we will enjoy together, should I be so fortunate as to live to be again with them. This evening a large bird called a Booby alighted upon the Jib boom, & immediately became stupid. One of the men went to him & caught him. His stomach was full of fish. Sailed 143 ms.—1156 ms.

Friday, 2d. Winds same as yesterday, fine weather. Our Latitude to day is 12°8' N. & Longitude 178°45' W. Sailed 188 ms.—1344.

Saturday, 3d. Our Latitude is 14°48' N. & Longitude 179°30' W. We have still fine weather, with a good breeze from NE. & NE. by E.

Sunday, 4th. Our Latitude is 17°04' N. & Longitude 179°50' W. Wind has been variable to day with occasional showers & calms. We have been enabled however to make a better course avaridging N. by W. It is our intention now to make some of the islands north of us, & add if possible to our Cargo a good lot of Green Turtles. In this I hope we may succeed. At noon this day we passed directly under the sun, consequently our bodies would show no shadow. The sun is now on her way from the north to the south. She passes over the Equator between the 22d & 23d of September. We passed under her between the 17th & 18th degree of N. Latitude, & verry near the same degree of Latitude we are now in. Distance sailed 2 last days 302 miles, whole dist.—1646.

Monday, 5th. Our latitude at noon is 18°51' N. & Longitude 179° 51' E. Winds from NE., with occasional showers. We crossed again during the last night the 180° of longitude, it being the *ne plus ultra* of longitude, so that we are now again in Eastern longitude. We have been keeping up a strict watch for several days & nights, & particularly during the last night for reefs & land—we being now in a part of the sea not much frequented, & where our charts are considered verry imperfect. This morning before day & about day light we saw & heard many sea birds flying & croaking around our vessel, which denotes a nearness to land. Dist. sailed 107 ms.—1753.

Tuesday, 6th. Latitude 20°48' N. Longitude 179°17' E. The weather is pleasant, altho we are directly underneath the sun. The breeze, almost constantly blowing from the NE., so tempers the air that it is positively delightful & exhilirating.

Our old cook has to day resumed his duties. Many of our chickens are beginning to pine, so we concluded to commence feasting upon them yesterday, & killed 4 & had a fine dinner. The time was when I considered I never could tire upon sweet potatoes, but the daily use of them since we left Wytaboo has changed my appetite. A little fresh good bread would now be one of the greatest luxuries I could get, particularly if greased over with a little cow grease fresh. We have plenty of Flour & butter aboard, but both so bad that they can scarce be eaten. Our meals for some time, excepting dinner yesterday, has been salt meat & sweet potatoes, with an occasional loaf of fresh bread, so heavy that it would sink in water as quick as a stone. Also hard bread full of small fine worms, & their webs, which I cannot eat. 123 miles.

Tomorrow at noon comes off one of Nature's most grand exhibitions, & we are awaiting most anxiously for the arrival of the time. I mean a total eclipse of the sun. Where our position will be at the time, we will not be able to see it totally eclipsed, but verry near it; that disirable spot is about on our track when going out in Lat. between 17° & 18°. This afternoon it became quite hazy & the wind fell off, almost to a calm, so that our progress was but little.

Wednesday, 7th. This morning we have witnessed the long expected & long looked for Eclipse. It was nearly total. There appeared to be about 1 in. on its northern side uncovered; it approached on its upper side & appeared to cross over its surface, leaving the above surface uncovered as it passed along. It became quite cool, darkened up considerably, tho' not as dark as I expected. It was truly a grand phenomenon, & has awakened within me many curious & serious impressions. This has been almost an entire day of calm weather, & I find I am becoming quite impatient to have the voyage completed. We find ourselves at noon in Latitude 21°52′ & Long. 179°52′ E. The small amount of breeze which we have is from SE., & we have been steering all day ENE. The atmospere this evening looks quite hazy, as tho a light fog rested upon the surface of the ocean. Clouds are flying considerably, with a few flashes of distant lightning. Dist sailed 73 ms.—1949.

Thursday, 8th. Our Latitude is 22°50′ N. & Longitude 178°28′. Distance sailed 118 miles & from Wytaboo 2067. Wind from SE. It arose in the night & has continued quite a breeze during the whole day. We are now enabled to make a good course, & also good speed. Course by compass NE. by E. This [day] one of our finest, largest & fattest hogs died suddenly; the cause we could not ascertain. She was with pig, & not far from her pigging time. Yesterday we feasted upon a pair of old tough Ducks. They were roasted & stuffed with our hard bread, in which I found cooked worms, which destroyed my relish for it. Another of our Hens died to day. The sea has been quite rough all day & our vessel tossed & pitched considerable. During the forenoon it made me quite sick.

Friday, 9th August. Our Latitude to day is 24°11′ N. & Long. 176° 13′ W. Our course by compass has been NE. by E. Distance sailed to day 157 ms.—2224 ms. Wind from SE. Being now far enough to the Eastward to be free from the fear of the changing of the wind, we at noon changed our course to N. by W. by compass, to make direct for Clarks Islands & reef or, as they are sometimes called, Pearl & Hermes Islands. Our Otaheite sailor & our Spaniard cook skinned a hind and fore quarter of the Hog that died yesterday, & have roasted it to day & are feasting sumptuously upon it. It has been squally during the evening with rain.

Saturday, 10th. We are today in Latitude 26°01′ N. & Long. 175° 50′ W., having sailed since noon yesterday 112 miles, whole distance from Wytaboo 2336 ms. Wind has been from SE. & light with squalls of rain. Our Otaheitean has saved the life of an old chicken cock by killing him just before he died, & eating him for his supper. We have a few companions, sea birds, some of whom are almost constantly with us. A small bird about the size of our Martin but shaped & coloured like our swallow, called the sperm whale bird, from its resorts being in the same region of that fish. It with another bird called [blank in MS] about the size & shape of our whippoorwill can be seen constantly skimming over the surface of the water. These two with another fowl called the Boatswain, or Tropic bird, have been our regular companions ever since our departure for home. Occasionally other birds show themselves but no new ones. This morning a Man of war hawk sailed high up in the air by us, most majestically, & verry slow. This evening a stinker made his appearance flying around the vessel, the first we have seen north since we left. Yesterday morning we crossed the line of the Tropic of Cancer & are now again beyond the march of the sun. We notice sensibly the evenings & mornings getting cooler.

Sunday, Aug. 11th. At noon we find ourselves in Latitude 27°38′ N. & Longitude 176°05′ W. This morning the number of birds has increased verry much & all appear to come from ahead. Some small striped land birds like snipes are also seen, all of which denote our nearness to land, & also that it is ahead. The winds are light & from WSW., clouded & squally with rain. After our observations were taken at noon we felt verry uneasy for 2 hours, fearing we would not be able to make land. We have 3 accounts of its position, & they all differ: viz. Morrell's, our chart, & epitome. And it is exceedingly doubtful whether any of them is correct.[1] The islands here are verry seldom visited, the navigation being extremely dangerous, & nothing upon them worth going to them for. We kept a man at the mast head constantly on the lookout; the land being verry low cannot be seen further than 6 or 8 miles from mast head. Two oclock had passed & still no land; we were now further north than two reports located the islands & still were not to be seen. We all felt very uneasy, not knowing positively what was wrong, & fearing some that the error might be in our chronometer. But soon we were releaved from our suspense by the cry from aloft, "Land & breakers ho! 3 points off our lee bow." We all sprang up at the same moment, electrified with joy, & went upon deck to look, altho' we could not see it without going aloft. This was about 10 minutes past two oclock, & were sailing at the rate of 4 knots per hour. Soon we were near enough to see the white crests of the breakers from deck, as they broke & foamed as far as the eye could reach. We could also see a bare looking island raising its bald head behind the breakers. These islands with the reefs around it [are] considered verry dangerous for vessels to sail near, in consequence of their lowness & extensive reefs. These Islands are called Pearl & Hermes, named from two British whale ships, the *Pearl* & the *Hermes*, that were wrecked here near 30 years ago.[2] They are called also Clarks islands & reef. We

[1]The reference here is to Benjamin Morrell, *A Narrative of Four Voyages, to the South Sea, North and South Pacific Ocean, Chinese Sea, Ethiopic and Southern Atlantic Ocean, Indian and Antarctic Ocean* (New York, 1832), pp. 218-219, 226. The "epitome" may be Charles Wilkes, *Narrative of the United States' Exploring Expedition, during the Years 1838, 1839, 1840, 1841, 1842. Condensed and Abridged* (London, [1845]).

[2]*Hermes* and *Pearl* were wrecked on the same night, Apr. 26, 1822, about ten miles apart.

sailed up along the reef on the SW. side, untill we were somewhat beyond the island, when we hove to, & the Capt. & three of the men let
down the boat & pulled for the Island. They were over 1 hour pulling
before they landed. They found it a verry small island or sand bar not
1 mile in circumference, & covered with coarse grass & a vine bearing
[a] prickly pod. It was covered with birds & nests, also a few hair seal,
but no Turtle nor the signs of any. They killed 10 or 12 seal, & brought
aboard their livers & hearts, from which we made several excellent
meals. I consider them equal to Beef's liver. No other part is considered eatable, & they were of course left upon the beach. A heavy
sacrifice of live for so little meat. They were verry fat & would weigh
each about 500 lbs. They were verry tame, & suffered our men to come
upon them without moving themselves & knock them in the head. The
birds were also equally tame, & suffered themselves readily to be
caught.

Fish were verry plenty around the island, & large quantities could be
readily caught with a hook & line. In coming off they caught one small
Green Turtle on the reef. There is no doubt but that in the proper Season many turtle might be taken here, which season is June when they
come ashore to lay their eggs.

There are also many Pearl & other handsome & valuable shells to be
had here, but our visit being for turtle & the prospect seeming poor for
them, we concluded to leave immediately, so that by 6 oclock we
were again under full sail with wind from the North. We directed our
course for Bunker hill island, as near as the wind would permit us to
go. Whilst we were laying to, immense numbers of fish, albicores, skip
jack, & sharks were swarming around us. We could see another small
island, apparantly about 1 mile north from the one on which our men
landed, & about the same size, and they supposed it must have been
on it the crew of the wrecked vessels landed. They saw two spars, the
only evidence of shipwreck visible, from which we took several copper nails. Morrell in his journal states that there are several of these
islands, or sand [s]pits as he calls them, extending north on the reef,
and when he was here in 1825 the hulls of the wrecked vessels were
still visible, & that the islands were entirely bare of vegetation, being
composed of lava & pumice stone & sand. He also states that the reef
extends NW. 70 or 80 miles, & that these islands were covered with sea
elephant & turtle the whole year. This account induced us to visit
them. I did not go ashore, intending to go the second trip, but as it
turned out, I feel verry sorry I did not go. The men picked up a few

verry pretty shells, & I am confident many curious specimens of shells & other things could have been collected upon this unfrequented spot. We have sailed this day 97 miles—& whole distance sailed from Wytaboo 2433 miles. By our observations we make the Southern island to lay in Lat. 27°53′ N. & Long. 176°04′ W. And the southern extremity of the reef leading south from it in Lat. 27°50′ N. & Long. 176°04′.

Monday, Aug. 12th. Our position to day is in Latitude 27°43′ N. & Long. 174°54′ W., having sailed this day 100 miles, whole dist. 2533 miles. Wind is verry variable, shifting around from E. to NW. frequently. The weather is most delightful in temperature. We have had frequent calms to day. I saw Dolphin for the first time in my life playing & swimming around the vessel. They are a beautiful fish. We threw our lines & caught a couple of excellent fish about the size of shad called *yellow tails* by the sailors.

Tuesday, 13th. At noon to day we are in Lat. 28°32′ & Long. 174°18′ W., having sailed the last 24 hours only 61 miles, whole distance 2594 miles. This is the poorest day's sail we have yet had, nearly the whole of it being made this forenoon, having a fine breeze ever since day light from SE. We find we cannot make Bunker H[ill] island without tacking, & succeeding so badly at the last islands, we have concluded not to waste the time, but are now steering for our destined port. The day before yesterday, whilst laying to opposite the islands, in attempting to step over a small hatchway in the stern of vessel, she rolled, which made me miss my step, stepping on my toes; my foot slipped back, & I fell down. I caught upon my side & groin, & bruised myself verry much both on my shin bone & in my groin. The surface was broken & scraped off & the flesh much injured. It is now much swelled & verry painful. I much fear a bad sore on my shin.

Wednesday, Aug. 14th, 1850. We are now in Latitude 30°44′ N. and Longitude 171°45′ W., having sailed 202 miles, whole distance 2796 miles.

We have had an excellent breeze from SE. which has borne us along with great rapidity. It is cloudy & threatens storms & rain. The Sea is also verry rough which tosses about our little vessel exceedingly. She is also occasionally struck in the bow, with a wave or roll of the sea, which stuns & jars her as tho' she was struck with an immense rock, & altho it seems momentarily to impede her progress, still she rides proudly over all.

Thursday, 15th. We find our position is in Latitude 32°35′ N. & Longitude 169°39′ W., having sailed 176 miles the last 24 hours—2972. Wind has fallen off some but is still from SE. & SE. by E. A large school of porpoise, Black fish & some others amused us for some time during the forenoon playing around the vessel.

Friday, 16th. We are to day in Latitude 33°49′ N. & Longitude 167° 21′, having sailed 154 miles, whole dist. 3126 miles. Wind is still from SE., but has almost left us. This has been a verry pleasant day, the air sufficiantly cool to be pleasant. We have watched for a long time to day the passing of *Portuguese men of war,* the surface of the ocean here being verry liberally supplied with them. They are a small animal of a gelatinous structure, of smooth upper surface, & below studded with innumerable long slim feet or feelers, verry thin except its centre, which is thickened some where the feet are inserted. On its upper surface is raised a transparant sail, with which it sails gaily over the surface of the ocean. Its colour is a rich purplish blue. It is capable of stinging or burning the skin with its feet when handled. I attempted a drawing of it on the other side, but it is poorly executed.[3]

Saturday, 17th. We are in Latitude 34°33′ N. & Longitude 165°40′ W., sailed 111 miles, whole dist. 3237 miles. We have been becalmed this day completely, laying perfectly still most of the time, & catching Portuguese men of war. The water seems to be completely filled with a substance looking like hair & rotted moss, also various kinds of insects called red eyes & bright eyes, sea eggs &c. These things Capt. Pease tells me all indicate that a calm has existed here for some time. I hope it is not a true prognostic this time, particularly if it is to remain so.

Sunday, 18th. We are in Lat. 34°59′ N. & Long. 164°35′ W. Sailed 74 miles, total 3311 miles. We have still but verry light winds, with occasional calms. It has been my expectation for some time that we would be in Port on the 1st of Sept. & I backed it in a conversation with Kissam by a bottle of wine. But these calms make me think of changing my notion. This evening I looked upon one of the most brilliant & charming sunsets my eyes ever beheld. Beautiful landscapes, with lakes & rocks & islands & mountains, were painted in coulours more brilliant & more natural than any painting I ever saw.

[3]The sketch of the Portuguese man-of-war has been cut from the manuscript.

Monday, 19th. Our position is in Lat. 36°09′ N. & in Long. 163°22′ W. Wind more variable from E. by N. to SE. by S. & verry light with calms. It was quite clouded over this morning, & many clouds have been flying all day. Sailed 102 miles. Total 3413 miles.

Tuesday, Aug. 20th, 1850. We find to day our Latitude [is] 36°49′ N. & Longitude 161°08′ W., wind from SE. to S. by E., & blowing a fair wind all day. We have sailed this day 144 miles. Total 3557 miles.

Our old companions, the island birds that have been with us constantly, have now all left us. A few Boobys or Stinkers are the only ones we now see. One of the men threw out a line yesterday, having a hook & some pork on it, & hauled one aboard. They are verry easily caught in this way, the hook catching them in the crook of their upper bill. Our hogs are still dying one every few days; they seem to take diarrhoea, many of them, & are carried off. Others die from disease in the urinary passages. We yesterday have changed their food by giving them a slop of flour. We have eaten up all our chickens & ducks but 3 or 4. We have been living rather sumptuously for some time. Having discovered some valuable uses to which we can apply the cocoa milk, we are now taking advantage of them. Viz. it is an excellent substitute for cream in tea or coffee. It answers all the purposes of eggs & milk in making custards or pies. We have made some excellent pumpkin pies with it. It answers as a good substitute for cream or milk & butter in making light short cakes, some of which we have had baked from verry indifferent flour, as good we all pronounced them as we ever ate. And I have no doubt if its use were extended to other cookeries, it would be found a valuable article in that department.

Wednesday, 21st. Our Latitude to day is 36°46′ N. Long. 157°44′ W. Day's sail 204 miles. Total 3761 miles. Wind has been blowing a fresh breeze all day, & our sailing has been fine. We have had several squalls, with some rain. The air is quite cool, altho the wind to day is from the South.

Thursday, 22d. We are in Latitude 36°35′ N. & Longitude 154°16′ W. Day's sail 209 miles. Total 3970 miles. Noah & myself have engaged ourselves for 2 days past getting out canes from a cocoa nut stick I procured upon the Island of Upolu. It makes us 16 beautiful canes. My health is now good tho I suffer much inconvenience from my sore shin. It appears as tho' it may remain sore for some time. My spirits are also good, although they are somewhat depressed at times, when I think of my family, & also the closing up of this expedition. I expect to loose money & also to have trouble with Perry, the captain. He is one of those down east Yankees who I find out is ready for any course to get out of a scrape. He is far from being the man I expected him to be. Wind has been from the South & moderate.

Friday, 23d. We are now at noon in Latitude 36°29′ N., and Longitude 152°01′ W., having sailed to day 136 miles. Total 4106 miles. Wind has been verry variable, generally from the west. I have been indulging much in the idea to day of going home by Cape Horn, provided it becomes necessary for me to return home this fall. I would purchase a vessel in San Francisco & leave there about 1st of October, at which time I expect hands will be willing to work their passage home, take the vessel to N. York & sell her at good profit.

Saturday, 24th. Our position at noon this day is in Latitude 36°35′ N. and in Longitude 150°45′ W., having sailed 76 miles. Total 4182 miles. The sky is frequently clouded over, & strong breezes & rain both threaten; still we are in an almost constant calm. Our vessel moves with the slightest air, or we would lay motionless.

Sunday, 25th. Our Latitude is 36°35′ N. & Long. 149°29′ W., having sailed 76 miles, total 4258 miles. Wind still verry light from N. & W. Several of our Hogs have had pigs since we left, but they were either born dead or were destroyed by the other hogs immediately after they were born. We used the precaution of putting some sows by themselves, & last night a verry small one had 3 pigs which are fine lively fellows. We have penned her by herself.

There is an animal living & growing upon the coral reefs around the Islands we have visited which is quite an article of commerce. Thousands of dollars is realized annually from it. It is called the *sea slug, tripang* or *biche de mer*, a name given to it by the French. It belongs to the genus *holuthuria* of naturalists, and is an unseemly looking animal, of a dirty brown colour, hard & rough, & possessing scarcely any animation or power of locomotion.[4] Its medium size is about 6 inches in length, & 2 or 3 in girth. It appears like a large stupid worm, generally more or less coiled. When I have been examining the shores &

[4]The *bêche-de-mer* or trepang is a holothurian or sea slug. Its dried flesh was especially esteemed by the Chinese.

shallow reefs for shells &c., the natives, many of whom would always be with me, would frequently pick them up & hand them to me, or pitch them towards me in sport. They do not eat them, or consider them eatable, & I believe it was the only animal I saw in the water that they did not eat. These animals are caught, & gutted & dried in the sun, & afterwards smoked over a wood fire, when they are fully prepared for Commerce. They are then taken to China, where they are sold for the consumption of the aristocracy of that country. They prepare a soup from them which is considered a great luxury, almost equal to that prepared from the *edible bird's nests*. They are worth there from $15 to $150 per hundred pounds owing to the quality. Morrell in his voyages describes another mode of preparing them, viz. after opening them, boil them a short time, not too much or little he says, then bury them 4 hours in the earth, & afterwards boil them again for a short time, & then dry them either in the sun or over the fire. Those dried in the sun command the best price, but is the most tedious mode of preparation.

Monday, 26th. We are now in Latitude 36°18′ N. & Long. 147°56′ W., having sailed 96 miles. Total 4354 miles. Wind during the day fair from N. & N. by E. We have not sailed the last 3 days further than one good day's sail. To day the wind breezed up, & we have all been in much better spirits. We are all extremely anxious to terminate the voyage.

Tuesday, Aug. 27th. Latitude 35°48′ N. & Longitude 146°20′ W. Distance sailed 111 miles. Total 4465 miles. We have been more completely becalmed today than at any other time during the voyage thus far; the sea for a greater part of the day has presented a perfectly smooth & mirrored surface, not a wave or ripple to disturb its calm repose. Towards night however clouds began to rise in all directions around us, & soon the sky was completely covered. The wind commenced rising & all hands looked out for a squall. It appeared to shift from all points of the compass & kept the men at the ropes most of the time shifting the sails to meet them. It however passed off with no rain, & but little continued winds.

The natives upon Wallace's Island are now turning much of their attention to the growth of the sweet potatoe, & their soil yields an excellent article. When there, King John told me his men were then daily engaged in planting, that he employed the most of his time among them, encouraging them & enjoining it upon them as their interest & duty to raise plenty, so as to be enabled to furnish all vessels that may come there with a supply or cargo. Before we left he told me they now had sufficient planted to load several vessels, & that they would be ready to dig them in four months. Formerly they raised but one crop each year. Now he will so plant them as to have them for Sale the whole year round, their climate being well adapted to their growth the whole year. They select a sandy loose soil & raise up quite a hill, in which they plant the fresh shoots of the potatoe. They take root readily & grow rapidly. They generally produce a good crop, though I was informed that some patches presenting a fine appearance by the luxuriant growth of the top, when examined, yielded scarcely any, it appearing that the whole growth was in the top. They ask two Yards of cloth or 1 lb. Tobacco for a basket of them containing from 2 to 3 pecks. They also sell a great many Uphelas. They are a root that appears to rank between the sweet & Irish potatoe, having a strong bark like rough skin, with a verry white mealy body. Its taste is also between the Irish & sweet potatoe. Its colour is a dirty brown, & shape like the sweet p[otato]. It grows wild, & in its cultivation but little attention is paid to them. Their top is a small vine growing from 10 to 30 feet long & covers completely the bushes in its neighbourhood. We found them verry scarce on the other islands we have visited. They value them about the same as sweet potatoes.

Wednesday, Aug. 28th. Latitude this day is 36°02′ N. Long. 144° 48′ W. It being nearly a calm all night, we made during it but little progress. The wind however this morning commenced blowing & we have had quite a moderate breeze all day, from the SE.—S. & SW., so that we have been enabled to sail our course. Sailed this day 94 miles. Total 4559 miles.

Thursday, 29th. Latitude 36°47′ N. Longitude 142°27′ W. Sailed the last 24 hours 145 miles. Total 4704 miles. Wind fallen off, from SSW.

Our Green Turtle is still alive, & about as active as when we first took him. I am told he will live so for several months. He neither eats or drinks. I am also told by Capt. Pease that a species of land Tarrapin is found on the Gallipagos Islands, that will weigh 600 pounds, that it is as much as 6 men can do to carry one of them suspended on poles. They are most excellent for eating; whalers eat large quantities of them. He says he has taken them there & kept them 8 months or so on his vessel & that they were then as active & apparantly as healthy as when first taken aboard. Some of them will eat & drink in small quantities, but they generally neither eat or drink any thing. He says whalers have informed him that they have had them aboard upwards of a year, without eating or drinking & still active & healthy.

Friday, 30th. Latitude 37°19′ N. Longitude 140°35′ W. Sailed the last 24 [hours] 117 miles. Total 4821 miles. This has been another day of slow sailing, it being almost a regular calm air from S. & SE. It seems that we are in a Latitude of calms, and Capt. Pease is firmly of the opinion that were we in Lat. 32° or 33° we would now have fair winds. Unfortunately for us, we have a Capt. who considers himself omniscient & were even an angel to arise & tell him he was wrong, accompanied by arguments or reasonings that no one else could doubt, he could not be convinced. Many examples of his weakness in this particular I might give. It is sufficient to say & to know that this feeling is conclusive evidence of a man's ignorance & complete incapacity to take charge of any business. There is a degree of confidence which every man should have in his own opinions, when formed with care, & upon a good basis. Still, all experiance proves that notwithstanding all our care when our *best* judgment is exercised, we are liable to be in error, & are often enlightened & benefitted by listening & paying regard to the opinions of others.

August 31st. Latitude 37°40′. Long. 139°30′. Wind verry light, varying from S. to W. Sailed 71 miles. Whole distance 4892 miles. We had an increase in our family of pigs last night, a large sow having 8. And this afternoon another one produced a family of 5. We now have 15 young pigs, having lost one of the first litter.

September 1st, 1850. We are to day at Noon in Latitude 38°05′ N. & Longitude 137°18′ W. We have had fair wind generally from WNW. Sailed 134 miles. Whole dist. 5026 m. This afternoon about 4 oclock a sail appeared ahead, & soon after dark we passed her about 1 mile off to windward. Our men called her an H[ermaphrodite] Brig, a vessel similar to our own. She heads for San Francisco, but passing her in the night, we could not speak her or ascertain her name. One thing is proved to us, that no vessel thus far in our voyage has proved itself able to sail with us. This evening the clouds gathered in the north &

with a kind of mist & fog the heavens were soon overspread. The wind arose & blows quite a strong breeze, so that our vessel is dashed along at the rate of 7 knots per hour. It has grown verry cold. I have put on socks & neck handkerchief for the first, & been compelled to button up my coat close.

Sept. 2, Monday. Our Latitude to day is 37°24′ N. & Longitude 134°22′ W. Sailed 182 miles. Total 5208 miles. Wind steady from N. by E. & blowing quite a breeze. The sea has been during the night & all day in great commotion, waves occasionally dashing across our vessel & rising to great heights all around. Our vessel is constantly wet with running & rushing water upon the deck. I have been sea sick all day & kept my berth most of the time. It has grown much colder. I have put on my overcoat. It is still quite clouded over, with an occasional mist or rain, & some fog.

Tuesday, Sept. 3. Latitude is 36°09′ N. & Longitude 130°06′ by dead reckoning, not being able to get an observation. These calculations I have no confidence in; they give us too little longitude & make us too far to the east. They were made by the omniscient Capt. & to dispute them to his face would be an insult not easily settled. I showed him an error in his calculations on his slate a few days ago, & I verrily supposed he would have burst with rage. His calculations he said were right, he made no errors, & I could not teach *him* navigation. I have since writing the above given my views to the mate, & it has resulted in placing our Long. in 130°56′ W. which is no doubt nearer correct. My sore shin has given me much trouble, & a good deal of uneasiness. I have been poulticing it for several days with lye poultices.

We are now nearing San Francisco, being only about 8° off. And I feel much like going home immediately. My family, I have no doubt, have a great deal of anxiety about me, & I feel as if it was my duty to be with them. The winds have almost entirely fallen off, being now from NE. Old ocean is still in great commotion, tho the sailors tell me she is quiet compared with her situation during a severe gale. Sailed 219 ms. Total 5427.

Wednesday, 4th. Our Latitude by Log book is 35°58′ N. & Longitude [129°]51′ W. We are still encircled with clouds & a misty semifoggy atmosphere, no wind. Sailed 66 miles. Total 5493 miles. No sun for observations.

Thursday, 5th. We find ourselves by observation to day in Latitude 36°03' N. & Longitude 128°36'. It is still clouded over, excepting a short time about mid-day, just long enough to enable us to take observations. Wind is from NW., tho so light as scarce to be called wind. Sailed 76 ms. Total 5569 ms.

We are now within 6° Long. of San Francisco. And had we a good breeze only for 2 days, we would be in Port; but at the rate of our present Sailing, we will be out yet 6 or 7 days. We have been out of salt meat for some time & having been living upon potatoes & bread we were getting verry tired of our living. Last evening we killed a small pig & have been feasting upon him to day most sumptuously. A large school of Sperm whales & also one of Porpoises were in full view for some time this afternoon. Two verry large Fin back whales came close to our vessel just before dark. They were longer than our vessel.

Friday, 6th. We having no observation have calculated our position again by the log: Latitude 36°46' N. & Longitude 126°19' W. We succeeded at 4 oclock P.M. yesterday in getting an observation & found an error in our Longitude of yesterday, it being 128°54' in place of 128°36'. Sailed 143 ms. Whole dist. 5712 ms.

We have been much amused to day catching Porpoises, altho unsuccessful. Capt. Pease made a rough iron for gigging them in the morning, & during the day we had many opportunities of using it, as large schools of them were every few hours playing around the vessel. He struck only one, & bent the iron on his spine, so that it did not get a hold. I am told that when one of them is injured so that he bleeds, the others immediately follow him & devour him. Many land birds are flying around us to day. Several small striped sand snipes have taken up their lodging upon deck, run about & pick up crumbs & are so tame as to suffer themselves to be caught by the hand, & are sometimes almost trodden upon. The wind has been from NW. The sky has been clouded over all day, & the atmosphere damp & foggy. My calculations of distances sailed daily have been made for degrees. Consequently in high Latitudes they overrun true miles. I have now made up the number of full miles sailed since leaving Wytaboo, which untill noon this day amounts to 5146 miles.

Saturday, Sept. 7th. This morning at the break of the day, I was aroused by the cry of "Haul in! Haul in! Help! Help!" I jumped up in my berth & soon ascertained that no person was overboard, & that no accident had happened, only that Capt. Pease had cast his Iron into a

Porpoise, & that he & young Merrill were trying to haul it in, but owing to the speed of the vessel they could not do it. They held to it for some time, but it finally tore loose & left them, leaving their iron & the water covered with blood. It left, the balance of the school in full pursuit, & no doubt would soon be devoured by them. It is this morning still clouded over, cold & damp & misty, with occasional flakes of snow falling.

There are many birds now to be seen. A swamp blackbird has shown himself & has been flying & chirping around the vessel for some time. We also see kelp floating in considerable quantities. These things all denote a nearness to land. But at 8 oclock this morning, I carried up the reckoning, which makes us yet 128 full miles off, & our course to the Fort N. 54 E. by compass. True course N. 75 E. This is verry near correct, provided our chronometer time is correct. Our Latitude by log at Noon is 37°23′ N. & our Longitude is 124°46′ W., having sailed 83 full miles, total 5229 full miles. Or 100 miles, total 5812 miles by chart.

Sunday, 8th. Last night has been the most severe upon us of any since we left. Soon after dark the wind arose untill it became a strong gale. The ocean soon began to roll & heave, & seemed to become covered with immense heaps of liquid fire. The men were all called upon deck, & most of the sails taken in, those that were not were reefed, & still we dashed ahead with tremenduous speed. The wind was from N. & NW. Our position being uncertain, having made no observations for several days, it was considered most prudent, the night being dark & foggy, to tack & not venture too much. So several hours were consumed in this way. Our course being NE. by N., we stood SW. by S. & returned again, so that by break of day we found land ahead & on our lee bow. The question now to be solved was, where are we? Our omniscient Capt. knew exactly; he saw the rocks or Farralone Islands, & a ship coming out of the bay. This corresponds *exactly* with *his* reckoning; he says he has had so much experience in keeping dead reckoning that he makes no errors. I made out our reckoning which places us about 39 miles North of the harbor. Time will soon tell who is right. He has now given up his ship seen to be a rock covered with Guano, & his islands to be a neck of land making out. In looking upon the chart he has concluded that we are probably in Bodega bay, & has now worked out reckoning again & forced the conclusion to correspond with this position, & blames the watch for not reporting correctly the run during the night to him. He has now committed himself to two points & if the last proves incorrect, he must fly again. Time will again soon tell the course & conclusions of the *Humbug*. His feelings seem now to be much agitated & mortified, & he tries hard to whistle it away. I mentioned my opinions of our position to the men, which he heard & which has added to his mortification.

The matter in dispute is now, at half past ten, decided. We have approached & are just now passing the Fort & settlement called Ross, located on a neck of land standing out on the N. side of Port Bodegas, so that we made land about 10 miles north of Ross or Port Bodegas. The Captain's agony is now great; his countenance is the picture of mortification, & his every act betokens great distress of mind. I am confidant that sooner than be exposed as he considers himself in his ignorance, or to have his mistake or want of accuracy exposed, he [had] rather see the vessel go down. This disposition he has shown on several former occasions, & at one time it came near proving a wreck to us.

The point we first made land was in Lat. 38°35' N. & Long. 122°45' W. At noon we were in 38°05' Lat. & Long. 122°40'.

We passed a large Barque about 2 oclock on her way to San Francisco, called the Delphos from Boston. We passed her opposite Reys point, & soon left her far behind. We now sailed down the coast in fine style, passing in view of several wrecks along shore. We were hailed by a pilot boat a short distance from the mouth of the harbor or bay, wishing to know if we wanted a pilot. We answered, "No." They answered us, we must pay half-fees. That is $25. We passed several vessels going out of the harbor, some to Panama, others to other ports. We came to anchor opposite [blank in MS] about sunset —intending to hunt out a location tomorrow to moor our vessel. We were soon boarded by 3 reporters for the different papers for news, description of our cargo &c.[5] They each left us papers. We gave them some cocoa nuts & spent the evening in reading the news. We have a bad account of the markets for such articles of produce as we have. Our prospect is bad indeed, & we shall doubtless loose each of us near $1000. The weather feels to us extremely cold; we all are shivering & shaking as tho' we were in the midst of one of our coldest winters.

[5]The San Francisco *Daily Alta California* and *Daily Pacific News* for Sept. 9, 1850, list the arrival of the brig *Rodolph,* Perry, from Vaitupu, Friendly Islands, cargo consigned to master, but give no further information regarding the cargo or voyage.

1️⃣⓪

SAN FRANCISCO—VOYAGE TO ACAPULCO—
JOURNEY ACROSS MEXICO

©

Monday, 9th Sept. This morning early we were boarded by the Harbor Master, who designated to us a berth for the vessel. Also a custom house officer called a Boarding master, requiring a statement of cargo &c. for duties.

The pilots also boarded us for their fees. Immediately after breakfast, the Capt., Kissam & myself put off for the city. We passed around the point, & searched for Clark's point, but it was concealed by late improvements so much that we could with difficulty point it out. We then went on intending to land at Long Wharf, but here the changes were still greater. Other wharfs had been erected near & adjoining it, on which rows of ware & storehouses were erected, some extending much farther out, & Long Wharf itself extended many rods, so that the old wharf could scarcely be recognized even when standing upon it. We here left our boat, with the 2 men that pulled us up, & made tracks as fast as possible for the post office. We passed along, but found every street & corner new to us. We soon ascertained that this part of the city had been burnt all down since we left, & is now entirely rebuilt & new streets formed, so as entirely to change the appearance of this part of the city.[1] The old & first built houses being all burned, they have replaced them with much better ones, & in some places most splendid edifices are erected. Some of the streets are also changed & new ones made, which is also a great improvement. Not a vestige of the effects of the fire is now to be seen, the whole of the ruins being cleared off & improved. We passed on untill we came near the

---

[1]During the absence of *Rodolph* on her voyage to the South Seas, there were two major fires in San Francisco, one on May 4 and the other on June 14, 1850.

office, when we discovered we must have some money. We turned immediately in search of some acquaintance from whom we could borrow. We returned to Montgomery Street & Mr. Kissam found an old acquaintance, a Mr. Johnson, from whom we borrowed $5—I having previously examined the Ward House for the Gov. & found he had left it. I now felt anxious to see him, & particularly to know if he was here & alive & well. I ran in to Burgoine's bank, knowing they could tell me, having previously enquired of several others. Mr. Plumbe here politely informed me that he was still here, & well, & that his office was one square below, & upon the next cross street.[2] I immediately went as directed, & found his office & him in it, apparently looking just as I left him. Here was also Adam Johnson & Mr. Munford, the Gov's partner. I was immediately informed that all at home were well. He had no letters for me. He also informed me that I. Castell & Mr. Lewton of Cadiz had returned home a few days ago, & also Dan'l Jones a short time since. I now felt truly rejoiced, at first finding that all at home were well & that Mr. Shannon was still here & also well. I repaired immediately to the Post Office with Mr. Kissam, & placed myself in the ranks for a letter. Here I stood between 2 & 3 hours before I reached the window, & witnessed many amusing scenes, some trying to steal a march into the ranks near the windows, others hissing, crying "Pull him out," they begging quarters, making excuses, pleading sickness, having waited hours &c. &c. All no go, no quarters here, compelled to yield & slide out, much ashamed. Others trying to buy berths, &c. &c. All proving & elucidating the fact that the only sure mode of getting along easily & successfully in this world is to enter upon its duties through the right door & pursue the plain open path of duty & honesty, & you will eventually succeed in accomplishing your object. I obtained 2 letters, one from my wife & one from I. Craig. They were both verry pleasant letters to recieve, for the reason that they contained no bad news. I now feel much anxiety removed. We returned to the vessel before sundown. The bay being rough I got quite wet.

Tuesday, 10th Sept. This morning by daylight our men were at work raising our anchor for a moove. We were soon under sail & in

[2]Burgoyne and Co. was established on June 5, 1849. In 1850 the firm was doing business at the corner of Washington and Montgomery streets in San Francisco. The San Francisco *Daily Alta California* on Sept. 9, 1850, noted that the panic in the money market might safely be presumed to have ended and that Burgoyne and Co. had already opened its doors to pay depositors. The firm failed on Feb. 23, 1855.

about one hour we were safely moored a short distance above & out from the old Long Wharf. Whilst on our way up we were run into by the Steamer McKim & thrust around & against another Steamer & broke to pieces her boat. Our own vessel is also somewhat injured, one of her shroud chains being broken off. We passed up the passage marked out for us by the Harbor Master, & notwithstanding, he now says we must pay for the broken boat. No justice in this.

After breakfast we all went ashore & spent the day looking around. The Governor gave me a Daguerreotype likeness of my wife, which he had received from home by the way of Oregon. It is an excellent likeness & every time I look upon it, I feel like speaking out to her, & embracing her. I have one I brought with me but it is a poor one. We find to day that our vegetables will bring us but little in this market, but that our hogs we will do well with. I think we will be able to get about 5 cents per lb. for our vegetables & about 35 cts. per lb. for Hogs. I see the market houses here full of vegetables of the finest quality. Turnips larger than any I ever saw at home, also [trem]enduous Beets, Tomatoes, Roasting Ears of Corn, Pumpkins, squashes, & [MS illegible] of an excellent quality & size. Irish and sweet Potatoes, &c. &c. This morning an officer was sent aboard to remain with us untill our cargo is all discharged, for the purpose of collecting duty. Mr. Kissam left this afternoon for Sacramento to see Mr. Bayley before we dispose of our Cargo, he having left word to inform him immediately after our arrival.

Wednesday, 11th. Went ashore to day & walked through the Streets untill verry tired. I see great changes & many improvements every place I have been. Are great many works—hands are employed upon the Streets, making gutters, Side walks, filling up Streets & levelling them. I see they are covering many of them with boards 2 In., which is the only plan to avoid mire holes in the winter; the gutters they line & cover also with boards. There are many extensive fancy stores, containing immense quanties of rich fancy goods, with which they make quite a gaudy display in their windows & in front of their Stores. I saw also an Ice Wagon going the regular round, its price 30 cts. per lb. Gambling houses are still numerous, but I do not see as many persons frequenting them as formerly.

I am informed by persons situated so as to judge pretty correctly, that the amount of Gold collected by miners is much greater this season than last, but that the amt. gathered by each individual on an average is less, there being a much great number mining this year than last. Gold dust is now plenty in market, & Gold Coin scarce. Dust will only bring $16 per oz. I visited with the Gov. yesterday a Gentleman who had some Specimens of Gold ore from the South, which promises fortunes to many, if it turns out half as well as is expected. The gold exists in verry small particles in Granite & Hornblende rock, & is procured by grinding or breaking it up. The specimens were considered poorer than the average, & it is supposed they will yield about $10 for each pound of rock. There are now several persons there exploring the country, & are expected to return in 2 or 3 weeks. And if successful in the search, it is the intention of the Gov. to embark into the business again when there will be no uncertainty in the business. I will also join him if possible. If it fails, I have now concluded to return home without further delay. A great change has taken place here in business since spring. I see nothing worth engaging in, to pay me for absenting myself longer from home. All kinds of business appears to be overdone. Many heavy failures are now occurring. And daily laborers appear to be doing better than merchants or traders. They can clear from 20 to 25 dolls. per week.

Saturday, Sept. 14th. Mr. Kissam returned last evening, & brought with him Mr. Bayley. He now is ready to return to the States if this vessel was disposed of, & he wishes to sell out to Mr. Kissam & myself. I do not feel disposed to go into it. We sold nothing yet but our Turtle. We sold it to day for 62½ cts. per pound; it weighed only 17 pounds. We have concluded to sell out all here & have been trying the market. We are offered 19 cts. per lb. live weight for our Hogs, & will probably let them go on Monday. This morning we discharged all our Seamen. To day we overhauled all our sweet potatoes & find that they have kept much better than we expected. We have not many of them on hands having lived off them fearing they would spoil.

Tuesday, 17th. This morning when we arose after day break & looked out upon the city, we discovered it apparantly all in a blaze. It had taken fire about 4 oclock & still continued to burn with fearful rapidity. We went ashore & found it raging between Portsmouth Square & the Graham house, & before it was checked it burned down about 4 squares. Estimated loss between $500,00[0] & one million of dollars.[3]

Monday, 30th. Our time has been spent up to this date in making [sales] of our Cargo, having disposed in amount about $1500.00 worth. We sold the Hogs principally for 12 cts. per lb. live weight. Our Cocoa nuts at [from] 5 to $10 per hundred, Yams ¢5 per lb., Oofelas from 6 to ¢8, & sweet potatoes ¢6. Mr. Bayley sold the vessel last week to a Capt. [F]isher, a friend of Perry's, & intends sending Perry back on another voyage. She is delivered to them this day & I have taken my final leave of the Rodolph, in whose Cabin I have spent many pleasant, & a few unpleasant days. I have taken up my board at the Sweeney house on Commercial Street, costing me about $2.50 per day for board & lodging.

We have taken from the Brig & stored about [MS unclear; figure is either 10 or 15] tons of Yams as we suppose & 1500 Cocoa Nuts. Kissam & myself are to be employed in selling them. I have now concluded to return home as soon as I get through with the disposal of the Cargo.

October 24th, 1850.[4] I have this day purchased a ticket in the

[3]The fire of Sept. 17, 1850, broke out about 4 A.M. near the Philadelphia House on the north side of Jackson Street near the Washington Market. Most of the buildings between Dupont, Montgomery, Washington, and Pacific streets were burned. They were chiefly wooden, one-story structures, and much less proportionate damage was sustained than in San Francisco's three previous major fires. Losses were estimated at $250,000 to $500,000. Frank Soulé, John H. Gihon, and James Nisbet, *The Annals of San Francisco* (New York, 1855), p. 290.

[4]At this point the organization of the journal becomes complicated. It will be noted that there is a break of nearly a month since the last entry. During this time Osbun apparently gave up the notion of joining Shannon in another mining venture and decided to head for home. The entry for Oct. 24 comes from a section of two sheets of paper of a different color from that of the rest of the book, bound in at the end and headed "Homeward Bound." Then the entry for Oct. 26 is to be found in the main body of the text following that for Sept. 30. After that the entries for Oct. 27, 29, 30, 31, Nov. 1, and Dec. 4 come from the "Homeward Bound" section. Meanwhile, in the main body of the text, the account following that for Oct. 26 begins in narrative form, is in Osbun's hand still but is rather shaky, and is in a different color ink than the rest of the book. Another blank notebook exists in which the narrative from Oct. 24 until Osbun's arrival at Chilpancingo is written in a hand and in ink which are apparently contemporary with the main body of the journal. This second version has been used in this edition in preference to that in the later hand and ink. The differences between the two are minor. This version in the second notebook, however, does not continue as long as the copy. Therefore, from Jan. 15, 1851, until the end of the account of the trip in Mexico and for the entries of Feb. 19, 20, and 21, 1851, the copy in later ink and hand have been used.

Barque Eureka, bound for Reallejo & Panama.[5] I gave for it $70. She was advertised to sail yesterday, but as it is customary with all sail vessels, she will not get off for several days after her advertised time. She is quite a comfortable looking vessel inside but is no doubt a poor sailer. I have selected her because there are upon her many of my acquaintances & neighbors from Ohio. I am now boarding at her expense at the Sacramento House & live well.

There is considerable excitement here now on account of the presence of several cases of cholera in the city & also upon the vessels lying in the harbor. One vessel has just arrived from Sacramento City on its way to Reallejo, having many cases aboard & 6 or 7 deaths.

Saturday, Oct. 26th. We have only just finished & closed up our Sale of Cargo, & found in closing up our Yams many of them rotten, injured from much handling. On the 24th I took my passage on the Barque Eureka bound for Reallejo & Panama, there being upon her many of my acquaintenances from Ohio. This being my principal reason for giving her the preference over many other much faster sailers, now up for the same ports.

Sunday, 27th. The passengers becoming impatient and unmanageable, in consequence of the delay in starting, the owner ordered the vessel to be shoved out into the bay this afternoon & before she was ready for sailing. I was up town when she shoved off & had to get a boat to take me aboard.

Tuesday, 29th. Yesterday I went ashore & spent there a portion of the day, in bidding farewell to my acquaintenances. This morning early a Pilot came aboard, & conducted our vessel out to sea; he left us at the entrance about 2 oclock & we put off under a light breeze, having aboard about [blank in MS] passangers, many of whom are now on sea for the first time.

Wednesday, Oct. 30th. Last night was a restless night among our passengers, all seeming to be more or less affected with sea sickness

---

Except that the narrative beginning from Oct. 24 somewhat parallels the entries which immediately precede it, these rather confusing materials, when rearranged in what seems to be proper order, move along without obvious break.

[5]The bark *Eureka* cleared San Francisco on Oct. 21, 1850, for Acapulco with 120 passengers and a crew of 16. For further information on this interesting and eventually unfortunate vessel, see Robert Samuel Fletcher, *Eureka: From Cleveland by Ship to California, 1849-1850* (Durham, N.C., 1959).

& diarrhoea, & to day a great many of them are confined to their berths. I have myself some diarrhoea, & have kept close to my berth. We have had a fair wind all day & made pretty good progress. It has been clouded over & no opportunity for observations.

Thursday, 31st. Last night was squally & quite an excitement among the Sailors, getting in the sails. I was called up about midnight to visit the sick; a passenger had been sick for several days with diarrhoea & attended by a Physician aboard. He getting worse, they wished me to prescribe for him. I sent for the Doctor, held a consultation, & decided that he must die, but we would check his diarrhoea if possible. I gave him an injection, but he died in a few hours afterwards; he was at the time pulseless & cold. This morning the Sailors sewed him up in his blankets, & fastened heavy weights to his feet, & after a service by Mr. Lambdin he was in the usual way committed to the bosom of the Ocean. His history I have not yet learned further than that he has a wife & is from the state or Territory of Wisconsin. To day several new cases have fallen under my charge, & among others the Mate of the vessel. There will no doubt be several other deaths before many days pass. By an observation at noon we are Lat. 33°30′.

Friday, Nov. 1st. Last night another of our passengers died from diarrhoea, & this morning he was consigned to his watery grave before our breakfast, with the usual ceremony. To-day many of the passengers became alarmed & I have been kept verry busily employed visiting & prescribing. The passenger who died this morning was from Missouri, came across the plains last summer, & altho he has been much sick, has with him about $1500. Coming to this country for a fortune looks to me now much like rushing into a house on fire [to save something]. You may most likely find it, if you work your way successfully thro [the] flame & Smoke, & after your pile or load is collected & upon your back, [all] may be lost, & life with it, during the exertion to get it away. What will not the love of gold stimulate man to undertake?

Wednesday, December 4th. We have during the last month put in our time upon the Eureka in rather an unpleasant manner. Most of the passengers have been sick, & I have had a verry busy time of it among them administering & prescribing.

No more deaths have occurred tho [several have been on the] verge

173

of the grave. We now have but 2 persons aboard seriou[sly] sick; to day I had a large sail spread for an aw[n]ing on dec[k] & have them taken above. I have been myself verry sick & took 2 emetics before I recovered, tho I still am verry bilious. We are now in about Lat. 12° & Long. 103° & completely becalmed. The wind for several weeks has been ahead, & we have by tacking made but little [progress] on our voyage. We are now out over one month, & with a poor prospect of getting into port. Our provisions are beginning to grow short, & daily allowances are beginning to stare us in the face. We have had many heavy Showers of rain with which we have filled up our Casks with water so that this great necessary of life will not be the first [to] give out. We have strived hard to make the port [of Acapulco] but cannot as yet do it. Passengers are now giving vent to long Complaints.

[*January 4, 1851*]. The Barque Eureka left the City of San Fran-cisco in California on the 24 of October 1850 with her crew & [blank in MS] Passengers bound for Realejo & Panama, being myself one of the passengers, the officers & owners assuring the passengers that the voyage would be made in about 30 days. During the voyage the chronometer became useless either from the ignorance or carlessness of the Captain. And when we arrived at the Bay of Acapulco we found to our surprise that we were in an error of six degrees in our Longi-tude, making us 360 miles further west than we supposed ourselves to be. Another important error in the voyage has been a disire to sail south for the purpose of taking the Southern trade winds. For this object we sailed as low as 7 degrees North Latitude, & to 130 degrees west Longitude.

We are now, Jan. 4th, 1851, at the port of Acapulco after voyag-ing 72 days. To this place the voyage is usually made in 20 days, & was made in that time by vessels sailing at about the same period with ourselves. And had we coasted it down we doubtless would have made it in the same time.

During all this time we have had no storms, & excepting the first week, we have had little else than a succession of calms, & when fa-vored with a breeze it seemed always to come from an unfortunate direction. We have during this voyage experienced all the dismal & horrid feelings which will arise in the mind when death from starva-tion stares us in the face. And had not Providence in his great kind-ness sent us rain to replenish our water casks, & Boobys, Sharks, Por-poises &c. to satisfy the cravings of hunger, this whole lot of passengers & crew would long ere this time be sleeping their last sleep in the quiet bosom of the Pacific, or upon the decks of the illfated Eureka. We have been on short allowance both in bread & water [blank in MS] days & this day will consume the last of our stock. We are however in sight of land & have been for 3 or 4 days, but were unable untill yesterday to make it, when we sent a boat ashore & procured a fine calf which has made us one excellent meal. At noon, when our observations were taken, we find ourselves in the Latitude of Acapulco & opposite the mouth of a Bay, but still our Capt. is unwilling to acknowledge it as the bay of Acapulco. We are now about 6 miles off.

Immediately after dinner a boat was dispatched to examine & then return before we would get too far in & make a report. A slight breeze was blowing from the west & our vessel heading for the point. The masts & yards were now covered with men looking eagerly after the Boat; she soon disappears around a bend but does not return. The Capt., as we advance towards the entrance, now becomes much excited & declares we are wrong.

I ascended to one of the yards with a glass, & clearly could distinguish all the marks of the entrance as described upon the Chart except one, which was a small island in the entrance making two entrances to the bay, but this I considered could not be distinguished at our present position, & mentioned these facts to the Capt.; but he still persisted in his opinion. I now told him positively that it was my firm & decided opinion that this was the entrance. He then called to the pilot to hold her strait for it, & he would go in right or wrong. It proved right & Oh! what rejoicing there now is upon the decks of this unfortunate vessel. *Acapulco* is a port where plenty of fresh provisions can be obtained & a point where we can either take steam & try the water again or travel homewards upon *Terra firma*. When within the bay, we at supper consumed what little was left of our Salt beef & bread. And long before she came to anchor, I & a number of my associates were out in an Indian boat that came alongside & were soon on our way ashore. "Old Virginny" was struck up & keeping time with the oars, we made these old mountains echo the sounds of Joy, which so cheerfully issued from the mouths of a half famished crowd, just entering a port of plenty, untill our boat struck the sand in shallow water a few rods from shore, when in jumped a lot of Indians who bore us ashore as in triumph upon their shoulders. Once more our feet are resting safely upon our Mother Earth.

Oh how thankful we feel that our destiny is no longer linked to that vessel, we exclaimed as we looked back upon her, striving to make her anchorage, & we wondered whether it was possible that we should ever again commit ourselves into the hands of a single man upon another sail vessel on such a voyage.

We walked around the Plaza & gazed with watering mouths upon the numerous stands, where fruits in great abundance & of every variety produced in tropical climates were exposed for sale. I purchased some oranges & Bananas, & ate a few, intending however to be extremely prudent.

Soon the vessel came to anchor, & all the hungry crowd were ashore eating & devouring in unrestrained indulgence the luxuries exposed before them. They ran around as men half crazed, laughing & shaking hands every time they met as tho' they were old friends after an absence of years. The passengers generally took supper at the American Hotel kept by our American Consul. Their appetites tempted them to eat extravagantly of the good things spread before them, notwithstanding my cautions & reproofs. I concluded to eat no supper. Many of us went to see a performance at the circus, which cost us 12½ cts. The performance was verry ordinary, the visitors appearing to be generally from the lower class. Inside of their enclosure were many cake & fruit stands. I, feeling hungry, ate some of their cake & drank some pulque, which I felt the worse of eating verry soon afterward.

This evening I went to bed & slept soundly in a cot upon the porch of the American Hotel.

Sunday, 5th Jan. This morning several of us concluded to hunt for better & cheaper quarters. We looked around & selected the *"Acapulco House,"* took breakfast here, but soon concluded to leave this place. About 10 oclock I began to sicken & eat no dinner. We moved to a new house called the French Hotel, it being quite a retired & quiet house. Fare $1.50 per day. I here became verry sick & towards evening began to vomit, & vomited up much bile. A comfortable bed has been prepared for me by my companions & after drinking a little hot tea I retired for the night.

Monday, Jan. 6th. I find myself much better this morning, & understand that most of our Company during the day yesterday & last night have been similarly affected with myself. The weather here is extremely hot, the sun so oppressive that I took one short walk only, & then covered with an umbrella. This place is so completely hemmed in by Mountains, that the sea breeze makes no impression upon it. Our company have generally concluded to cross the country through Mexico to Vera Cruz. Some of them are buying Horses, to make the trip. And others have concluded to go in a train of Horses & Mules to the City of Mexico, & from thence to Vera Cruz in wagons. They are charged from 40 to $45 through.

Tuesday, Jan. 7th. Seven persons have concluded to travel together, viz. A. Higgins & P. McNeeley of Bridport, O., Wm. Mac Lambdin of Wheeling, Thompson, A. Booker & myself of Belmont Co., O. & D. M. McConnell of Peoria, Ill.

Higgins, Thompson, & McNeeley have each bought horses, saddles & bridles to day, & begin to show considerable anxiety to get off.

Wednesday, Jan. 8th. Messrs. Lambdin, Booker & McConnel have each supplied themselves to day with horses. All are now anxious to be off, & a portion of the company will start tomorrow evening & wait for the balance at *Venta Egedo*. I have spent the day in looking after a Horse, & also viewing the town & neighborhood. It is a verry ancient city; many of its improvements & churches, from their delapidated condition, show that many ages have passed away since their construction. It was formerly the principal port of entry for all the importations into Mexico, but now it is almost entirely superseded by Vera Cruz & other ports.[6]

The road from this place to the City of Mexico was first laid out by Cortez & we understand that it is generally bad. Merchandise & the products of the country are transported entirely upon the backs of Horses, Mules & Indians. No waggons or carriages are seen here. The population of this place is variously estimated at from 4 to 5,000, & is composed mostly of Indians & their mixtures, with a few pure blooded Castillians, French & Americans. They are remarkable for their cleanliness both in their persons & about their dwellings. The men & women generally dress in white linen, & their cloathing is gen-

---

[6]Acapulco, the finest port on the west coast of Mexico, was the American terminus for Spanish trans-Pacific trade by the Manila Galleon from 1565 until the end of the service in 1815. Acapulco was not, of course, a competitor of Vera Cruz. The latter port, on the east coast of Mexico, was the major port of the country from the Spanish conquest onward.

erally well & neatly made. The women wear mostly a chemise with long sleeves, a pettycoat & no stockings, with neat low shoes. The men wear verry neat shirts, pants & roundabout.

The streets are narrow & laid out with little regularity, but are kept generally verry clean. The Houses are one story & constructed generally of Stone & adobe, around the Plaza & for some distance from it. The outskirts are inhabited by Indians & is built up with reed huts thatched with grass or leaves of Cocoa nut. In the centre of the city & fronting on the bay is the *Plaza* or public Square surrounded by Hotels, Restaurants, public offices, Shops, Stores & a Church. In it is the customs house & a great number of Stalls & Sheds where are kept coffee, cakes, fruits &c. & every evening nearly its whole surface is studded over with gambling tables of various kinds brilliantly lighted up in the open air. There appears to be here a universal disposition to gamble, & I am told that all the money that can possibly be saved through the day in any way is here nightly gambled off. I observed whilst looking on that small cakes of Soap passed as currency among them.

One part of the plaza is used every morning for a market of vegetables, which they spread out upon the ground on mats. And another part for meat, which they cut up in Strings & sell by the yard. There is also in front of the church an old well still in use, said to have been dug by Cortez. At the lower end of the city stands their Castle or fort, said to be an excellent fortification & commands completely the entrance to the harbor & city. I did not get time to visit it. I understand it was much injured by an Earthquake in 1842 but is now repaired.

Thursday, Jan. 9th. I have succeeded to day in purchasing a Horse to please me for $50. This evening 4 of our company started to travel 4 leagues, there to wait for the balance of us to morrow. I have spent a busy day repacking my Trunks which I place under the care of Mr. Jno. Dawson, a young man of Guernsey Co., Ohio, & one chest. The chest belonging to Mr. Lambden in which I have placed Gills, Silks & a few other things. I have arranged all for my early departure tomorrow morning.

Friday, 10th. We arose before day this morning, fed our Horses, saddled & bridled them & mounted with our blankets & mat sacks under us, proceeded to the Plaza where we partook of a fair breakfast of coffee &c. & by sun up were fairly upon our road. We travelled for several miles in an easternly direction along the base of the mountain & the shore of the bay, when we came to a ravine. We here left the waters of the Pacific & took our course through the depression in the mountain.

Here for the first time we see *Cactus* of immense size growing in all directions. Timber is small but the undergrowth, consisting of bushes, vines, & low varieties of Cactus, grow luxuriantly & make it entirely impossible to travel out of the road. The road is over a rough & hilly country untill we arrive at the valley of Egedo, is so much cut up with travel & rain, & covered with rocks, that it is almost impassible! We passed but few shanties on the road, & they appeared to live from the profits arising from the sale of Pine Apples, Oranges & Pulque. We observed crosses erected frequently on piles of Stone, & upon a large rock we saw quite an establishment of the kind, the cross being ornamented with a wreath of leaves & flowers, & appeared to be much resorted to. Here the road forked, & we unfortunately took the one on the right, which proved the wrong road. We soon overtook some Indians, but for the want of a little Spanish could get no information from them. After travelling two or three miles we came to a Rancho, where its accomodating owner, knowing what we wanted, pointed to us our direction, & made us understand that we could take a path & go to our place much nearer than by returning. He sent a little girl to put us on the right way. Similar mistakes are no doubt frequently made here, from the readiness with which our friend comprehended our desire. Just before entering the path & before crossing a branch of the river, we passed by an Indian hut, & feeling dry we called for a green Cocoa nut to drink. We made them understand by pointing to the tree & going through the motions of drinking. They quickly understood us & calling for a boy near, sent him to climb a tree & procure 2 for us, for which they told us we must pay one real. Whilst he was gone, we dismounted & conversed with the ladies as well as we could. One of them was making a Chemise from fine linen, & we were much surprised at the neatness & beauty of the work; we were satisfied that it could not be excelled by our most accomplished seamstresses.

From here we travelled several miles through a valley of verry rich land, tho but little of it is under cultivation, to the town of Venta Egeda. Here we arrived at about 10 oclock, being at a distance of 4 leagues from Acapulco.

We find here 4 of our companions waiting for us, viz. Lambdin, McNeely, Thompson & Booker. These, with Higgins, McConnell &

myself, 7 in all, makes up the number of our Company. McNeely being quite unwell during the morning, we conclude to remain here untill morning & make an early start. We stopped at the first house in the village, in consequence of being able to procure plenty of corn &c. for our horses. We here learned the fact that every house was a house of entertainment in the whole country. That is, that we would be as well entertained at one house as at another. Our meals would be given to us upon a matt spread upon the ground, & our seats along side upon a level with the eatables. We soon had our Landlady at work preparing for us some dinner and at 11 oclock we seated ourselves to a pile of *Tortillas*, a pair of hard fried Eggs for each, & some Beef Stewed up with a goodly proportion of *chile,* so hot that no complaints could be made for want of Pepper. The *Tortillas* are prepared by boiling corn in lye untill it is quite soft & the hull removed; it is then mashed upon a stone & patted into verry thin cakes, & baked upon a thin clay pan or griddle, without any salt or other substance in their composition. After dinner Thompson & myself took a stroll through the woods with a gun for a few hours, but found no game. We saw evidences of some verry old settlements in the neighborhood, large orchards of Fig trees surrounded by Cactus fences &c., all in a neglected condition, also Lemon trees growing among the bushes, full of fruit, & bushels rotting upon the ground. On our return we found McConnel absent in hunt of his mule. He had left him unfastned with the rest of our animals for a short time, & he had started on the back track at a rapid gate. He followed him near 4 miles, when he met an Indian woman who informed him by signs that she met him, caught him & had tied him to a tree. Thompson & myself had also joined in the pursuit, following him by the drag of the [lariat].

After returning, McConnell & myself again started on a hunting expedition down the river in quest of some spotted squirrels which he reported having seen sporting upon the trees, but we could not find them. We hunted on however & entered a field in which were some Indians at work saving corn; we noticed here a rich crop of superior & highly flavored tobacco, also Cotton in full bloom, which I took to be a native Hybiscus growing wild, it being the first I ever saw. The flowers were beautiful. Here were also extensive fields of Plantain & Bananas. We tried to procure some milk but were told we could get none untill morning. It appears that Mexicans milk their Cows but once a day & then in the morning. We returned about dark, ate a little supper, spread our blankets upon the ground under the branches of a tree &

retired for the night, having previously engaged an early breakfast at a neighbouring house to consist of wheat bread, coffee, chockolate & chicken. In this village, having an Indian population of from one to 200, we find an Englishman located keeping a grog shop & a kind of a house of entertainment, & calling himself Doctor ———. He introduced himself to me as a Doct. & enquired if I had never heard of him. He came here he says following cholera as it passed through Mexico from Vera Cruz, & treated successfully thousands of cases of it; he considers that he has immortalized himself, & is much astonished that his fame had not reached me & California. Mr. Lambdin expressed much surprise that the people had survived the two plagues, first the cholera & then this Doctor. He considers them doubly visited & doubly scourged. He tried to shave us by getting us to move our quarters to his rooms. We enquired his prices & found them more than double what was customary. He also insisted upon my supplying myself with medicines, & when entering a village on my route, to let it be known that I was a Physician & I could make a great deal of money. "Bye the bye," says he, "I have a pair of nice convenient Saddle bags, just the thing you need, which to accomodate you I would sell. Look here," says he, "at this massive gold headed cane. It was a present to me, in addition to a large fee, from a Gentleman in the City of Mexico for valuable services rendered his daughter whilst labouring under cholera." His manner was verry pompous & his dress foppish. I have generally found, both here & on the Isthmus & in California, Yankees or persons speaking the English language must be avoided in business transactions if we have any regard for our pockets.

Saturday, 11th Jan. I arose just before day & proceed to the house of our Indian neighbour where we had engaged our breakfast, & found Thompson there ahead of me. He had them up, & they were busy preparing our breakfast. We fed our Horses, & ate an excellent Mexican breakfast, consisting of good wheat light cakes, &c. &c., & were upon the road soon after sun up. We rode this morning through quite an extensive & rich valley & some of it under good cultivation. On the top of a low range of Mountains at the distance of 4 leagues we stopped at a small Indian village, & took our dinners. Our Landlord & Landlady appeared to be quite important personages. He was a Saddler, or a worker in Leather generally. She was verry talkative & verry sociable.

We made our dinner upon Eggs & Tortillas. Whilst the dinner was being prepared, a trade was struck up for a pair of spurs, of Mexican dimensions & manufacture. McConnell tried to exchange a fine large bowie knife for them, but could not do it. He paid $5 in gold for them. In his haste in starting he forgot his knife & went near 1 mile, when, recollecting it, he returned but was unable to get it. They pretended 'no intende', could not understand, & being alone (the balance of the company being all ahead), he could not force them. Just before night & after travelling verry slowly we arrived at the village of *Dos Aroyo,* a distance of 8 leagues from our lodgings last night. This is also an Indian village containing from 40 to 50 houses & a church built upon a mountain spur. A good portion of the road over which we have travelled to day has been verry rough & mountainous. Many of the mountain slopes are covered with a rich soil, on which fine crops are raised altho verry steep. This region is celebrated for its corn.

We had supper spread for us as usual upon matts, on the ground, without knives or forks; we paid for it 62½ cts. ea.

We spread our blankets in the yard by our Horses, & slept comfortably. Before going to rest we took a stroll through the village, & found the church lighted up, with a band of music playing in one corner of it, verry merry & lively tunes. Their instruments were a violin, guitar, & bass drum. Their performance was verry fair, indeed quite good for such ragged specimens of human nature. We also saw several crowds assembled in different parts of the village, some of them playing on the ground games at Monte, others singing & playing on Guitars preparatory to a regular Fandango. We were informed that a fandango would come off at our stopping place for our benefit if we desired it & would be at some expense to procure eatables & something to drink, but we declined the honor, preferring to have a night's rest in our *comfortably* fixed beds. Intending to start verry early, we furnished ourselves with some light wheat cakes & sugar for our breakfast on the road. They danced & sang in the neighborhood untill near morning.

Sunday, 12th Jan. We arose & started before daylight this morning, & at the distance of 6 leagues came to the village of Los Pocules (pronounced Poswalos) containing a few filthy Indian houses. We here procured some corn for our Horses, a little milk & tortillas, which with our bread & sugar we ate a dinner that barely satisfied the cravings of hunger. Three leagues on the decending side of a mountain further on we entered the town of Venta la Perro, a village built up with but 2 or

3 Indian huts. Being much oppressed with the heat, we here stopped a short time to rest, & were much amused at the efforts of some travelling natives to trade Horses with us. They seemed verry careful always to ask more boot money than their horses were worth. They show off their horses to great advantage, & praise in extravagant terms all his good qualities. We have met to day an unusual number of trains of pack mules, some of them numbering as high as 100 in a train. The road in many places is so completely blocked up by them that it caused vexatious detentions in getting by them. Four leagues further we came to *Venta Pala Gordo*, where we put up for the night. This place is the residence of 3 families who live in the most miserable & degraded manner. We called for Supper & about one hour after dark were supplied upon the ground & upon a dirty mat, with some tortillas, chockolate, stewed kid & soup as hot as fire with chile, & eggs. It was a rich spectacle to witness our company seated around this humble meal upon the ground, hungry, & devouring with great apparant relish such humble fare. The natives supplied us with ample light for the occasion by burning torches of pitch pine, & seemed to enjoy themselves verry much in waiting upon us. They appeared to be much surprised at the quantity of provisions we consumed. We in general eat at one meal what would be sufficient to amply supply three times the number of Mexicans.

After supper we spread our blankets under a shed, & streched ourselves after a weary day's ride of 13 leagues, expecting a good night's rest. But we were much disappointed; soon after midnight we were aroused by the cries of a boy 10 years of age who had been bitten by an insect of some kind. He continued crying the balance of the night. I arose before day, not knowing what was the matter, & went to him, inside an old outhouse, & found an older brother waiting upon him, & endeavoring to hold him, he being then in spasms, & in great apparant agony. He made the little fellow bare to show me where it had bitten him on the belly, but I could discover no particular wound. He appeared to be much swollen.

We have travelled to day over several lofty spurs of mountain & looked upon scenes & prospects of the most grand & magnificent character. We crossed the river *Rio Gordo* upon a bridge made by throwing timbers across, & floored with raw hides covered with sand, & enclosed by cane reeds. We here see the ruins of a bridge built by the Spaniards from hewn stone, which must have been a beautiful structure. It has been designed & executed by men skilled in their profession. We supposed from its apparant age that it was a work of Cortez or of his age.

Monday, 13th Jan. Being disturbed by the boy, we arose, routed the cooks & had breakfast prepared & eaten by sun up, so that we have made an early start. The boy still seems no better, & no one excepting his small brother seems to feel any interest in him, not even so much as to leave their beds in the night to see him.

From this place to the small neat Indian village of Colorado, distant one league, is a beautiful valley producing all the tropical fruits, & meadows of most luxuriant grass covered with large droves of Horses & Cattle. It is surrounded with lofty barren mountains, which contrasted with the rich & productive soil of the valley, raised in my mind ideas of terrestrial paradise more vividly than any spot I had ever seen. Here is a Hacienda, with its fields of Sugar Cane, bananas, plantains, oranges &c. cultivated on a small scale, the whole of it nearly lying in a state of nature. This spot as I looked upon it, secluded from the world, with its picturesque scenery, & its power of universal production, would be a retreat invaluable to one tired of the world or disgusted with the restraints & formalities imposed by fashionable civilization. In this village I stopped & obtained a large bowl of new milk warm from the Cow for 6 cts., the first that we were able to get since leaving Acapulco. It was excellent. Four leagues further, upon an elevated mountain flat we came to a genteel town, *Dos Caminos.* Here is established the first toll gate, & here also we came up to the 2d train of mules with our companions who started several days before us. Three leagues further we came to the valley & *Hacienda de Buena Vista*. This is a rich & extensive valley well watered by artificial streams conducted from the surrounded mountains. The Hacienda is a verry large & ancient building of a verry imposing appearance, surrounded by a great number of Indian houses tenanted by Indians who do the labor upon the farm. Its appearance reminded me much of our slave plantations in the South. Before leaving the valley & at the distance of about one league further, we came to a village where we stopped to feed our horses & to get some dinner. Where we procured feed for our horses, we were unable to get any thing for ourselves. Mr. Lambdin scoured the village & succeeded in getting a widow to bake us some tortillas, & we purchased eggs from an Indian who was carrying a load upon his back to Acapulco. These we got boiled & made a fair dinner.

We now passed out of this valley over a range of mountains of the most rocky & precipitous character whose almost perpendicular surfaces were covered with various species of blooming Cactus, & we occasionally passed by caverns deep & rocky, the bottoms of which we were always unable to see. Altogether the scenery &c. to day has been more grand & interresting than any we have seen since we left, & more so than any I have ever witnessed. Three leagues further & 12 from our lodging place last night we come down suddenly into the valley & to the *Hacienda de Acahuizotla*, where we put up for the night. Here is a Hacienda, a sugar mill, a distillery, a verry old & venerable looking church, a blacksmithshop, & several other houses, & all in successful operation.

We here find the train stopping & occupying the principal houses. Some of our Horses now need shoeing, and the blacksmith has agreed both to shoe them & lodge us. He also keeps merchandise & grog to sell on a small scale. Such specimens of Horse shoeing I never expected to see; Nails large & strong enough to fasten rafters upon a house with enormous heads were used. We visited the Sugar house, & drank freely of the cane juice as it flowed from the press. It being the first opportunity of the kind we ever had, we thought it delicious. We also obtained a plentiful supply of Cakes of Sugar, finding it an excellent article to increase variety in our meals. We here spent quite a pleasant evening with our old companions, talking over the different scenes that have occurred since entering Mexico. One of them related a difficulty he had at the first place he lodged at, in making them understand what he wanted. He & his companions wanted chicken for their meal, but entirely failed in communicating their desires to their worthy landlady by gestures or conversation, untill fortunately one of their company suggested the idea of imitating a chicken crowing. This Snyder performed to admiration & in an instant the whole household were out in pursuit, & but a short time elapsed before the pot was filled & boiling. Here we were also entertained & bored by a drunken Mexican, who was extremely liberal in his *treats*, carrying around his glass to our crowd. He frequently alluded to the Mexican battles, & laughed at their defeats, saying "Mucha fandango at Cerro Gordo" &c. &c.

Tuesday, Jan. 14th. Arose long before day & started, for the purpose of keeping ahead of the train, it being difficult to procure sufficient for so large company to eat in any one place at one time. We travelled through several rich vallies & by several extensive Haciendas of great wealth & beauty, having extensive fields of Sugar Cane, Sugar Mills & aquaducts for irrigation, constructed at great expense & labor.

We also passed through several verry ordinary Indian villages, at one of which, called Mazatlan, we stopped & procured some bread & milk & feed for our Horses. Here we were overtaken & passed by a portion of the train. At the distance of about 4 leagues we decended into the valley of Chilpansingo. Here flows a large stream during a great portion of the year but it is now about dry, and also a large comfortable looking Indian village, in a gro[ve] at a short distance from the road. We here travel up the creek & along the valley in a northernly direction for the distance of four leagues further, when we arrive at the interresting City of *Chilpansingo*. This valley is long, narrow & verry rich. The fields are many of them well cultivated, & but verry few of them are enclosed. During the summer & whilst their [crops] are growing, they herd their cattle, for the protection of their crops.

About 12 oclock we entered the city & were truly surprised to find a city of such beauty & magnitude in this portion of Mexico. Its population numbers from 15 to 20,000, & is a city of considerable wealth. Its houses are constructed in the Mexican style, generally two stories in height, & built either from stone or adobe. Each town or city in Mexico of any importance has its plaza, or public square, which is always more or less ornamented in accordance with the wealth & taste of its citizens. We find here quite a large plaza, with a fountain of pure mountain water conducted from the neighbouring mountains springing up in the Centre of a basin built of cut stone in its centre, which is the public watering place for the city. The streets & sidewalks are well paved & kept verry clean. We find here on the sidewalks surrounding the plaza, a fine market of fruits, of every variety common in tropical regions: cakes, milk, tortillas, with trinkets & finery of every kind worn by them. They have also large stores of dry goods [hard]ware & groceries. There are here no regular taverns. We stopped at a *maison,* or public stable, where we put up our horses, & called for our dinners at an adjoining house.

Jan. 15th. We arose early and long before daylight were upon the road. We were much perplexed this morning whilst travelling before it was light in fear that we were on the wrong road and we travelled near 2 leagues before we felt we were on the right track. We then hailed some ladies lying under the branches [of] a large tree who told us we were right. We discovered them by their loud laughing and talking to themselves before we came up. Feeling still in doubt, we hailed several huts before we found one tenanted. We had an amusing mode of ascertaining the locality of dwellings; it was to raise a general yell which aroused the dogs. We then made for them and between our yells and the barking of the dogs we at last succeeded in getting up a fellow who told us satisfactorily we were right. We then travelled on, satisfied, 4 leagues until we came to the *Venta del Topilote*, a double Indian house occupied by a few Indians who kept a store of whisky and a Tavern. We waited here two hours and got for breakfast Chicken, beans, cakes chocolate and coffee and again started on and travelled 3 leagues further to Venta Mescala, a store situated on the north bank of the Mescala river. Our travelling thus far to day has been the whole road in a narrow valley and a good portion of it in the beds of dry streams. There has been a great variety of Acasia and other magnificent flowering trees and s[h]rubs, also most beautiful varieties of Cactus and some of immense growth. We have seen to day the Cactus made a common article for fencing. The train unexpectedly catching up with us here, we after supper and at about sundown after feeding our horses concluded to go ahead. We consequently started and travelled 2 leagues over a spur of mountain into a valley, and it getting late we concluded to tie up our horses and stop for the night in a vacated field in which was some grass. We spread our blankets, lay down and slept well.

Thursday, Jan. 16th. We arose at break of day and put off and travelled about 2 leagues over a broken country and came to the small town of Coacayula. We here found out we were on the wrong road tho not much out of the way. We observed it first by the crowds that gathered around us immediately on our alighting and staring at us. We stopped at a store, procured corn for our horses and had breakfast furnished by a neighboring female, the most active, businesslike woman we have seen in the Country. Thompson now acknowledges that Mexicans may possibly belong to the human family, a fact he has all along denied. She in good time spread upon a table a fair meal, tho without knives and forks. She brought us our Chocolate before any thing else was prepared and we were forced to drink it immediately or drink it cold with the ballance of our breakfast. We had Bread, Tortillas, Frijoles and Eggs. We like not the appearance of the people here and keep a good lookout. A boy was sent with us to show us the road and he went to where it forks about two miles. We were then in anoth[er] extensive and rich valley in which we travelled 4 leagues and arrived at the beautiful City or Puebla of Cocula. Here we stopped and dined at another store, the residence of a rich man and much of a gentleman. The Plaza here is ornamented in its centre with a fountain of water and a large stone reservoir. The yard was full of ornamental flowering Trees, Orange and Lemon. Our kind landlord invited us to take of them as many as we desired and we helped ourselves liberally. I was here taken for a Padre in consequence of my bald head, which produced considerable merriment among us. As soon as we allighted, crowds collected around us bringing in horses to sell and proposing trade. Whilst passing out from this place we had some difficulty in getting upon the correct road and in making our enquiries we have fully declared, when it is in our power to do so, to ask the females for information. They have invariably given us the truth.[7]

Wednesday, 19th. Fair wind with a fair run came at soundings at noon in Lat. [blank in MS].

Thursday, 20th. Have been verry impatient, wind falling off, made small run, in evening opposite light house 45 miles below SW. Pass, and 10 or 12 miles from shore, also becalmed with occasional flashes of lightenind, now begin to think much of home, all hands speculating much about doings on shore and at home.

Friday, 21st. Arose this morning and find ourselves surrounded by muddy water and at about 9 oclock, being surrounded by dense fog, came to anchor. [In] course of an hour fog cleared off and suddenly the light house and steamers and shipping were exposed to view NE. of us about 2 miles. In about 1 hour a Steamer came to us and took us in tow. She brought us around into the Pass and lashed to her side a ship, the Monterey of Boston, and off we dashed once more in fresh water. An oyster Boat came along side and we purchased a good supply raw, roasted and some excellent soup.

---

[7]At this point there is another gap in the journal. What follows was apparently written on shipboard between Vera Cruz and New Orleans as Osbun's vessel was coming to the mouth of the Mississippi River.

LETTERS

From Dr. Albert Gallatin Osbun, Yuba River, California, July 14, 1849.
No address, salutation, or close.[1]

I am about 15 miles from the mouth of the Juba, on a bar formed by the mouth of a ravine. The water rushes by us with the speed almost of a race horse. The river runs literally upon a bed of gold. The truth is, *gold is plenty* here. Myself, James Barnet, and a young Spaniard, are working hard. We worked one week and made nothing—we then bought a cradle; the next day we rocked out 7 ounces of gold, worth here $112, and at home $154. It is now nearly two weeks since we purchased it, and we since then have gathered about 4 pounds. The average amount here is 1 ounce per day at this time. But as soon as the waters get down we expect much more. The richest deposits of gold are in the beds of the rivers, and it will be from one to two months yet before they will be exposed. I expect to work hard until our company arrives, when I will commence trading with the Indians. Or I may locate upon a ranch or farm close to the diggings. We have sent in a proposition for one which I expect we shall get.[2] It contains 7 square leagues of land, with 2 good adobe houses &c., and 3000 head of cattle and 1200 horses. With this ranch we can carry on a bold business at mining. It has several hundred Indians dependant upon it, and they work pretty well. I am here, and glad I come, and that I am here. I do not wish myself back; but if I were at home and knew what I now know, I would come. This place is healthy, with prudence, though by working in the hot sun I have seventeen patients on hands.

---

[1]*The Belmont Chronicle, and Farmers, Mechanics, and Manufacturers' Advocate*, St. Clairsville, Ohio (hereafter cited as *Belmont Chronicle*), Nov. 2, 1849.

[2]The reference here is probably to Reading's Ranch. See diary entries for Sept. 12 and 22, 1849.

LETTERS

From William A. Booker, Camp Comfort, near San Francisco, August 13, 1849, to William M. Booker.[3]

Dear Father:—

After a passage of 145 sailing days and 162 on water, on the 6th of the present month we came to an anchor in the Bay of San Francisco, about one hundred yards from the shore. Nothing of particular interest or any way exciting taking place on the voyage, not a soul, rope, or spar, or any of the ship's rigging having received the least particle of injury. We doubled the Horn with royals and studding sails set; the weather was very cold for some two or three weeks, with a continual fall of rain or snow. We were in sight of land almost daily from the time we first hove in sight of the main land of Tierra del Fuego until we anchored in the Bay of Valparaiso, where we lay for ten days watering and unloading and taking in cargo and Chilian passengers (22). After leaving this port we had a fine run until we came to the line, after which we caught strong head winds from the east north east, in the very direction we wanted to run, making us run north west by west and south west by west, carrying us far to the westward of our port of destination, detaining us about twenty days.

Father, I do not know what to say as regards the prospect here. I am too much excited under present circumstances to give you a full and correct statement of things as they actually are, and the b'boys are gabbling and laughing so that I cannot keep an idea a second. But of one thing rest assured, that this is the greatest country in the world; as frivolous and absurd as the accounts of the gold in this country may be, it is still twice as good as represented, and new discoveries are daily made, but those things I wish you to keep and let none but my dear wife know. Shannon and the party that came by Panama have accumulated some three thousand dollars worth of the precious metal in the last month, and have been exploring the country the greater part of the time; but when they did mine they averaged from 2½ to 3 oz. per day each. I have seen various chunks of gold from the size of a small marble up to the size of a goose egg, and a man came down from the mines this morning with one hundred and twenty thousand dollars that he had dug in one month at the lately discovered mines, where we start for tomorrow. Rents and lands are most extravagantly high in this city and country; all kinds of trade are dull in this place, excepting lumber, and that sells at from three to four hundred dollars a thousand. Every thing else I can purchase as cheap as in the States. Patents are worth nothing here—gold-washers are all a humbug; what we brought we will not take off the ship—if

[3]*Belmont Chronicle*, Nov. 2, 1849.

190

we do it will be to heave overboard. No person should purchase any preserved meats of any kind, as they are all a hoax, and as few clothing as possible, and them made out of the best of materials, good heavy substantial goods, corduroy or beaverteen, and a few hickory shirts, and a few flannel for winter and evening wear. I shall write to you by the next steamer. Give my best respects to all inquiring friends, and love to my wife and yourself. All well, and have been since we left home—fat as pigs.

Your son, truly and with respect,

WM. A. BOOKER

P.S. Since I wrote the above, the Governor informed me he had something for me in his trunk, but that his mind was so taken up with the mining business that he had entirely forgot them; but I went down along with him and received them, and amongst other things, which I am very thankful for, I found a letter from you in which you give me some most excellent advice, of which I had long ago made up my mind to follow, and am very thankful for any news or instructions you can give. As regards the gold business, you no doubt have heard; if not, I hope the fore part of this letter is sufficient to convince you of the mineral wealth of this country. To be sure, there are some men who come here and do not make one red cent. But who are these men? The idle, dissipated, and gambling men are the ones. From this I would not have you infer that the mining business is hard work, but quite the contrary. To-day whilst walking from the agent's to our tents I came across a man whom I had seen in the army, and has been at the mines. He has been very fortunate in the mining business, only having mined six weeks and brought down forty thousand dollars of the ore. This is correct, as I saw his bills of deposit, and four chunks about the size of my fist. As you request, I shall most certainly have some to send home in a short time, and I want you to act as my agent in all money matters. But first of all let my wife, who alone I would possess wealth for, receive the whole amounts I send, if she wants it, of which I in another advised her of. I understand we shall be divided off in squads of four or five, and shall not see one another only at the expiration of the month. As for stealing, it is a thing not done here—I see all kinds of things lying about here, and nothing is touched. They hung a man up at Stockton a few days ago for stealing seventeen dollars. Poor show here for a thief. I must stop by saying this is no agricultural country—all fol de rol.

W.A.B.

Last portion of a long journal-letter from Daniel Jones, dated San Francisco, August 17, 1849. The greater part of the letter concerns the voyage from New York to San Francisco. This runs through the BELMONT CHRONICLE *for October 26 and November 2, 1849.*[4]

6. [Aug.] This morning about sunrise (but we saw no sun, it was so very dark and foggy) we found ourselves, to our unspeakable delight, in front of the harbor of San Francisco, and could see the coast range of mountains looming up in the gloomy horizon. A great many whales were spouting around us, and vast numbers of pelicans and other birds flying to and fro over the waves. We soon entered along with 5 other ships, between the high headlands (about 1 mile apart) that form the great portals to this magnificent harbor. As it grew lighter, and we penetrated inland, I remarked that the encircling mountains wore nearly the same barren aspect that we observed at Valparaiso. Soon, on turning a cliff, we came in sight of the city of San Francisco, and the hundred ships that lay at anchor there.

The town stands on the declivity of a mountain slope. It looks, with its small houses, like a creature of yesterday. We anchored a mile from shore, amid the host of deserted vessels. Very soon our ship was surrounded with skiffs and boatmen, who asked $1 per man to take us on shore, $2 each to bring us back. Young Shannon went on shore for a short time. Mr. Cahoon, the Director of the Company, came on board. He came in a skiff, hired at the expense of the company, at $10. The skiff got adrift—he called to some persons in a boat to catch it—they did so, and in ten minutes returned it, charging and receiving $5 for their services. These things opened my eyes in amazement. Mr. Cahoon stated that his men had all been more or less sick—that there was much sickness in the placers—that his men had on an average made ½ oz. per day each. Soon after anchoring, we were saluted with three cheers by a crowd on a neighboring ship—what should it be but the Isabel, which we met near the equator, on the Atlantic side! She arrived yesterday. The vessel on which Jack Irons embarked has not yet arrived. In the evening young Shannon came on board with the letters, papers, &c., which were sent by the Governor. I was extremely pleased to hear that you were all well—but I fear I shall not have time to reply to all at this time. We learned that the Governor was not in town, but up at the mines—but that he will be down in a day or two.

7. [Aug.] This morning we all went ashore in the ship's boat, having all our baggage with us. We hauled it in a hand-wagon up an eminence on one side of the town. Through the kindness of young Frazier and a Mr. Estyle,

[4]Quoted section from *Belmont Chronicle*, Nov. 2, 1849.

we were loaned two tents, which we pitched. We were then waited on by a young man who was sent down by the Governor to wait for us. He supplied us with some money to live on, and we had a supper of California beef, which we got for 18 cents per pound. After supper I strolled over the town, observing things, and trying to get all the news. There is no house in town as good as Mr. P.'s, but the best one rents for one hundred and forty thousand dollars per annum. The gambling houses are numerous, and there I saw immense quantities of gold and silver: they are thronged at all hours. The state of things here is really extraordinary, the prices are enormous for everything, and everybody seems to have plenty of money. All kindreds, tongues and people are here represented. I saw even Malays and Chinese. But really I cannot spare time to enlarge on these matters. I tell you once for all, that you are not to discredit any stories of the prodigious prices and wages here. The town is a very disagreeable place, the wind blowing hard off shore all day, and raising clouds of dust. I wore my overcoat.

9. [Aug.] Yesterday morning Nutting, Gilliland and myself got a job of digging in a cellar. We worked ten hours, and each man got $5 a day. Nutting and I worked this day also at the same wages. One of our men got $12 a day for laying brick. We would have got more, but there are just now so many ships arriving with passengers who wish to work a few days before going up to the mines that wages have fallen some. On our return from work we had the immeasurable satisfaction of meeting the Governor at the tents. He looked better than I ever saw him, and was in fine spirits. The meeting, you may be sure, was full of pleasure. The news he gave us, of his explorations and mining, was very encouraging and entirely gratifying. Our expectations are very brilliant. If we are lucky enough to retain our health, we shall in all probability do very well. The Governor has a very poor opinion of California as an agricultural country, and what I have seen of it around the bay leads me to think that the reports of Col. Fremont are quite extravagant.

I will, however, suspend my opinion until I see the interior. The Governor has been over the whole country to select a proper location for us, which he has succeeded in doing, and he says it is a healthy one. There can be no doubt that fever and ague and other fevers are prevalent in the valleys of the Sacramento and San Joaquin (pronounced by the Spaniards San Hawkeen). In our location Dr. Osbun and the other men have been perfectly healthy. I think I shall be able to endure my share of the fatigues incident to this enterprise.

11. [Aug.] Some of the men went on board to-day, to help get our freight, and put it on board of a brig bound up the Sacramento, to Sacramento City. Freight from the latter place to the mines is still very high. Mr. Cahoon paid

42 cts. a pound, but it is now somewhat more reasonable. We will be compelled to sacrifice everything not indispensable—even our beds must be emptied of their contents, and our trunks thrown away. We submit to these things willingly. I made this day $5 at the same job at which I worked before.

12. [Aug.] This morning Gilliland, Mulvany and myself were deputed to go up the river with that part of our freight already on board the brig. Had not all the sailors ran off, we might have had all our goods out by this time—as it is, some of the company must remain to secure the remainder of them. In the afternoon we embarked and set sail. Before dark we cast anchor at Venetia, a little contemptible town on the shore of the third one of the triple Bay of San Francisco. At this place, the government has commenced a navy yard.[5] This day, although we were in full view of the shores, we saw no timber worthy the name. The country is all mountainous, parched and brown, and is covered, according to the accounts we heard, with wild oats, ripe and yellow. We saw some cattle on the hills.

13. [Aug.] This day we commenced the ascent of the Sacramento, which is difficult on account of the numerous low islands; the shores of the river are also low, being little higher than the water. In the rainy season the whole adjacent region must be overflowed. The shores are becoming lined with rushes and a few live oaks—these latter look very like old overgrown apple trees. We went on shore to hunt and roam over the hills, as our vessel got stuck in the mud, where she must remain until high tide. The hills are covered with rich soil, which at this season is parched into dust—the grass is all withered. We saw no game but some small birds and snakes.

In the bottom, between the stream and the hills, I found a wild rose in bloom, and some other flowers. The bottom is somewhat swampy, and is covered with bushes and grass.

14. [Aug.] The water remains low. We now see many willows and a variety of other trees, small and unknown; also rushes and wild grape vines bearing grapes which are not yet ripe are frequently seen climbing over the trees. The river, thus adorned with green shores, looks quite beautifully from the mast head.

I have had a fine view of the country. The hills have disappeared, and as far as the eye can reach the surface is perfectly flat.

You can trace the meanderings of the river to a great distance by the strips of timber that grow on its shores. I should say that this country could

---

[5]Benicia, of course, is the town referred to. In 1849 it was recognized as the military and naval headquarters of California. Early that year Commodore Thomas ap Catesby Jones had brought the Pacific Squadron there for a visit. Mare Island, at the other end of Carquinez Strait, was purchased for use as a navy yard in 1853.

be easily irrigated, and would produce good crops—and I think rice could be profitably cultivated—but that it will ever be a real healthy country, I very much doubt. It is exceedingly warm this day, and mosquitoes are innumerable. Saw many vessels and sail boats to-day. I am surprised that this river in the wilderness (for we have not seen a house since we left the bay) has so soon become the highway of a large commerce.

15. [Aug.] The shores, as we proceed, are gradually rising above the stream. Timber the same. Saw an Indian village, consisting of a few huts made of rushes. We now begin to see the open groves of oak that Fremont speaks of. They very much resemble apple orchards, only the trees are larger.

16. [Aug.] The shores of the river become more elevated, and it cannot be denied that the country looks very picturesque from the mast head. Passed Suttersville—a town without a house—and at sundown we cast anchor in the city of Sacramento. I think this will become a large place. Primeval trees shade it now—but there have been many frame houses and canvas ones erected within the last six months. Prices here are all prodigious —for instance dried apples sell for 80 cents per pound.

I must now conclude this letter, or I may not get it in the steamer. I will write whenever I have an opportunity—but as we will be far from San Francisco, you must not expect regularity.

17. [Aug.] This morning I arrived with the rest of the men, and we are all busy. They did not get out all our freight, and say that Capt. Durfey is now giving $1 an hour for hands. We are not now in sight of the Sierra Nevada (pronounced Searraw Navawthaw) but we shall soon be among their mighty peaks.

The Brooklyn has at last arrived, some of her passengers having died at sea, and four since she landed, of scurvy. Many more sick. Jack Irons' ship not yet in. For any of you to think of coming to this country next year, to live, is quite out of the question. Before you could raise anything to eat you must spend thousands for the necessaries of life—and to build a house would cost an immense sum.

From Joseph W. Mulvany, dated San Francisco, August 21, 1849.[6]

Dear Brother:

Left New York on board the Jno. G. Coster, Capt. Durfee, and had been severely ill, as you know, for a year. We were sea-sick, and such scenes never presented themselves to one unaccustomed to sea-life. But my health

[6]*Belmont Chronicle,* Nov. 2, 1849.

began to improve as soon as we crossed the equator, and was materially improved by salt water bathing, which entirely cured me of night sweats and cold feet. When I arrived in Valparaiso, May 28th, weighed 180 lbs., having made 20 lbs. clear gain in 3 months, of solid flesh. I would not take a fortune and be in the same state of health that I was a year ago, altho' we are now on allowance of water on ship-board, at 2 qts. a day for cooking and drinking, and every thing we eat is very salt. Abner Barton is very well and was not sea-sick.

July 30. The winds had been unfavorable for three weeks. You cannot imagine the anxiety there was to get here. When any one came down off the quarter-deck, the cry was "how is she heading," and this is the last cry at night & the first in the morning.

Our list of rations per day was as follows: daily allowance, bread 14 ounces, sugar 2 oz., with a little tea or coffee, and on alternate days, pork and beef, beans and cheese, butter, pickles, rice, molasses, raisins and dry fruit in small quantities. We divided off in messes, as the negro cooking aboard was intolerable, good and bad provisions being mixed together. There are four of us in a room—Abner Barton, Jno. Gilleland and D. Jones, are my room-mates. Jones and myself were cooks. The others drew rations, and cleaned the rooms. You may fancy we had some great dishes.

There was 79 of us in the 2d cabin, and 14 in the first, and we were mostly young men, having had no difficulty with each other, but on a long voyage the idea was to make the time pass away pleasantly.

Our ship is as fine a one as ever sailed around Cape Horn. She draws 17 feet water. She has 2 captains, 2 mates, 18 sailors. Until we crossed the equator, we had averaged 200 miles a day. Off De la Platte river we had a severe storm for 2 days on the 17th and 18th of April. We passed between the Falkland islands and Patagonia in lat. 54 deg. 48 min. S., long. 64° W. On May 1st we made Staten island, the first land seen in 65 days, and we passed along pretty much in sight of land until we reached Cape Horn, which was the 8th of May. We met an English brig here bound to Van Dieman's land; she had one side of her bulwarks knocked in. We cleared the capes in 4 days; the weather then became cloudy, and was like December with us. Some mornings the decks had 2 in. snow on them, and not dry for four weeks. The days were 8 hours long & the sun was at twelve o'clock 15° 35 min. above the horizon. All the capes we saw were covered with snow; the Horn is said to be 3000 feet high and of solid rock.[7] Our lamps were taken from us for fear of fire below.

[7]Cape Horn headland is 1,391 ft. high.

On the 19th of May we had passed Terra del Fuego and San Diego Ramiez, which is 81 m[iles] S. of the Horn, and looks like a high range of mountains with high peaks covered with snow. After a succession of storms, and hardships on the part of some who volunteered with me to take our part as watch to aid the sailors in times of gales, until the 21st. We then had a pretty day, and this is the first day since we left La Platte that the men could lay about on deck. This was in lat. 75° 22 min. W. On passing around the capes, we saw a great variety of birds and caught many with hooks and lines. We caught a number of the Albatross; one measured 10 ft. from tip to tip of the wings. We caught a Dolphin, the most beautiful fish I ever saw, about 3 ft. long.—We saw a number of sharks and whales.

On the 23d we came in sight of the island of Mochan, in lat. 38° 3 min. When we got in Valparaiso bay, we dropped anchor beside an English ship of war, of 84 guns and 800 men; she was great company for us for she had a band of music aboard. The city had a bad appearance from the bay, and is not much better when within it. It is in a cove, on the N. side of the mountains, having three main streets for business, of 2 miles in length. The rest is nothing but mule paths, with little huts built of mud along the passes up the mountains. The ravines that come down into the bay are very deep, and built up along the banks where one would think nothing but a goat could get to them. The people think a great deal of the Americans, and showed us much hospitality, making us eat and drink with them whenever they would catch a number of us together. Their business hours is only from 8 to 1 o'clock, then they fandango it till midnight. Their manners are a good deal like the Mexicans. We could see from the vessel the Andes range of mountains, said to be 100 miles distant, covered with snow. One very high peak is said to be a volcano.

The weather was very fine, being the fall of the year to them; there were plenty of oranges, apples, grapes, &c. in abundance, and onions six inches in diameter. We lay here ten days and took aboard 20 passengers, Chileans, bound for the mines. There was great excitement about California. We saw a good deal of gold from the mines. We sailed out on the 7th, crossing the tropic of Capricorn on the 11th of June, long. 80° W. and crossed the equinoctial line on the 26th, being 3 months south of it, & crossed it in lon. 108° W. On the 30th, a man named Evans died of Dysentery, caused by eating fruit at Valparaiso. It was a hard sight to see him thrown overboard, but he was soon forgotten; I believe I never heard his name three times afterwards. The captain discharged the 2d mate and a sailor who, it is said, tried to raise a mutiny at the Horn and stabbed the first mate.

July 1. There was a large water spout near us; a body of water about the size of a hogshead; when they strike a vessel, they are apt to do great harm.

July 4. This was a great day. The captain gave us a fine dinner, and as much liquor as all could drink. We had an oration, and the Declaration of Independence read. It went off very pretty. We were here becalmed about a week, in lat. 12° N., 116° W. long. On the 8th the sun was vertical; the thermometer at 70 with cold north winds. At only 900 miles E. of the Sandwich islands, in long. 135° W., having been detained by head winds, or we should have been in San Francisco on the 20th July. We were nearly all starved, and I lost 20 lbs. in weight in the last month. On the 6th of Aug. one of the passengers caught a shark, 7 ft. long, with a large hook baited with pork. This day we saw land at 2 o'clock in the morning, and you may be sure there was no more sleep this night. We had been 60 days out of sight of land. On the 7th we entered the Bay of S. Francisco, the entrance being a mile wide; here we met the sweet sound of the birds, and the grass looked green; every thing began to look like home; and seeing the men so much rejoiced till the tears were running down each others cheeks. We sailed up the bay about 4 miles; it was the most beautiful sight I ever saw. We dropped anchor about 10 o'clock about a mile from the city. There was about 200 vessels laying here, and many of them looked perfectly deserted. You can believe all you have ever heard about the bay. The Captain says it was the best he was ever in; he had been at sea all his life.

We went ashore and pitched our tents in a grave-yard in a very cool place, and in view of the city. One hotel as large as Smith's rents for $140,000; ground rent for a tent 80 to $100 a month. I was offered $25 a day by the Harbor Master to aid in receiving vessels.

9th. Gov. Shannon arrived in good health and spirits. I was never more pleased to see any one than I was him. There was a general rejoicing in camp. He seemed very glad to see us all, and that we looked so well, and all living, which was more than he expected to see. On the 10th and 11th we had to get off our freight ourselves, on a brig to Sacramento city, 180 miles up the river, for every sailor left the ship the day after we landed. The captain could not get any help at $1 an hour for discharging cargoes. I was sent with Gilleland and Jones with the brig that had our freight, for Sacramento. The river having 8 ft. water, and the pilot not knowing the river very well, we run aground several times, and lay there until the tide rose, which gave me time to go ashore with my gun to see the land. I saw some good land, a great deal of it rolling and would make beautiful farms. This land is covered with wild oats, with no timber except along the water, and that is very poor.

Arrived at Sacramento, where I met Mr. McKnight, of Sandusky city, Ohio, who gave the Governor and me a cordial invitation to tea, which was accepted. Here is the handsomest place for a city I ever saw, and vessels can lay right up against a bank and unload. The river for 40 miles below is from three to six fathoms, and not more than 200 yards wide. It has three branches. Two months ago there was but two houses here, and now there are 200, built in tent fashion. We pitched our tents here, and sleep in them, or in carts, &c. It is very pleasant here. We have gum-elastic blankets which keep us dry. We cannot take any thing with us from here but what we really need.

19th Aug. We leave here to-morrow for the Juba river, where I hope we will be successful. You can believe all you have ever heard about the mines. The Governor said this morning that there was over $100,000 arrived here yesterday from the upper mines. It is only worth here $15 the ounce. I saw a great quantity, some lumps that weigh a pound.

I have a few words to say to my friends that want to come to Calafornia. Now, if they would as soon die as live, I say try it, and if they reach here with good health, no doubt but that they will be well rewarded. One man told us there was 40 of them started from Independence, Mo. and 10 got here; their suffering was from hunger and cold. There have been a good many vessels reported lost on their way here, and I think there will be many a good man find a watery grave. Doctor's fees per visit, one ounce of gold in this place, and there is much fever and dysentery at the mines. The cheapest rhubarb a dose is $1 in weight of gold.

Isaac Giffin has called in to see us several times—he looks very well, and is getting $75 a day for surveying. He wishes to be remembered to you and his relatives.

As we were about going to Juba river, Gov. S[hannon] told us that he might change his location. There is a company here of 12 from Kentucky wants to join us and go to King's river, the extreme southern mines 200 miles from here. Only three small companies have been there yet. All were killed by the Indians but two. One man who arrived yesterday said there were five more killed last week. He said gold was very plenty, and a company of 40 strong would be able to get along with care. We are now going to Juba river. If the ones he left there are doing well, we will stay; if not, we will return and go to King's river. It will be a hard undertaking, but these upper mines are filling up very fast. We want to get where there is no white men. All the company wish to be remembered to their friends.

199

James Langley, Sacramento City, California, August 31, 1849, to Samuel H. Hutchinson.[8]

Dear Sir—I have been called upon by Mr. John C. Johnson to record the death of Mr. James R. Hutchinson. He died this afternoon at 2 o'clock of Dysentery; which complaint he had been afflicted with at this place for the last eight or ten days. He arrived at San Francisco on the 6th, after enjoying excellent health all the way. He was attended by a Mr. Johnson, of Utica, N.Y., the physician that accompanied him in the ship from New York to this place.

Governor Shannon, who had been with him since his arrival, departed from this place three days ago for the upper country, and before departing called upon me and requested that I should visit and attend Mr. Hutchinson, in connection with Mr. J. C. Johnson. I have done so, and can assert that all a brother could do, was done by Johnson—his watchfulness, care and attention being manifested on every occasion.

I thought proper two days ago to call on a very scientific physician, and an aged and successful one, Dr. Miller, of Ky. He was of opinion that there was still a ray of hope for the deceased; and my intimacy with the doctor induced him to do all that was in his power, but without effect. We will on tomorrow morning (Sunday) at 9 o'clock bury him at Sutter's fort, two miles from this place. We have engaged every necessary means to give him a decent burial, and we will also have the funeral rites performed at the grave.

Mr. Johnson has taken charge of Mr. Hutchinson's effects, and stored them at this place, and he requests the deceased's father to write to him directed to "Shannon Company, San Francisco," as Mr. Shannon has made arrangements to have his letters forwarded to this place by express, he, Johnson, being desirous to know what disposition he shall make of the deceased's effects.

Mr. Johnson, who is now overwhelmed with grief at the loss of his friend, will write you at a future period, and until then you will allow me to say that we sincerely sympathise with you over our absent friend, and your unfortunate but now happy son.

I remain your obedient servant,

JAMES LANGLEY,
Late of New York City

———

[8]*Belmont Chronicle*, Nov. 9, 1849.

From Abner Barton, dated Vernon, California, September 21, 1849.[9]

Dear Father—

It is with pleasure that I take this opportunity of giving you a short account of my travels since I left home, and what I have seen in California. We left N.Y. on the 1st of March; arrived here on the 6th of August. *** We remained at San Francisco about two weeks, when we left for Sacramento City, where we tarried about a week, and then left for the Juba river, where we went to work; and the few of us who were able to work averaged from 1 to 3 ounces per day, and on the upper bar or Yamboo's bar one of our boys dug 7 ounces in one day. While we were on this river, which was 3 or 4 weeks, 10 of the company were left on the lower bar, and out of the 10 not more than 3 were able to work; the most of them had the Diarrhaea, and 2 the California fever, but they got well. John Gilliland died on the 8th of Sept. of Diarhaea, and James Hutchison died of the same disease on the 1st Sept. The California Fever and Diarrhaea are very fatal, and is prevailing all over the country. While we were on the Juba river I saw companies of 7 and 8 persons that were unable to even take care of each other. We left the Juba on the 15th for Vernon; and arrived on the 19th, which is at the entrance of the Juba river into the Sacramento, and 25 miles above Sacramento City. We intend to start to-morrow, if the Governor comes up from Sacramento City, up the Sacramento river about 250 or 300 miles, where no white man has been; it is on the head waters of the Sacramento—Isaac Given and J. Frazier and 8 or 10 other persons will accompany us. We expect to remain there all winter, and it may be that we will not get back before next June, for the rainy season commences about the 1st of January, and the waters will be so high that we cannot get back. We will take provision, &c. to last us. Now I will tell you something about the gold region. There is plenty of gold here but a man has to work hard to get it. Gold is found all over the country, along the creeks and rivers, and up in the mountains there are dry diggins where all the large lumps are found. I have not seen or heard of any lump weighing more than 2 pounds and such are very scarce. The gold is found generally in fine particles. Some men have struck on rich spots and made fortunes in a little while, and others have left as poor as Job's Turkey.

From Sacramento City out there is a plain for 30 or 40 miles; the land is not very good, only in spots, and when you come to the mountains they are so rough and high that they will never be worth anything. There is scarcely any water on the plains.

The land is not worth much; there is very fine timber on the mountains,

---

[9]*Belmont Chronicle,* Dec. 21, 1849.

but none hardly on the plains. Game is plenty, such as Elk, Deer, Antelope, Wild Cattle, Bear, Panther, Wild-cat, Wolf, hare Rabbit, and all sorts of wild animals and fowls. I have not been out hunting much, but I have shot 5 Deer and a great many Hare. Yesterday 7 of us went up to a swamp about 3 miles from here, and I shot 3 Elk that would average 400 pounds neat, and saw hundreds, some that would weigh 800 lbs. The other boys shot several. I went out a few nights before and shot 3 Deer and 2 Hares in about an hour. But notwithstanding all this we have seen hard tmes, and of the hardest kind. I have not slept in a house since we left N.Y. We sleep on the ground wherever we happen to be. While we were on Juba river the Indians stole some of our goods, and some from the Chilians. We went up and caught their Chief and brought him to the Alcade, but he got away. Several tribes collected together about 300; there were but 17 of us, and we laid on our guns about a week, expecting an attack every night. They were only 3m. from us. I expect we will have hard times where we are going.

If a man steals any thing at all, he is shot, if caught, and if he kills any person he is hung. Several have been hung and shot, since I have been here. The Indians have been very bad, and a great many had to be shot, and that has cooled them down.

One of our boys was down at Sacramento City a few days ago; and saw one of the Wheeling company who said that Wm. Drennon got drowned in the Platte river.

I will tell you how things sell here. I have seen good horses sell at $800 and $1000, mules from $150 to 300, Brandy $8 to $20 a gallon, Pickeled Pork $1 per pound, Beens $1 per pound, Onions $8 per pound, Pine Boards are worth $600 to $1000 per thousand, and every thing else in proportion; this is at the mines, and where mining is very good they are worth more.

It is very warm here; the thermometer has stood at 120°. It is warm until about midnight, and then it is quite cold till daylight.

I would like to have some of my young friends come to this country, but if they ever do start, tell them to prepare for hard times, and tell them there is plenty of gold here, and, if they will take my advice, they will stay at home for their own good health.

The Governor and several of the boys have the Fever and Ague; at present I am well, and have never seen a sick day since I left home, and that is more than any of the company can say. I am going to send you $2 worth of Gold of my own digging; I dug it in about half an hour. I would send more, but I can't conveniently. Gold is worth but $15 per ounce here, and at home it is worth $22½.

Your gold digger, ABNER BARTON.

From Platoff McNeely, dated San Francisco, February 18, 1850.[10]

Dear Father:

Here I am at last, in the land flowing with milk and honey, and relative to which letter after letter has been perused, and as this is my first attempt, I shan't promise that it will be a very lengthy epistle; in fact I could no more describe the city, the doings, the "Elephant" (which I have come so far to see), and divers other matters than I could fly.

We arrived in the Bay on the 16th [February] after a tedious passage of 55 days in length, and found John Patterson, A. Higgins, Capt. Hill, J. R. Justiss, and all gone up the River, and I presume are by this time up to their eyes in gold dust.

We sailed from Panama on the 23d Dec. and for the first few days made little or no headway. We at length however got a faint breeze which carried us clear of the bay of Panama, into the glorious old Pacific, and after running south several hundred miles for the purpose of striking the trade wind, which was necessary to ensure a quick passage, we struck our course running west or thereabouts until passing Cape St. Lucas, and then varying, for there we found winds both favorable and unfavorable, and for near two weeks they were so adverse that it was as much as the old tub could do to hold her own. We at length, however, got a slant wind, as the old tars would say, which sent us on our course. We had what might be termed a lucky passage, no sickness, or at least but little, and that was a few cases of the Panama Fever, brought on board at the time of sailing from Panama. No deaths, and when we landed all were well and able for their rations. Our fare was as good as I anticipated before going on board. We had plenty of salt meat, both pork and beef, rice, tea, sugar, molasses, beans, &c. We also, in addition to the above bill of fare, had fresh fish, shark meat, &c. You may judge that I had my share of the above luxuries, when I say that I can pull down 172 lbs., which is a gain of considerable since leaving the states. My health is good, never a day's sickness since I left home.

Now for the Elephant, relative to which, I shall endeavor to give a faint description. On casting anchor in one of the best harbors in the known world, I got on my best plated, which by the by was scanty indeed, got over the side of the vessel into a small boat, paid the fellow $1 to pull me to the shore, a distance of fifty yards. On arriving in the main part of the city or plaza, I concluded to await and take a peep at the animal before proceeding further. I tho't before seeing the town that I had a pretty fair idea of it, but ye gods, if ever poor mortal was roped in the working of imagination, it was me.

[10]*Belmont Chronicle,* May 3, 1850.

I think it exceeds any thing in the shape of a city man ever beheld. Well, as I before have said, after looking at the beast in, I think, about his grandest dimensions, off I put through the city in quest of some one of my acquaintances, and whom should I first meet but our worthy citizen, Col. Johnson. Mighty glad to see him was I. From him I ascertained that Art., Capt., and the rest of the boys were up the river. I, however, with his assistance managed to scare up what remained of Old Belmont in this place, and which I found in the persons of Gov. Shannon and C. Arick. The Gov. is in good health, and doing, I am told, a good business. Last week he made the round sum of $2,000 in one case, a suit between the passengers of a vessel to this port, and the owners of the same, particulars I did not ascertain; not being interested, I did not enquire. C. Arick is well and hearty, has a contract from the city for furnishing timber to make a Pier or Wharf in front of the city. He commences operations in a few days, and if he succeeds it will be a handsome operation. He gets $27,000.

Col. Johnson tells me that in a few days he will start for the regions of heathenism. He first heads for Trinity River. Doct. Osbourn[11] is also here; he has been sick and looks bad, but is fast recovering.

Gambling is carried on to an alarming extent in this place. Thousands are lost every night in these places; every other door on an average leads into a gambling house, that is, in the main part of the city. Each house has three or four musicians placed in a part of the room playing their mightiest for the purpose of attracting custom. I have visited a number of these rooms, and find them all liberally patronized. The gamblers are making the most money, and no mistake. Money seems plenty & it requires plenty for a man to keep his head above water. I had, on landing, to within a trifle of $300, which is as much as I need until making a raise in the mines, if such is to be my luck. The accounts from the mining districts are favourable, but it requires the severest toil to make money. I may stand the hardships and I may not, one thing I do know, and that is, I can stand it as well as two-thirds I find going there. I shall give it a strong trial at all events. The wages for day laborers in this place at present is $6. C. Hicks and Lewis Eyre have both got employment with Arick, at, I believe, the above rate. Mechanics are getting from $12 to $20 per day. Living in this place for any length of time, a man must have a large pile or else he finds himself out at the toes in double quick order, for instance, I pay for breakfast $1, dinner $1.50, Supper $1, Lodging $1, and which is the cheapest to be had.

I think, considering all things, that I was fortunate in getting here at this

[11]Osbun.

season of the year. The mining season has just set in, the weather is delightful. The rainy season is over, &c. From the condition of the streets, I was half inclined to the opinion that Bridgport had a pretty fair rival in the production of the article called mud; it is however drying up very fast, which is not the case with old Bridgport, methinks.[12] Everything looks as though it had been deluged with the above commodity.

It is unnecessary for me to give you the prices of any thing in the market, in fact, it would be ridiculous to attempt it, so fluctuating is the market. Flour per cwt. is worth, at this time, $6, and by the manner in which things run, may, by this time next week, bring $15, and again, it may be below its present value; at least I am informed that such is the case by the knowing ones. For Newland & Kerr's especial benefit, I will here state the prices of lumber. Plank is dull sale at any price. Scantling is more saleable, worth from $100 to $135 per thousand; heavy timber $200; such as is used in wharfing and is the most in demand, at present, the prices range from $65 to $200 per 1000; what shingles are bringing I now disremember although I enquired.

I have not had a letter as yet from home. I left Panama before the arrival of the mail in which I was expecting a letter. I was at the P.O. on my arrival at this place, but did not get any. I presume if any were mailed they were directed to Sacramento city, for which place I shall start either to-day or to-morrow. Theodore Fink of Wheeling received 2 letters, from which I understood that there was likely to be a severe winter in the States.

I understand that Gen. Wier of St. Clairsville was to start to this country with a company of men. If such is the case, I am sorry to hear it, for there is not a doubt but that it will be a failure. There has not been a single company from the States that has done any good—all smashed up. Two men are as many as can do well together at mining.

Sacramento City, Feb. 20th, '50.

I commenced the above letter, and had not sufficient time to conclude it before leaving San Francisco for this place.

On my arrival (came on the steamer Eldorado, and for my passage paid $25, a distance of 180 miles, and $2 a meal)—I found John Patterson and Jack Castell and a great many of my acquaintances. Art is in the Diggins, in company with W. B. Wakeman. They have, so Cap. tells me, just commenced operations, with what success I know not. Capt. was up—tried his luck, and which resulted in his obtaining nearly 50 cts. He returns in a few days. I will leave this place in the course of a few days and will land, don't know where. I am going prospecting with my pack on my back. May find Art, may not. Don't care much which. It is every man for himself, I find.

[12]McNeely's home was in Bridgeport, Ohio.

Jack desires me to say that he has not written to any one, and don't intend to—reason why—he has not received any letter from home. I had hoped to have received a letter at this place, but was disappointed. If any were sent I shan't be able to get them, as I will be in the mines for a length of time to come. J. Frazier is up at the mines, as are also the rest of Shannon's company, excepting Jack Castell and Dan'l Jones; Jack is pleading at the bar, gets per month, so he says, $200. Jones is working at his trade and can make per day from $12 to $20.

I am in haste and shall conclude by a word or two to such as talk of coming to California. To those who are doing well, and enjoy the advantages of comparative ease and comfort, the enjoyment of the social circle, and the endearments of home, to such, my advice is stay where you are. But if a young man, used to hard labor, and wants very much to see the Elephant, this is the country.

I have endured hardships, but nothing in comparison, as yet, to what I had in Mexico.

In haste,
P. M'NEELY.

From John C. Johnston (or Johnson), dated Fremont, California, 1850.[13]

I am enjoying good health, weigh about 200 lbs., and can do the work of two darkies of our color (himself and nephew).

When I was in Sacramento I saw Governor Shannon, who has purchased some lots, and was improving them. His partner, Mr. Thompson, in his business, is an excelent carpenter and a very fine man. I hope they will prosper in business; this place is found from its location to be a point for trade and travel to the mines, being situated at the west side of the Sacramento at the junction of Feather river. The valley has been overflowed since I came here, but the water is subsiding and the rains ceased.

Gov. S. has released his company, and all are doing for themselves. All separated in peace and harmony. One of the men one day dug a pound and a half of gold, but the rain drove them away from the mountains. Not one of us has been sick. The work of gold-digging is dirty, hard, and requires the strongest constitutions. You are exposed to water and mud. I have got a few pounds of the "critter," and will shortly send specimens for "pins," in the natural state, picked out with my knife on the river Stanislaus.

I am going north, where the people live in tents—and there is plenty of snow on the mountains. Flour is 25c lb., pork 45, sugar 37, beef 31, mo-

---

[13]Quoted from the Wheeling [Virginia] *Argus* in the *Belmont Chronicle*, Aug. 9, 1850.

lasses 2.50 gall., onions 1.37 a lb., potatoes 50c., boots 1 to 3 oz. gold a pair, washing clothes $6 a dozen.

There are some fine families here and pretty girls. I have heard but one sermon since I left home.

I have gold from large pieces of many pounds, some with quartz rock, down to particles as fine as sand, and many beautiful specimens of my own digging, but too rough to send in a letter.

Capt. John Patterson is here and I saw him and Mr. Higgings—both well.

From J. C. Conwell, dated Sacramento, California, May 12, 1850.[14]

I am enjoying better health than when I left home. Some of the boys are making money like dirt. Between 1500 & 2000 persons arrived here the last two days, just from the States. At one place, bound for Trinity river, about 120 men went over every day. A party of four of us, Joseph Mulvaney, Abner Barton, James Alden, and myself, left Fremont, April 15, bound up to Trinity, and finding the waters too high to work to advantage we stopped on Clear Creek, 50 miles this side where the "diggings" are tolerably good. But the gold is very fine and hard to collect without quicksilver, and as we had nothing but the common rockers which are used in the mines, I come back to procure quicksilver, machines, retorts, &c. You have no idea of the expenses here. My trip from April 15th until I get back to the mines will be over $1000, besides a very laborious journey. I have now walked 200 miles over the second time, and to-morrow morning shall start on my third trip.

I understand that Dr. Henry Mulvaney has arrived in San Francisco, having seen a man who conversed with him yesterday. He was well and was inquiring for Gov. Shannon's company. But I guess he'll find them like the beard on a boy's face—a good deal scattered.

A man has to live here a year to get the run of things. When I came here last August I wished myself in any place but California. The Sun scorched and blistered my back thro' my shirt; the months of October, November, and December were rather pleasant, and I could stand to work all day in the shade, at a moderate rate. From that time until April, the whole valley is covered with water and mud. But this is one of the best grazing countries I ever saw. Blue grass and clover and wild oats grow the whole winter and in April and May are up to a horse's back for hundreds of acres and as thick as it can stand. There is a great abondance of good elk, gristly bear and salmon; deer, antelope, &c., are so common that they are not worth mentioning. The Sacramento river is one of the finest rivers in the world for fish.

[14]Quoted from the Wheeling [Virginia] *Argus* in the *Belmont Chronicle,* Aug. 9, 1850.

I have never advised any one to come here but a man with a family can do well. One woman with good health can make more than two men. A good boarding house, [I] would guarantee, would make one's fortune in a summer. People may say what they please about California being a rough and uncivilized place, but it is a country for all that. In the city of Fremont there are about 50 families who have settled as permanent residents. So don't toil out your best days while the grasshoppers are stoopshouldered and nipping the grass, but come where you can get a farm, my uncle, of your own and plenty of stock on it in a short time.—Boarding at the houses on the roads $1½ a meal, lodging $1 a night, drink 50 cents and cigar 25 cents, and crowded houses at that.

I send some flowers from the mountains to show what the climate is, and they grew within 100 yards of the snow that lay 10 feet deep.

APPENDIX A

PERSONS

Only those names of persons mentioned in the text of the diary or in the letters printed in the *Belmont Chronicle* about which some additional information is available beyond that contained in the body of the text itself are included here.

Allen, Colonel. Presumably Col. R. T. P. Allen, who sailed from New York for Chagres in the steamer *Falcon* two days after the Shannon Party sailed in *Crescent City*.

Barton, Abner. Presumably from St. Clairsville, Ohio. A letter from him, dated Sept. 21, 1849, at Vernon, Calif., and addressed to his father, was published in the *Belmont Chronicle*, Dec. 21, 1849.

Bayley, A. S. (also spelled Bailey in the diary). Listed in the ship's papers as owner of the brig *Rodolph,* Nov. 20, 1849. At that time his address was Coloma, Calif.

Booker, W. Augustus. Presumably from St. Clairsville, Ohio. A letter from him, dated Aug. 13, 1849, at Camp Comfort, near San Francisco, and addressed to his father, William Booker, was published in the *Belmont Chronicle,* Nov. 2, 1849. His name was included in the list of the Shannon Party published in the same paper on Feb. 23, 1849, and he was referred to as a passenger from San Francisco to Acapulco in *Eureka* in the same paper, Feb. 21, 1851. He may be the same person as the A. Booker mentioned by Osbun as a companion in the Acapulco–Vera Cruz trip in 1851.

Castell, John. From Wheeling, Virginia. Included in the list of the Shannon Party published in the *Belmont Chronicle*, Feb. 23, 1849. A native of England, he had been admitted to United States citizenship in 1840. He was then a resident of St. Clairsville, Ohio. The "Castle" mentioned in the diary may well be the same man.

Collier, Colonel. Col. James Collier of Steubenville, Ohio, was appointed Collector of the Port of San Francisco in 1849.

Fisher. Presumably Alvin Fisher, who came to California in the same ship as Osbun. See Helen Irving Oehler, "Nantucket to the Golden Gate in 1849," *California Historical Society Quarterly,* XXIX (1950), 169, 171.

Gilleland, John. Presumably from St. Clairsville, Ohio. An original member of the Shannon Party.

Gilman, C. On the Yuba with Shannon and Alvin Fisher, July 4, 1849. Mentioned by Winslow as "a very worthy and intelligent gentleman of Baltimore" and the leader of a mining company of which he had come to California as pioneer. See Helen Irving Oehler, "Nantucket to the Golden Gate in 1849," *California Historical Society Quarterly,* XXIX (1950), 171.

Greenwood, Old. Presumably this was Caleb Greenwood, who came to California in 1844 with his sons Britain and John. He claimed to be 83 years of age in 1846. See Hubert Howe Bancroft, *History of California* (San Francisco, 1886-90), III, 766.

Higgins, Arthur. A passenger in *Eureka* from San Francisco to Acapulco, and a companion of Osbun on the trip across Mexico.

Hutchinson, James R. Presumably from St. Clairsville, Ohio. Died at Sacramento, Aug. 30, 1849.

Ibbitson, Robert (spelled Ibbotson in the Osbun diary). Presumably from Wheeling, Virginia.

Jelly, Andrew (spelled Jelley in the Osbun diary). Presumably from St. Clairsville, Ohio.

Johnson, John C. (also spelled Johnston in letters in *Belmont Chronicle,* Aug. 10 and Aug. 17, 1849). Presumably from St. Clairsville, Ohio.

Johnston, Abner (spelled Johnson in the Osbun diary). Appointed Sub-Agent for Indian Affairs on the Sacramento and San Joaquin rivers, Apr. 14, 1849. Relieved of his position in January 1852. Apparently from St. Clairsville, Ohio. A letter of his dated City of the Great Salt Lake, Aug. 30 and Sept. 1, 1849, was published in the *Belmont Chronicle,* Jan. 18, 1850.

Jones, Daniel. Presumably from St. Clairsville, Ohio. His journal of the voyage from New York to San Francisco was published in the *Belmont Chronicle,* Oct. 26 and Nov. 2, 1849. He returned home from California before Sept. 9, 1850.

Lacy, Robert (spelled Lacey in the Osbun diary). Presumably from St. Clairsville, Ohio.

Lambdin, William McK. (also spelled McLambdin in the Osbun diary). Presumably from St. Clairsville, Ohio. Referred to as "The Rev." in the *Belmont Chronicle,* Feb. 21, 1850. An advertisement of C. S. Lambdin and Co., South Wheeling, Va., dry goods, groceries, queens ware, and hardware, appeared Mar. 16, 1849, ibid.

McNeely, Platoff. From Bridgeport, Ohio. A letter of his to his father, dated San Francisco, Feb. 18, 1850, appeared in the *Belmont Chronicle,* May 3, 1850. He had arrived from Panama on Feb. 16. He was listed as a passenger in *Eureka,* Feb. 21, 1850, ibid.

Morrell, (Captain) Benjamin, Jr. Author of *A Narrative of Four Voyages, to the South Sea, North and South Pacific Ocean, Chinese Sea, Ethiopic and Southern Atlantic Ocean, Indian and Antarctic Ocean* (New York, 1832). The description of Pearl and Hermes islands contained in Second Voyage, Ch. vii, was apparently the section chiefly used aboard *Rodolph.*

Mott, Daniel (spelled Motte in the Osbun diary). Presumably from St. Clairsville, Ohio.

Mulvany, Joseph W. (also spelled Mulvaney in the Osbun diary.) Presumably from St. Clairsville, Ohio. A letter from him, dated San Francisco, Aug. 21, 1849, appeared in the *Belmont Chronicle,* Nov. 2, 1849.

Mumford, Col. J. D. (spelled Munford in the Osbun diary). Listed in Charles P. Kimball, *San Francisco City Directory,* 1850, as a counselor with offices on Jackson between Montgomery and Sansome sts.

Nutting, Lyman. From the State of Maine. Included in the *Belmont Chronicle* list of the Shannon Party, Feb. 23, 1849.

Peck, D. Listed as a member of the Shannon Party but as not expecting to go to California until the autumn of 1849. *Belmont Chronicle,* Feb. 23, 1849.

Perry. Listed as captain of *Rodolph* in newspaper notices of her return to San Francisco from the voyage to the South Seas.

Plume, John V. (spelled Plumbe in the Osbun diary). Partner in Burgoyne & Co., bankers and commission merchants, Montgomery St., San Francisco *Pacific News,* Jan. 26, 1850. In view of the circumstances of Osbun's meeting with him in Burgoyne's Bank on Sept. 9, 1850, this seems a likelier identification than E. Lee Plumb, who was listed as a merchant with offices on the Jackson St. Wharf in Kimball, *San Francisco City Directory,* 1850.

Reading, Pierson Barton (ca. 1816-68). Came to California in the Chiles-Walker Party in 1843. Obtained a grant of land on the upper Sacramento River in 1844.

Ross's Boys. Possibly sons of John Ross of Cadiz, Ohio, whose farm was purchased by Dr. Osbun in 1845. Dr. Osbun's daughter Sarah stated in her old age that Dr. Osbun's mother was a "full cousin" of the Ross family.

Schmidt, Carl William E. Missionary in Samoa for the London Missionary Society, 1848-57.

Shannon, William. From Missouri. Included in the *Belmont Chronicle* list of the Shannon Party, Feb. 23, 1849.

Shannon, Wilson (1802-77). Born at Mt. Olivet, Belmont County, Ohio. Attended Ohio University, Athens, Ohio, 1820-22, Transylvania College, Lexington, Ky., 1823. Studied law and admitted to the bar, 1830. Prosecuting Attorney, Belmont County, 1833-35; State Prosecuting Attorney, 1835; Governor of Ohio, 1838-40, 1842-44; U.S. Minister to Mexico, 1844-45; member of House of Representatives, 1853-55; Governor of Kansas Territory, 1855-56. Engaged in practice of law in Lawrence, Kansas, 1856-77.

Steel, Clemen F. (also spelled Stelle in the Osbun diary). From Pennsylvania. Included in the *Belmont Chronicle* list of the Shannon Party, Feb. 23, 1849.

Stevenson, Jonathan D. Came to California in 1847 in command of the regiment of New York Volunteers. Settled in San Francisco as a real-estate agent after 1848. For some years he was especially interested in developing New York of the Pacific.

Weber, Charles M. (d. 1881). A native of Germany, he came to California in 1841. Weber was the founder of Stockton.

Weller, John B. (1812-75). Congressman from Ohio, 1839-45. Served as lieutenant colonel of an Ohio regiment in the Mexican War. Appointed by President Taylor to the commission to settle the Mexican boundary, 1849. After reaching California, he resigned in 1850 and devoted himself to law and politics. He was a member of the U.S. Senate, 1851-57, and Governor of California, 1858-60.

Wheeler, James. From Ohio. Included in the *Belmont Chronicle* list of the Shannon Party, Feb. 23, 1849.

APPENDIX B

◎

PLACES

Only those names of places mentioned in the text about which some additional identifying information is available have been included in this list. Maps of the California gold region and of the Pacific Islands have been prepared to accompany the text, and these should be consulted in connection with this list. Places whose location is a matter of common knowledge have not been listed.

Achilles Island. Ellice Islands. Identified as the same as Vaitupu or Tracy Island.

Bear Creek, Calif. A tributary of the Feather River. Shown on some maps as Bear River.

Bryant House, San Francisco. On Clay St. side of Portsmouth Plaza. Col. J. J. Bryant was the proprietor of the largest and best-conducted hotel in San Francisco. It was called the Bryant House in April 1850, when the proprietor was running for sheriff. Formerly it was known as the Ward House. It was a favorite place of resort for politicians. Frank Soulé et al., *The Annals of San Francisco* (New York, 1855), p. 270.

Bunker Hill Island. Bunker Island, not Bunker Hill Island, has been identified with Jarvis Island. It was reported by Kotzebue as having been discovered by an American on Jan. 11, 1815.

Central House, San Francisco. On Washington St. near Montgomery St. A. Staples and Co. were proprietors in July 1850.

Chagris. Properly spelled Chagres. A village at the mouth of the Chagres River on the northern coast of the Isthmus of Panama.

Chain Islands. Tuamotu Archipelago. Chain Island is the same as Anaa Island.

Chilpansingo, Guerrero, Mexico. The town's full name is Chilpancingo de los Bravos, and it is also known as Ciudad Bravo. It is 11 miles from Acapulco and 198 miles from the City of Mexico. It is the capital of the State of Guerrero.

213

Clarks Islands or *Pearl and Hermes Islands*. Not far from Midway Island, Pearl and Hermes Reef is a well-known location, but no available Pacific Ocean sailing directions identify them with such a location as Clark's Islands.

Clarks Point, San Francisco. Clark's Point was at the northwest end of Yerba Buena Cove. The rocks there formed the only practicable landing place for small boats at low tide before wharves were built. After the cove had been filled, its location was approximately at the intersection of Broadway and Battery St.

Clear Creek, Calif. A tributary of the Sacramento River. Reading's Ranch was located on Clear Creek, and Pierson Barton Reading discovered the first gold in Shasta County on Reading's Bar in Clear Creek in 1848. It became known as Clear Creek Diggings, and in October 1849 there were three or four hundred miners congregated there. It became known as Horse Town in 1851.

Cotton Wood Creek, Calif. A tributary of the Sacramento River. The Reading adobe stood on the west bank of the Sacramento just south of Ball's Ferry and near the mouth of Cottonwood Creek.

Falealupo, Savaii Island, Samoa. Felialupo Road is the designation in modern sailing directions.

Fannings Island. Fanning Island is a coral atoll lying about 152 miles north of Christmas Island.

Farraloni Islands, Calif. The Farallones Islands lie off the mouth of San Francisco Bay.

Fort Ross, Calif. Established by Ivan A. Kuskof for the Russian-American Fur Co. in 1812. The buildings and equipment were sold to Sutter in 1841.

Foster's Bar, Calif. A famous mining camp on the North Fork of the Yuba River. William M. Foster, a survivor of the Donner Party, mined on the west bank of the Yuba between Willow and Mill creeks early in 1849. He built a store there, and the men of the camp cast 1,500 votes in 1850. It was known as the roughest and toughest spot on the Yuba.

Fremont, Calif. A town on the west shore of the Sacramento River opposite the mouth of the Feather River. Established by Jonas Spect in March 1849, it was superseded by Washington when the Feather River became navigable to Marysville after the winter storms of 1849. It disappeared in 1851.

Gitune. Properly spelled Gatun. A village eight miles up the Chagres River from its mouth.

Gordons Ranch. William ("Julian") Gordon was the first white settler in what became Yolo County. He was the grantee of the Quesesosi or Jesús María Ranch, Jan. 27, 1843. It was located on Cache Creek.

Gorgona. A village on the Chagres River, 39½ miles above its mouth. Travelers usually left the river here for the land journey of about 20 miles to Panama.

Graham House, San Francisco. A hotel on the northwest corner of Kearny and Pacific sts. A four-story wooden building, it was shipped out knocked-down from Baltimore. In April of 1850 it was purchased for the city hall of San Francisco.

Happy Valley, San Francisco. An area roughly bounded by Market, Folsom, 1st, and 3rd sts. Apparently the term was loosely applied and might refer to almost anything south of California St. and for several blocks inland.

Hock Farm, Calif. Established by John A. Sutter in 1841 on the west side of the Feather River and below the region which was to become Yuba City. It was named after an Indian village. Sutter lived there from 1849 to 1865.

Ides Ranch, Calif. William Brown Ide bought the Rancho Barranca Colorada, on the west bank of the Sacramento River, from Josiah Belden in 1847. He built an adobe there in 1849 about two miles north of the site of the town of Red Bluff.

Johnson's Ranch, Calif. William Johnson came to California in 1840. In 1845 he bought part of the Rancho de Pablo, which had been granted to Pablo Gutiérrez, an employee of Sutter. On Bear Creek four miles above its confluence with the Feather River, it was well known as the first settlement reached by overland immigrants after crossing the Sierra.

Juba River, Calif. Properly spelled Yuba River.

Knights Ranch, Calif. William Knight of Indiana settled on the Sacramento River in 1843. His ranch became known as Knight's Landing, and a town by that name was laid out in 1850. After the discovery of gold, Knight moved to the Stanislaus River, where he operated a ferry— Knight's Ferry. He died there in 1849.

Long Wharf, San Francisco. An extension of Commercial St., it was completed in 1849, to a length of 800 feet. The construction of Long Wharf was the first important step taken to overcome the difficulties of landing goods on the tidal flats or at Clark's Point. By October 1850 it had reached a length of 2,000 feet.

Manonoo Island, Samoa. Spelled Manono in sailing directions. It is enclosed within the sea reef of Upolu Island.

Mooa, Wallis Island. Spelled Mua in sailing directions. The parish of St. Joseph was on the southern end of Uvea, or Wallis Island.

Mormon Island, Calif. The site was first known as Mormon Diggin's because of the discovery of rich gold deposits here in March 1848. On the American River a short distance above Folsom, it was the first major strike after Coloma. Mormon Island was created when diggers cut a channel to uncover gold deposits.

New Grenada. Properly spelled New Granada. The republic within which lay the Isthmus of Panama. Later it became the Republic of Colombia.

New York of the Pacific, Calif. Col. Jonathan D. Stevenson acquired part of Los Médanos Rancho in 1849 and had William T. Sherman lay out a townsite which he named New York of the Pacific. It was at the confluence of the Sacramento and San Joaquin rivers. The real-estate venture was not successful. The locality was known as Black Diamond from 1863 to 1909, and thereafter it became Pittsburg.

Nicholas Ranch, Calif. On the Feather River. Nicholaus Allgeier, a German, came to California in 1840 as a trapper for the Hudson's Bay Co. He received a tract of land from Sutter in 1842, where he built a hut. It was known as Nicolaus' Ranch. He operated a ferry beginning in 1846 and a hotel from 1849. Nicolaus was the seat of Sutter County in 1850-51, 1852, and 1854.

Nye's Ranch, Calif. Michael C. Nye came to California in 1841 in the Bartleson Party. He became naturalized in 1844 and received a grant of the Willy Rancho on the Yuba River. In January 1849 he bought the Cordua Ranch, which became known as Nye's Ranch. It was bounded on the west and north by the Feather River, on the east by the Sierra, and on the south by the Yuba River and Sutter's land.

Oahtooah Island, Samoa. Spelled Upolu in sailing directions, although variants are Ojalava, Oahtooha, Ojatava, and Opoloo. It is 36 miles west of Tutuila. Apia is a reef harbor on Upolu.

Olosingah Island, Samoa. Variant spellings: Orosenga, Oloosinga, and Orisega. Called Leoné by La Pérouse. It lies between Manua and Tutuila.

Oregon House, Panama. J. J. Landerer, proprietor in November 1849.

Otaheite Island. Commonly spelled Tahiti.

Pitt River. Properly spelled Pit River. One of the two principal streams which form the Sacramento River.

Platte River. The reference is to the Rio de la Plata in Argentina.

Plaza, San Francisco. Otherwise known as Portsmouth Square. Bounded by Washington, Kearny, and Clay sts.

Pleasant Valley, San Francisco. The region generally between Folsom, Bryant, 1st, and 3rd sts.

Port Bodegas, Calif. On the coast of Sonoma County. The modern version of the name, Bodega Bay, was established by the United States Coast Survey in 1850. The text would indicate that Osbun thought that this place was the same as Fort Ross, which is not the case.

Portsmouth Square, San Francisco. See entry for Plaza.

Reading Ranch, Calif. Pierson Barton Reading came to California in the Chiles-Walker Party in 1843. Through Sutter's friendship and influence, he received a grant of some 26,000 acres in December 1844 from Governor Micheltorena. It was the most northerly grant made in California and consisted of a strip of land three miles wide extending 19 miles along the west bank of the Sacramento River from the mouth of Cottonwood Creek at the head of Bloody Island in the south to Salt Creek in the north. The towns of Anderson and Redding were later established on it. Reading took possession in August 1845. In October 1849 Wilson Shannon negotiated for the purchase of the ranch. The price set by Reading was $10,000. The sale was not consummated.

Red Bluffs, Calif. The site was apparently known as Red Bluffs in 1849, the name coming from the Barranca Colorada Rancho, which in turn was named for the reddish-hued high cliffs along the Sacramento River. John Myers, the reputed first settler, was said to have built a hotel on the site of the present town of Red Bluff in the fall or winter of 1849.

Reys Point, Calif. Properly spelled Point Reyes.

Rincon Point, San Francisco. The southeast end of Yerba Buena Cove. Near the intersection of the present Folsom and Spear sts.

Rock Creek, Calif. A tributary of the Sacramento River from the east between Deer Creek and Mud Creek, or a tributary of the Sacramento River just west of the present town of Redding.

Rose's Bar, Calif. On the Yuba River 18 miles east of Marysville. Jonas Spect discovered gold at the place later known as Rose's Bar on June 2, 1848, the first discovery in Yuba County. John Rose, who came to California from Scotland in 1839, opened a store at Rose's bar in the fall of 1848.

Rottomah Island. Also known as Rotumah, Rotuam, and Grenville Island.

Sacramento House, San Francisco. Located on Broadway near Clark's Point, Jeffrey & Co., proprietors, by *Bogardus' Business Directory . . . May, 1850*, p. 6. Bancroft places it in June 1850 on the east side of Kearny St. between Clay and Sacramento (*History of California* [San Francisco, 1886-90], VI, 203).

Salailua, Savaii Island, Samoa. Spelled Salealua in sailing directions.

Salt Creek, Calif. A tributary of the Sacramento River from the west. Near the present site of Redding.

San Diego Ramirez Island. An island to the southwest of Cape Horn. It is properly known as Diego Ramirez Island.

Savaii Island, Samoa. Westernmost and largest of the Samoan Group. Captain Edwards of *Pandora* called it Chatham Island. Called Saviè and Oteewhy by La Pérouse and Pola by Kotzebue.

Sinorian Camp, Calif. Probably the reference is to Sonorian Camp, established in the summer of 1848 by a party of Mexican miners. The name was changed to Stewart and then to Sonora in 1850.

Specks, Calif. The reference is to Jonas Spect's ferry across the Sacramento River at the mouth of the Feather. This was at the town of Fremont. Spect lived here until 1856.

Stockton, Calif. Charles M. Weber purchased the Rancho del Campo de los Franceses in 1845. The town, at the head of Weber Slough, a tributary of the San Joaquin River, was named in honor of Commodore Robert Field Stockton, U.S.N. It was laid out in 1849 and incorporated in 1850.

Suisson Bay, Calif. Properly spelled Suisun Bay.

Sutter's Fort. John Augustus Sutter settled on the present site of the city of Sacramento in 1839. He began construction of a fort in 1841. The settlement was properly named New Helvetia, but in popular usage it was Sutter's, Sutter's Fort, or Fort Sutter.

Tobago Island, Bay of Panama. Properly spelled Taboga Island.

Toomalooah Island, Samoa. Apparently this is the Tau in the Manu Islands of modern sailing directions. Earlier it has been variously called Manua Island, Omanooau Island, and Opoun Island.

Tootooilla Island, Samoa. Modern sailing directions spell it Tutuila.

Vaitupu or *Tracy Island.* Ellice Islands.

Wallas's Island. Osbun says the native name is Uvea or Uva'ah. Sailing directions give the spelling as Wallis Islands and the native name as Uea.

Wambo's Bar, Calif. On the North Fork of the Yuba River. Spellings vary to Wambough's, Wambos, and Yamboo's.

Ward House, San Francisco. On the Clay St. side of Portsmouth Plaza. Later it became the Bryant House.

Webster, Calif. A "paper city" on the east bank of the Sacramento River about 10 miles south of the mouth of the American River.

Williams Ranch, Calif. John S. Williams came to California in 1843. He took charge of Thomas Oliver Larkin's ranch in Colusa and built the first adobe in Colusa County in 1847. He was succeeded in 1849 by Charles B. Sterling. It was the site of the Fourteen Mile House on the River Road on the west bank of the Sacramento River between Colusa and Shasta City.

Witaboo Island. Also spelled Wytebu and Wytaboo. Probably this is Vaitupu or Tracy Island.

Yamboo's Bar, Calif. See Wambo's Bar.

APPENDIX C

©

SHIPS

Ships mentioned in the text of the diary or in the letters printed in the *Belmont Chronicle* are listed here if any information about them is available beyond that contained in the text itself. There has been no attempt to give the entire career of the vessel but only such material as could be found as to her size and character, the outlines of her career, and especially the voyage or service in which she was engaged when mentioned. Where tonnage is given, it is "registered tonnage," which is a calculation of the "contents or burden" of the ship. From 1799 until 1864 in the United States this was arrived at by multiplying the extreme length of the vessel less three-fifths of the breadth by the breadth or beam and the product of this by the depth, and then dividing by 95. The quotient was taken as the legal tonnage, on which tonnage dues were to be paid. This space measurement of the vessel under decks is now calculated more accurately, and 100 cubic feet within the vessel is the equivalent of one ton. It is usually referred to as "gross tonnage" in contrast with "displacement tonnage," which is the weight of water displaced by the vessel, or her actual weight. Dimensions are given in the order: length, beam, and depth.

California. Wooden, side-wheel steamer. 1,057 64/95 tons. 199 ft. 2 in. x 33 ft. 6 in. x 20 ft. Side-lever engine. Diameter of cylinder 70 in., length of stroke 8 ft. Cost $200,082. Built by William H. Webb, New York, for the Pacific Mail Steamship Co.'s service from Panama to Oregon. Keel laid Jan. 4, 1848; launched Mar. 19, 1848. Cleared New York for the Pacific Oct. 6, 1848. Arrived San Francisco Feb. 28, 1849. Operated regularly between Panama and San Francisco between 1849 and 1854. Served as a spare steamer and made occasional voyages until 1866, when she was sold to Holladay and Brenham's California, Oregon and Mexico Steamship Co. She returned to Pacific Mail ownership in 1872 and was sold to Goodall, Nelson and Perkins in 1874. She operated in local coastwise service from San Francisco until the end of 1875, when her engine was removed and the hull sold to N. Bichard. Rigged as a bark, she engaged in the coal and lumber trades until she was wrecked near Picasmayo, Peru, in December 1894 with a cargo of lumber from Port Hadlock, Wash.

Crescent City. Wooden, side-wheel steamer. 1,291 tons. 233 ft. 7 in. x 33 ft. 11 in. x 22 ft. 8 in. Side-lever engine. Diameter of cylinder 70 in., length of stroke 9 ft., diameter of paddle wheels 33 ft. 6 in. Built by William H. Brown, New York, in 1847-48 for Isaac Newton, Charles Stoddart, J. P. Whitney and Co., and J. Howard and Son for the New York–New Orleans service. Entered the New York–Chagres service for J. Howard and Son, Dec. 23, 1848. Purchased by Charles Morgan and associates in January 1849 but continued under the management of the Howards. Passed to the control of the Pacific Mail Steamship Co. in October 1850 and was sold to the United States Mail Steamship Co. early in 1851. Ran regularly from New York to Chagres until the summer of 1852 and made one voyage there in 1853. Lost on a reef in the Gulf of Mexico in 1856.

Delphos. Wooden bark. 397 70/95 tons. 123 ft. 10 in. x 26 ft. 5½ in. x 13 ft. 2¾ in. Built at Kennebunk, Maine, in 1844. Owned 1844-59 by Thomas Curtis of Boston, Mass. Arrived at San Francisco Sept. 9, 1850, 193 days from Boston.

Eureka. Wooden bark. 372 88/95 tons. 137 ft. 5 in. x 26 ft. 7½ in. x 10 ft. 11½ in. Built at Black River (now Lorain), Ohio, in 1847. Originally brig-rigged but altered to a bark before she sailed from Cleveland for San Francisco via the Welland Canal on Sept. 25, 1849. She arrived at San Francisco on June 17, 1850, with 59 passengers. Callard & Co.'s Regular Line for Realejo, Panama, and Valparaiso was advertised in the San Francisco *Daily Alta California* on Oct. 21, 1850. She was to sail in this service on Oct. 23. She cleared on Oct. 26 and arrived at Acapulco on Jan. 5, 1851, with 120 passengers and a crew of 16. She was sold there by the master, and the crew was discharged. She was still at Acapulco on June 1, 1851. See Robert Samuel Fletcher, *Eureka: From Cleveland by Ship to California, 1849-1850* (Durham, N.C., 1959).

Huron. Wooden ship. 290 26/95 tons. 99 ft. 9 in. x 25 ft. 6¾ in. x 12 ft. 9¾ in. Built at Kennebunk, Maine, in 1827. Made three whaling voyages from Hudson, N.Y., to the Pacific and South Atlantic between 1832 and 1840. She was sold to owners in Sag Harbor, N.Y., in 1840 and made four whaling voyages from there to the South Atlantic and Northwest Coast between 1840 and 1848. In 1849 she was owned by Oliver E. Wade of Sag Harbor and twelve others. She departed Sag Harbor on June 20, 1849, carrying a cargo of brick and lumber. Arriving at San Francisco on Dec. 10, 1849, she was sold at auction there on April 13, 1850, for $1,300. Apparently she did not return to whaling.

John C. Coster (also spelled *John G. Coster, J. G. Costar, John C. Koster*). Wooden ship. 714 60/95 tons. 141 ft. x 33 ft. 6 in. x 21 ft. 9 in. Built at New York, 1841. Owned by Thomas P. Stanton, Nathaniel P. Durfey, William E. Howland, and John L. Aspinwall, 1847-50. Departed New York Feb. 24, 1849; Sandy Hook, Mar. 1, 1849. Arrived Valparaiso, Chile, May 28, 1849; departed June 7, 1849. Arrived San Francisco Aug. 6, 1849.

McKim. Wooden, screw steamer. 244 17/95 tons (1844), 376 77/95 tons (1858). 139 ft. 6 in. x 23 ft. 2 in. x 11 ft. 7 in. Built in 1844 at Alloways-town, N. J., as *John S. McKim.* Sold to the Quartermaster's Dept., War Dept., in 1846 for Mexican War service. Returned to private ownership in 1849, when she was purchased at New Orleans and sent to California. Arrived San Francisco Oct. 3, 1849. She engaged in service between San Francisco and Sacramento. In 1851 she made a voyage to Panama and was condemned at Acapulco, northbound in the summer of 1851. She arrived at San Francisco July 31, 1853, 62 days from Panama. She was broken up at San Francisco in 1858.

Monterey. Wooden ship. 422 5/95 tons. 123 ft. 6 in. x 27 ft. 4½ in. x 19 ft. Built at Medford, Mass., in 1846.

Oregon. Wooden, side-wheel steamer. 1,099 9/95 tons. 202 ft. 9 in. x 33 ft. 10 in. x 20 ft. Side-lever engine. Diameter of cylinder 70 in., length of stroke 8 ft., diameter of paddle wheels 26 ft. Cost $198,504. Built by Smith and Dimon, New York, for the Pacific Mail Steamship Co. Launched Aug. 5, 1848. Sailed from New York for San Francisco Dec. 8, 1848. Arrived San Francisco Apr. 1, 1849. In regular service between Panama and San Francisco until 1855. Made one voyage in 1856 with freight only. She was then placed in service between San Francisco and Portland, Oregon, and was still engaged in this trade when she was sold to Holladay and Flint in 1861. In 1869 her engines were removed and she was converted to a bark for the lumber trade. *Oregon* was sunk in the Straits of Juan de Fuca in 1880 in collision with the bark *Germania.*

Oris (properly spelled *Orus*). Wooden, side-wheel steamer. 210 61/95 tons (1842), 247 26/95 tons (1845). 158 ft. 7 in. x 21 ft. 6 in. x 7 ft. 6 in. (1845). Built at New York in 1842; lengthened in 1845. Operated between New York and Red Bank, N.J. Purchased by Howland and Aspinwall in 1848 and sent from New York to Chagres with passengers on Dec. 22, 1848. She was intended for service on the river between Chagres and Gorgona, or Cruces, whence travelers continued overland to Panama. She was too large to go more than 15 or 20 miles up the river, and her passengers had to make the rest of the trip in native dugouts or pulling boats. *Orus* was chiefly useful as a tender and tug at Chagres. Late in 1849 she was purchased by Cornelius Vanderbilt for service on the San Juan River in Nicaragua.

Panama. Wooden ship. 508 87/95 tons. 127 ft. 8 in. x 29 ft. 8 in. x 14 ft. 8 in. Built at Chatham, Conn., in 1834. In 1849 she was owned by Horace W. Carpentier, Russell S. Bodfish, and James Evanson, all of New York. She departed New York on Feb. 4, 1849, and arrived at San Francisco on Aug. 8, 1849. Among her passengers were members of the California Mutual Benefit Association of New York. She was still in San Francisco Bay on Sept. 9, 1850.

Panama. Wooden, side-wheel steamer. 1,087 31/95 tons. 200 ft. 4 in. x 33 ft. 10½ in. x 20 ft. 2 in. Side-lever engine. Diameter of cylinder 70 in., length of stroke 8 ft., diameter of paddle wheels 26 ft. Cost $211,356. Built at New York by William H. Webb for the Pacific Mail Steamship Co's service from Panama to Oregon. Keel laid Feb. 21, 1848; launched July 29, 1848. Sailed from New York for San Francisco Dec. 1, 1848, but returned under sail due to having broken her cylinder and cylinder top. After repairs, she sailed again Feb. 15, 1849. Arrived San Francisco June 4, 1849. *Panama* was in regular service between Panama and San Francisco from 1849 until 1853, made a single voyage in 1854, and was held as a spare steamer at Panama in 1856 and 1857. She was employed between San Francisco, the Columbia River, and Puget Sound from 1858 until February 1861, when she was purchased by Holladay and Flint. In 1868 Holladay and Brenham gave her to the Mexican government. She was renamed *Juarez,* armed with six guns, and placed in commission as a revenue and transport steamer.

Rodolph. Wooden brig. 123 5/95 tons. 79 ft. 3¼ in. x 20 ft. 8½ in. x 8 ft. 5½ in. Built at Nobleboro, Maine, in 1843. Originally schooner-rigged. Rig officially changed to brig Mar. 19, 1845. Operated as a coastwise packet. In January 1849 she was purchased by the Shawmut and California Co. for $3,500. Her new owners had her coppered, newly rigged, and stored with provisions for six months. She loaded mining machinery and consigned goods and sailed from Boston Feb. 8, 1849. On board were 16 members of the company, 18 passengers, 8 officers and crew, 2 cooks, and 2 stewards. She arrived San Francisco Sept. 16, 1849. The company dissolved before the vessel reached San Francisco. *Rodolph* was taken up the river to Sacramento, and on Nov. 20, 1849, she was sold to A. S. Bayley of Coloma for $5,000. After her charter by Osbun and Perry and the voyage to the Pacific Islands, *Rodolph* was sold to Alfred K. Fisher of San Francisco on Oct. 12, 1850. Her register was canceled on July 1, 1851, but the document bears no indication of the place or reason.

Senator. Wooden, side-wheel steamer. 754 87/95 tons (1848), 901.69 tons (1865). 219 ft. 5 in. x 30 ft. 4 in. x 12 ft. 2 in. Vertical beam engine. Diameter of cylinder 50 in., length of stroke 11 ft. Built by William H.

Brown, New York, in 1848 for James Cunningham of East Boston. *Senator* first operated from Boston to Portland, Belfast, Bangor, and St. John, N.B. Purchased by Lafayette Maynard in 1848 and briefly saw service on Long Island Sound in early 1849. Departed New York Mar. 10, 1849. Arrived San Francisco via Panama Oct. 27, 1849. She was placed on the run from San Francisco to Sacramento at once and remained in this trade until 1854, when she was purchased by the California Steam Navigation Co. and entered the coastwise trade to San Diego via intermediate ports. *Senator* operated in this service until 1882. During these years she was owned by S. J. Hensley, Holladay and Brenham, the Pacific Mail Steamship Co., and Goodall, Nelson and Perkins. Her engines were removed in 1882 and she was temporarily rigged as a barkentine in 1884 for the voyage to New Zealand, where she became a coal barge.

Splendid. Wooden ship. 392 38/95 tons. 110 ft. 6 in. x 28 ft. 2¾ in. x 14 ft. 1⅜ in. Built at Rochester, Mass., in 1835. She made nine whaling voyages from Edgartown, Mass., to the Pacific over the years 1835 to 1872. In 1849 she was owned by Albert Osborn of Edgartown (managing owner) together with 26 others from Edgartown, 5 from Chilmark, 4 from Tisbury, and one each from Nantucket and Fairhaven, Mass. She sailed from Edgartown on Sept. 20, 1849, carrying members of the Duke's County Mining and Trading Co. She arrived at San Francisco on Feb. 15, 1850, and was still in San Francisco Bay on Sept. 9, 1850. On Oct. 1, 1851, she sailed from Edgartown on a whaling voyage.

Tennessee. Wooden, side-wheel steamer. 1,275 1/95 tons. 211 ft. 10 in. x 35 ft. 8 in. x 22 ft. Side-lever engine. Diameter of cylinder 75 in., length of stroke 8 ft., diameter of paddle wheels 31 ft. Built by William H. Webb, New York, for the Savannah Steam Navigation Co. Keel laid June 20, 1848; launched Oct. 25, 1848. She sailed on her first voyage from New York for Savannah on Mar. 22, 1849. Purchased by the Pacific Mail Steamship Co. in October 1849 for $200,000 and sailed from New York for San Francisco on Dec. 6, 1849. Arrived San Francisco Apr. 14, 1850. She operated between Panama and San Francisco until she stranded in a dense fog at Tagus Beach, Bolinas Bay, California, on Mar. 6, 1853. Passengers, mail, and baggage were taken off safely, but *Tennessee* became a total loss.

INDEX

©